AL-SANŪSĪ'S

SHARḤ AL-MUQADDIMĀT

AL-SANŪSĪ'S SHARḤ AL-MUQADDIMĀT COMMENTARY ON THE PROLEGOMENA TO ISLAMIC THEOLOGY

شرح المقدمات

Imām al-Sanūsī

Translation with notes by

MUSA FURBER

Last updated: 11 March 2026

ISBN 978-1-944904-27-2 (paper)

Published by:
Islamosaic
islamosaic.com
publications@islamosaic.com

All praise is to Allah alone, the Lord of the Worlds
And may He send His benedictions upon
our master Muḥammad, his Kin
and his Companions
and grant them
peace

TRANSLITERATION KEY

ء	' (A distinctive glottal stop made at the bottom of the throat.)
ا	ā, a
ب	b
ت	t
ث	th (Pronounced like the *th* in *think*.)
ج	j
ح	ḥ (A hard *h* sound made at the Adam's apple in the middle of the throat.)
خ	kh (Pronounced like *ch* in Scottish *loch*.)
د	d
ذ	dh (Pronounced like *th* in *this*.)
ر	r (A slightly trilled *r* made behind the upper front teeth.)
ز	z
س	s
ش	sh
ص	ṣ (An emphatic *s* pronounced behind the upper front teeth.)
ض	ḍ (An emphatic *d*-like sound made by pressing the entire tongue against the upper palate.)
ط	ṭ (An emphatic *t* sound produced behind the front teeth.)
ظ	ẓ (An emphatic *th* sound, like the *th* in *this*, made behind the front teeth.)
ع	' (A distinctive Semitic sound made in the middle of the throat and sounding to a Western ear more like a vowel than a consonant.)
غ	gh (A guttural sound made at the top of the throat, resembling the untrilled German and French *r*.)
ف	f
ق	q (A hard *k* sound produced at the back of the palate.)
ك	k
ل	l
م	m
ن	n
ه	h (This sound is like the English *h* but has more body. It is made at the very bottom of the throat and pronounced at the beginning, middle, and ends of words.)
و	ū, u
ي	ī, i, y
ﷺ	A supplication made after mention of the Prophet Muḥammad, translated as "May Allah bless him and grant him peace."

CONTENTS

المُحْتَوَيَاتُ

TRANSLATOR'S PREFACE

[مُقَدِّمَةُ المُتَرجِمِ]

In the name of Allah the All-Merciful, the Ever-Merciful

THIS BOOK presents a translation of Imām al-Sanūsī's commentary on his *al-Muqaddimāt* (*Prolegomena*) – a work composed as a preparation for his *Umm al-Barāhīn*,[1] establishing the logical and epistemological foundations required for the conduct of *kalām*: the typology of judgements, the categories of rational necessity, impossibility, and possibility, and the conceptual framework within which the divine attributes can be rigorously demonstrated. It is prolegomena in the strict sense – not prefatory remarks, but the premises without which the argument cannot proceed. Readers who work through the commentary will find themselves equipped to engage with *Umm al-Barāhīn* and al-Sanūsī's own commentary thereon.

ABOUT THE PROLEGOMENA

Al-Muqaddimāt (*Prolegomena*) comprises thirty-three paragraphs organised into eight prolegomena. The first treats judgement (*ḥukm*, §1) and its tripartite division into legal, customary, and rational (§2); legal judgements are defined as divine address relating to the acts of the morally responsible (§3), their demand-forms – obligation, recommendation, prohibition, and reprehensibility – enumerated (§4), and the stipulative category with its subdivisions of cause (*sabab*, §7), condition (*sharṭ*, §8), and impediment (*māniʿ*, §9) distinguished; the

1 Yūnus Aḥnānah, *Taṭawwur al-madhhab al-ashʿarī fī al-gharb al-islāmī* (al-Ribāṭ: Manshūrāt Wizārat al-Awqāf wa-al-Shuʾūn al-Islāmiyyah, 1424/2003), 256.

customary judgement is defined (§10) and its four categories identified (§11); and the rational judgement (§12) is divided into the necessary, the impossible, and the possible, each in its immediate and speculative forms (§§13–16). The second prolegomenon sets out the positions of the Jabriyyah, the Qadariyyah, and the People of the Sunnah on volitional acts (§17) and defines acquisition (*kasb*, §18). The third and fourth treat the six varieties of shirk (§§19–20) and the seven roots of disbelief and innovation (§21). The fifth classifies existent things in relation to substrate and specifier (§22) and enumerates the six pairs of mutually opposing possibilities (§23). The sixth, seventh, and eighth define the divine attributes of capability, will, knowledge, life, hearing, sight, and speech (§§24–29); divide speech into declarative and non-declarative types and treat truth and falsehood (§§30–31); and close with a definition of trustworthiness (*amānah*, §32) and a brief doxology (§33).

The *Prolegomena* does not, however, treat propositions and argumentation. For this, readers will need to refer to Imām al-Sanūsī's short treatise on *manṭiq* and his commentary thereon.

Two commentaries on the *Prolegomena* are readily available. The first is by the author himself – translated here. The second is *al-Mawāhib al-Rabbāniyyah fī Sharḥ al-Muqaddimāt al-Sanūsiyyah* by Abū Isḥāq Ibrāhīm al-Andalūsī thumma al-Sirqasṭī (Egypt: Kasheeda Publishing, 2015/1436).

Two editions of the author's commentary are currently available: Anas Muḥammad 'Adnān al-Shurfāwī's edition (*Sharḥ al-Muqaddimāt*, Damascus: Dār al-Taqwā, 1441/2019); and an edition edited by Nazar Ḥammādī (Maktabat al-Ma'ārif, 1430/2009).

ABOUT THE COMMENTARY

The commentary serves the *Prolegomena* in several ways simultaneously. At the level of definition, al-Sanūsī parses each formula component by component, identifying genus and differentia and specifying what each clause includes and excludes; where a term admits of multiple senses – as with *jā'iz* – he resolves the ambiguity and fixes the intended meaning. He grounds the abstract categories in concrete examples drawn from both jurisprudence and rational demonstration, and where the *Prolegomena* gestures toward a proof he sets it out in full, as in the extended arguments for divine independence from substrate and specifier and the universality of the scope of the divine attributes. The commentary is also substantially polemical: the positions of the Mu'tazilah, the Jabriyyah, the Qadariyyah, the corporealists, and the dualists are presented and systematically refuted, often with named interlocutors. The treatment of shirk and disbelief expands into a detailed taxonomy of the historical communities and theological schools in which each variety is instantiated, and the section on the roots of disbelief and innovation develops into an extended epistemological account – of compound ignorance, vile imitation, and unguarded adherence to apparent meanings – that constitutes in effect a diagnosis of the errors the whole work is designed to forestall.

ABOUT THE AUTHOR

The author is Imām Abū 'Abd Allāh Muḥammad bin Yūsuf bin 'Umar bin Shu'ayb, al-Ḥasanī, al-Sanūsī, al-Tilmasānī. He lived from 830 AH/1426 CE and died in 895/1490. He was a master of outward and inward disciplines and authored books in at least thirteen disciplines, primarily in creed, logic, and sufism. He is best known for creed works, especially *Umm al-barāhīn* – also known as *Al-Ṣughrā* – a core theological text with scores of commentaries (including the author's own), meta-commentaries, and other derivative works. It remains studied throughout the Muslim world, from West Africa to the end of Southeast Asia. His other writings include *al-Kubrā, al-Wusṭā,* and *Ṣughrā al-Ṣughrā* – all oriented around *Umm al-Barāhīn* as their reference point.

ABOUT THE TRANSLATION

The initial translation of the *Prolegomena* was completed in mid-2023. The initial translation of the commentary was completed in July 2025 and revised in March 2026.

The base text for this translation is Anas Muḥammad ʿAdnān al-Shurfāwī's edition of *Sharḥ al-Muqaddimāt* (Damascus: Dār al-Taqwā, 1441/2019).

The edition's internal section headings have been replaced with a paragraph numbering system. The headings, while useful for navigation, interrupt the flow of al-Sanūsī's prose; the paragraph numbers serve the navigational function without this cost, and the table of contents maps them to the corresponding descriptive headings for readers who wish to locate a particular discussion.

Hadith texts mentioned or alluded to in the commentary have been referenced, primarily using Imām al-Suyūṭī's *Jāmiʿ al-aḥādīth*, in the edition prepared by a research team under the supervision of Dr ʿAlī Jumʿah, printed at the expense of Dr Ḥasan ʿAbbās Zakī, 13 vols.* *Sources for the majority of passages quoted from other works have also been identified and cited.

***

I would like to thank the individuals who supported this project. I would also like to thank...

May Allah bless the author of our text, those mentioned in the text or footnotes, those who contributed in any way to bringing it to English readers, and their fellow readers. And may He forgive the translator and protect readers from his copious shortcomings.

MUSA FURBER
CYBERJAYA, MALAYSIA
1447AH/2026 CE

AL-SANŪSĪ'S AL-MUQADDIMĀT

المقدمات

The Prolegomena to Islamic Theology

AL-MUQADDIMĀT

متن المقدّمات

بسمِ اللّهِ الرحمنِ الرحيمِ

In the name of Allah the All-Merciful, the Ever-Merciful

§١ الحكمُ: إثباتُ أمرٍ أو نفْيُهُ.

§1 A judgement (*ḥukm*) is the affirmation or negation of a matter.

§٢ وينقسمُ إلى ثلاثةِ أقسامٍ: شرعيٍّ، وعاديٍّ، وعقليٍّ.

§2 It divides into three categories: legal, customary, and rational.

§٣ فالشرعيُّ: خطابُ اللّهِ تعالى المتعلّقِ بأفعالِ المكلّفينَ بالطلبِ أوِ الإباحةِ، أو الوضعِ لهما.

§3 The legal [judgement] is the address of Allah (exalted is He) related to the actions of morally responsible individuals, whether in the form of a demand, permission, or stipulation concerning either of them.

§٤ ويَدْخُلُ في الطلبِ أربعةٌ: الإيجابُ، والندبُ، والتحريمُ، والكراهةُ.

١. فالإيجابُ: وهو طلبُ الفعلِ طلبًا جازمًا؛ كالإيمانِ باللّهِ ورُسُلِهِ، وكقواعدِ الإسلامِ الخمسِ.

٢. والندبُ: وهو طلبُ الفعلِ طلبًا غيرَ جازمٍ؛ كصلاةِ الفجرِ ونحوِها.

٣. والتحريمُ: وهو طلبُ الكفِّ عنِ الفعلِ طلبًا جازمًا؛ كشربِ الخمرِ والزنا ونحوِهما.

٤. والكراهةُ: وهي طلبُ الكفِّ عنِ الفعلِ طلبًا غيرِ جازمٍ؛ كقراءةِ القرآنِ في الركوعِ والسجودِ مثلًا.

٥. وأمَّا الإباحةُ: فهي إذنُ الشرعِ في الفعلِ والتركِ معًا مِنْ غيرِ ترجيحٍ لأحدِهما على الآخرِ؛ كالنكاحِ والبيعِ ونحوِهما.

§4 Four [legal judgements] are included under demand: obligation, recommendation, prohibition, and reprehensibility.

1. Obligation (*ījāb*) is the request to perform an act with decisiveness – such as belief in Allah and His Messengers, and the five pillars of Islam.
2. Recommendation (*nadb*) is the request to perform an act without decisiveness – such as praying the Fajr Prayer.
3. Prohibition (*taḥrīm*) is the request to abstain from an act with decisiveness – such as drinking wine, fornication, and the like.
4. Reprehensibility (*karāhah*) is the request to abstain from an act without decisiveness – such as reciting the Qur'ān during bowing and prostration.
5. Permissibility (*ibāhah*) is the divine legislation authorising both performing and foregoing an act – without either being preferred over the other – such as marriage, trade, and the like.

§٥ وأمَّا الوضعُ لهما: فهو عبارةٌ عن نصبِ الشارعِ أمارةً على حكمٍ مِنْ تلكَ الأحكامِ الخمسةِ.

§5 As for their being stipulated (*waḍ'*), it refers to the Lawgiver placing an indicator for one of those five judgements.

§٦ وهي: السببُ، والشرطُ، والمانعُ.

§6 They are cause, condition, and impediment.

§٧ فالسببُ: ما يلزمُ مِنْ وجودِهِ الوجودُ، ومِن عدمِهِ العدمُ لذاتِهِ؛ كزوالِ الشمسِ لوجوبِ الظهرِ مثلًا.

§7 A cause (*sabab*) is that whose existence entails existence, and whose nonexistence entails nonexistence – by its very essence. Such as the sun's passing the zenith for the obligation of the Ẓuhr prayer, for instance.

§٨ والشرطُ: ما يلزمُ مِنْ عدمِهِ العدمُ، ولا يلزمُ مِنْ وجودِهِ وجودٌ ولا عدمٌ لذاتِهِ؛ كتمامِ الحولِ لوجوبِ الزكاةِ.

§8 A condition (*sharṭ*) is that whose absence entails nonexistence, while its presence entails neither existence nor nonexistence – by its very essence. For example: the completion of a lunar year for the obligation of Zakāt.

§٩ والمانعُ: ما يلزمُ مِنْ وجودِهِ العدمُ ولا يلزمُ مِنْ عدمِهِ وجودٌ ولا عدمٌ لذاتِهِ؛ كالحيضِ لوجوبِ الصلاةِ.

§9 An impediment (*māniʿ*) is that whose existence entails nonexistence, while its nonexistence entails neither existence nor nonexistence – by its very essence. For example: menstruation as an impediment to the obligation of prayer.

§١٠ وأمَّا الحكمُ العاديُّ: فهو عبارةٌ عن إثباتِ الربطِ بينَ أمرٍ وأمرٍ وجودًا أو عدمًا بواسطةِ التكرُّرِ، معَ صحَّةِ التخلُّفِ، وعدمِ تأثيرِ أحدِهما في الآخرِ ألبتَّةَ.

§10 As for the customary judgement (*ḥukm ʿādī*), it refers to affirming a correlation between two matters – whether in existence or nonexistence – based on repetition, while allowing for exceptions, and with no causal influence whatsoever between them.

§١١ وأقسامُهُ أربعةٌ:

١. ربطُ وجودٍ بوجودٍ: كربطِ وجودِ الشبعِ بوجودِ الأكلِ.
٢. وربطُ عدمٍ بعدمٍ: كربطِ عدمِ الشبعِ بعدمِ الأكلِ.
٣. وربطُ وجودٍ بعدمٍ: كربطِ وجودِ الجوعِ بعدمِ الأكلِ.
٤. وربطُ عدمٍ بوجودٍ: كربطِ عدمِ الجوعِ بوجودِ الأكلِ.

§11 It has four categories:
1. Correlating existence with existence – such as the correlation of the existence of satiety with the existence of eating.
2. Correlating nonexistence with nonexistence – such as the correlation of the absence of satiety with the absence of eating.
3. Correlating existence with nonexistence – such as the correlation of hunger with the absence of eating.
4. Correlating nonexistence with existence – such as the correlation of the absence of hunger with the existence of eating.

§١٢ وأمَّا الحكمُ العقليُّ: فهو إثباتُ أمرٍ أو نفْيُهُ مِنْ غيرِ توقُّفٍ على تكرُّرٍ ولا وضعِ واضعٍ.

§12 As for the rational judgement (*ḥukm ʿaqlī*), it is the affirmation or negation of a matter without reliance on repetition or the stipulation of a stipulator.

§١٣ وأقسامُهُ ثلاثةٌ: الوجوبُ، والاستحالةُ، والجوازُ.

§13 Its categories are three:
1. necessity (*wujūb*),
2. impossibility (*istiḥālah*),
3. possibility (*jawāz*).

§١٤ فالواجبُ: ما لا يُتصوَّرُ في العقلِ عدمُهُ؛ إمَّا ضرورةً؛ كالتحيُّزِ للجِرْمِ، وإمَّا نظرًا؛ كوجوبِ القِدَمِ لمولانا جلَّ وعزَّ.

§14 The necessary (*wājib*) is that which the intellect cannot conceive as nonexistent. It is either immediate (*ḍarūrī*) – such as a body occupying space; or speculative (*naẓarī*) – such as the necessity of pre-eternity for our Lord (majestic and mighty is He).

§١٥ والمستحيلُ: ما لا يُتصوَّرُ في العقلِ وجودُهُ؛ إمَّا ضرورةً؛ كتعرِّي الجِـرْمِ عنِ الحركةِ والسـكونِ معًـا، وإمَّا نظرًا؛ كالشـريكِ لمولانا جلَّ وعزَّ.

§15 The impossible (*mustaḥīl*) is that which the intellect cannot conceive as existent. It is either immediate – such as a body being devoid of both motion and rest; or speculative – such as a partner for our Lord (majestic and mighty is He).

§١٦ والجائزُ: ما يصحُّ في العقلِ وجودُهُ وعدمُهُ؛ إمَّا ضرورةً؛ كالحركةِ لنا، وإمَّا نظرًا؛ كتعذيبِ المطيعِ وإثابةِ العاصي.

§16 The possible (*jā'iz*) is that which the intellect deems both existence and nonexistence conceivable. It is either immediate – such as our motion – or speculative – such as punishment of the obedient and rewarding the disobedient.

§١٧ والمذاهبُ في الأفعالِ ثلاثةٌ: مذهبُ الجبريَّةِ، ومذهبُ القدريَّةِ، ومذهبُ أهلِ السنَّةِ.

§17 The doctrines concerning volitional acts are three: the doctrine of the Jabariyyah, the Qadariyyah, and the People of the Sunnah.

فمذهـبُ الجبريَّـةِ: وجـودُ الأفعالِ كلِّهـا بالقدرةِ الأزليَّةِ فقـطْ مِنْ غيرِ مُقارَنَةٍ لقدرةٍ حادثةٍ.

The doctrine of the Jabariyyah is that all actions exist through the past-eternal capability alone – without concurrence with any originated capability.

ومذهبُ القدريَّة: وجودُ الأفعالِ الاختياريَّةِ بالقدرةِ الحادثةِ فقطْ مباشرةً أو تَوَلُّدًا.

The doctrine of the Qadariyyah is that volitional acts exist through an originated capability alone – whether directly or through causal generation (*tawallud*).

ومذهبُ أهلِ السنَّةِ: وجودُ الأفعالِ كلِّها بالقدرةِ الأزليِّ فقطْ معَ مُقارَنَةِ الأفعالِ الاختياريَّةِ لقدرةٍ حادثةٍ لا تأثيرَ لها لا مُباشَرَةً ولا تَوَلُّدًا.

The doctrine of the People of the Sunnah is that all actions exist through the past-eternal capability alone – with voluntary acts occurring in concurrence with an originated capability that has no effect, neither directly nor through causal generation.

§١٨ وأمَّا الكسبُ: فهو عبارةٌ عن تعلُّقِ القدرةِ الحادثةِ بالمقدورِ في محلِّها مِنْ غيرِ تأثيرٍ.

§18 As for acquisition (*kasb*), it refers to the originated capability's connection to an object of capability (*maqdūr*) in its substrate – without any effect.

§١٩ أنواعُ الشركِ ستةٌ:

١. شركُ استقلالٍ: وهو إثباتُ إلهينِ مستقلينِ؛ كشركِ المجوسِ.

٢. وشركُ تبعيضٍ: وهو تركيبُ الإلهِ مِنْ آلهةٍ؛ كشركِ النصارى.

٣. وشركُ تقريبٍ: وهو عبادةُ غيرِ اللَّهِ تعالى ليقرّبَ إلى اللَّهِ تعالى زُلْفَى؛ كشركِ متقدِّمي الجاهليَّةِ.

٤. وشركُ تقليدٍ: وهو عبادةُ غيرِ اللَّهِ تعالى تبعًا للغيرِ؛ كشركِ متأخِّري الجاهليَّةِ.

٥. وشركُ أسبابٍ: وهو إسنادُ التأثيرِ للأسبابِ العاديَّةِ؛ كشركِ الفلاسفةِ والطبائعيِّينَ ومَنْ تبعَهم على ذلكَ.

٦. وشركُ الأغراضِ: وهو العملُ لغيرِ اللَّهِ تعالى.

§19 The varieties of shirk (associating partners with Allah) are six.

1. *Shirk* of Independence: this refers to affirming two independent deities – such as the shirk of the Majūs [the Zoroastrians].
2. *Shirk* of Division: this refers to composing the deity from multiple deities – such as the shirk of the Christians.
3. *Shirk* of Approximation: this refers to the worship of other than Allah (exalted is He) as a means of drawing nearer to Him – such as the shirk of the early pre-Islamic Arabs.
4. *Shirk* of Imitation: this refers to the worship of other than Allah (exalted is He) in imitation of others – such as the shirk of the later pre-Islamic Arabs.
5. *Shirk* of Means: this refers to attributing causal influence to customary causes – such as the shirk of the philosophers, the naturalists, and those who follow them in that.
6. *Shirk* of Purposes: this refers to performing acts for other than Allah (exalted is He).

§٢٠ وحكمُ الأربعةِ الأوَّلِ: الكفرُ بالإجماعِ، وحكمُ السادسِ: المعصيةُ مِنْ غيرِ كفرٍ بإجماعٍ، وحكمُ الخامسِ: التفصيلُ؛ فمَنْ قالَ في الأسبابِ العاديَّةِ: إنَّها تُؤَثِّرُ بطبعِها.. فقد حُكِيَ الإجماعُ على كُفْرِهِ، ومَنْ قالَ: إنَّها تُؤَثِّرُ بقُوَّةٍ أودعَها اللَّهُ تعالى فيها.. فهو فاسقٌ مبتدعٌ، وفي كُفْرِهِ قولانِ.

§20 The judgement of the first four is disbelief, by consensus.

The sixth is disobedience without disbelief, also by consensus.

The judgement of the fifth is detailed: if someone claims that customary causes affect by their nature, consensus has been reported on his disbelief. But if he claims they affect through a power Allah (exalted is He) placed in them, then he is an immoral innovator – and there are two opinions regarding his disbelief.

§٢١ وأصولُ الكُفْرِ والبِدَعِ سبعةٌ:

١. الإيجابُ الذاتيُّ: وهو إسنادُ الكائناتِ إلى اللَّهِ تعالى على سبيلِ التعليلِ أو الطبعِ مِنْ غيرِ اختيارٍ.

٢. والتحسينُ العقليُّ: وهو كونُ أفعالِ اللَّهِ تعالى وأحكامِهِ موقوفةً عقلًا على الأغراضِ؛ وهي: جلبُ المصالحِ، ودرءُ المفاسدِ.

٣. والتقليدُ الرديءُ: وهو مُتَابَعَةُ الغيرِ لأجلِ الحميَّةِ والتعصُّبِ مِنْ غيرِ طلبٍ للحقِّ.

٤. والربطُ العاديُّ: وهو إثباتُ التلازُمِ بينَ أمرٍ وأمرٍ وجودًا أو عدمًا بواسطةِ التكرُّرِ.

٥. والجهلُ المركَّبُ: وهو أنْ يجهلَ الحقَّ، ويجهلَ جهلَهُ بهِ.

٦. والتمسُّكُ في عقائدِ الإيمانِ بمجرَّدِ ظواهرِ الكتابِ والسنَّةِ: مِنْ غيرِ تفصيلٍ بينَ ما يستحيلُ ظاهرُهُ منْها وما لا يستحيلُ.

٧. والجهلُ بالقواعدِ العقليَّةِ: التي هي العلمُ بوجوبِ الواجباتِ، وجوازِ الجائزاتِ، واستحالةِ المستحيلاتِ، وباللسانِ العربيِّ: الذي هو علمُ اللغةِ والإعرابِ والبيانِ.

§21 The roots of disbelief and innovation are seven.

1. Intrinsic Necessitation (*ījāb dhātī*): this is ascribing created entities to Allah (exalted is He) by way of causality or nature, without His volition.
2. Rational Moral Appraisal (*taḥsīn ʿaqlī*): this is the view that Allah's actions and judgements (exalted is He) are contingent upon purposes – namely, attaining benefits and averting detriments.

3. Vile Imitation (*taqlīd radīʾ*): this is following others out of tribal solidarity and fanaticism, without any pursuit of the truth.
4. Customary Association (*rabṭ ʿādī*): this is affirming a correlation between two matters – whether in existence or nonexistence – based on repetition.
5. Compound Ignorance (*jahl murakkab*): this is to be ignorant of the truth while also being ignorant of one's ignorance of it.
6. Adherence to Apparent Meanings (*tamassuk bi-ẓawāhir*): this is adherence in matters of belief to the mere outward meanings of the Qur'an and Sunnah – without distinction between those whose apparent meanings are impossible and those which are not.
7. Ignorance of Rational and Linguistic Principles: that is, ignorance of the rational principles by which one knows the necessity of what is necessary, the possibility of what is possible, and the impossibility of what is impossible – and ignorance of the Arabic language, that is, [ignorance of] its lexicology, syntax, and rhetoric.

§٢٢ والموجوداتُ بالنسبةِ إلى المحلِّ والمخصِّصِ أربعةُ أقسامٍ:

١. قسمٌ غنيٌّ عنِ المحلِّ والمخصِّصِ: وهو ذاتُ مولانا جلا وعلا.

٢. وقسمٌ مُفتقِرٌ إلى المحلِّ والمخصِّصِ: وهو الأعراضُ.

٣. وقسمٌ مُفتَقِرٌ إلى المُخصّصِ دونَ المحلِّ: وهو الأجرامُ.

٤. وقسمٌ موجودٌ في المحلِّ ولا يَفْتَقِرُ إلى مخصِّصٍ: وهو صفاتُ مولانا جلَّ وعزَّ.

§22 Existent things (*mawjūdāt*), with respect to a substrate (*maḥall*) and a specifier (*mukhaṣṣiṣ*), are of four categories:

1. A category that is independent of both substrate and specifier – namely, the essence of our Lord (majestic and mighty is He).
2. A category that is dependent upon both substrate and specifier – namely, accidents.

3. A category that is dependent upon a specifier but not a substrate – namely, bodies.
4. A category that exists in a substrate but is independent of a specifier – namely, the attributes of our Lord (majestic and mighty is He).

§٢٣ والممكناتُ المُتقَابِلاتُ ستةٌ: الوجودُ والعدمُ، والمقاديرُ، والصفاتُ، والأزمنةُ، والأمكنةُ، والجهاتُ.

§23 The mutually opposing possibilities are six:

1. existence and nonexistence,
2. magnitudes,
3. attributes,
4. times,
5. places, and
6. directions.

§٢٤ والقدرةُ الأزليَّةُ: عبارةٌ عن صفةٍ يَتَأَتَّى بها إيجادُ كلِّ ممكنٍ وإعدامُهُ على وَفْقِ الإرادةِ.

§24 Past-eternal capability (*qudrah*) is an attribute through which every possible being is brought into existence and brought out of existence – in accordance with the will.

§٢٥ والإرادةُ: صفةٌ يَتَأَتَّى بها تخصيصُ الممكنِ ببعضِ ما يجوزُ عليهِ.

§25 Will (*irādah*) is an attribute through which a possible being is specified with some of its possibilities.

§٢٦ والعلمُ: صفةٌ يَنْكَشِفُ بها المعلومُ على ما هو بهِ.

§26 Knowledge (*ʿilm*) is an attribute through which what is known is disclosed as it truly is.

§٢٧ والحياةُ: صفةٌ يصحُّ ممَّنْ قامَتْ بهِ الإدراكُ.

§27 Life (*ḥayāh*) is an attribute by which the one in whom it subsists is capable of perception.

§٢٨ والسمعُ الأزليُّ: صفةٌ يَنْكَشِفُ بها كلُّ موجودٍ على ما هو بهِ انكشافًا يُبَايِنُ سواهُ ضرورةً، والبصرُ مثلُهُ، والإدراكُ على القولِ بهِ مثلُهما.

§28 Past-eternal hearing (*samʿ*) is an attribute through which every existent is disclosed as it truly is – with a disclosure necessarily distinct from that of any other attribute.

Sight (*baṣar*) is like it.

Perception (*idrāk*), according to the view that affirms it, is like the two.

§٢٩ والكلامُ الأزليُّ: وهو المعنى القائمُ بالذاتِ، المُعَبَّرُ عنهُ بالعباراتِ المختلفاتِ، المُبَايِنُ لجنسِ الحروفِ والأصواتِ، المُنَزَّهُ عنِ البعضِ والكلِّ، والتقديمِ والتأخيرِ، والتجدُّدِ والسكوتِ، واللحنِ والإعرابِ، وسائرِ أنواعِ التغيُّراتِ، المتعلِّقُ بما يتعلَّق بهِ العلمُ مِنَ المتعلَّقاتِ.

§29 Past-eternal speech (*kalām*) is a meaning subsisting in the essence, expressed through various different expressions. It is distinct from the genus of letters and sounds, and is transcendent above part and whole, priority and posteriority, origination and silence, incorrectness and grammatical inflection, and all other types of change. It links to the same objects to which knowledge links.

§٣٠ والكلامُ ينقسمُ إلى خَبَرٍ وإنشاءٍ.

فالخبرُ: ما يَحْتَمِلُ الصدقَ والكَذِبَ لذاتِهِ.

والإنشاءُ: ما لا يحتملُ صدقًا ولا كذبًا لذاتِهِ.

§30 Speech divides into declarative and non-declarative types.

A declarative expression (*khabar*) is that which, by its very essence, admits of truth or falsehood.

A non-declarative expression (*inshāʾ*) is that which, by its very essence, does not admit of truth or falsehood.

§٣١ والصدقُ: عبارةٌ عن مُطابَقَةِ الخبرِ لِمَا في نفسِ الأمرِ، خالفَ الاعتقادَ أم لا.

والكذبُ: عدمُ مطابقةِ الخبرِ لِمَا في نفسِ الأمرِ، وافَقَ الاعتقادَ أم لا.

§31 Truth (*ṣidq*) is the declarative statement's correspondence to what is in reality, whether or not it agrees with one's belief.

Falsehood (*kadhib*) is the declarative statement's non-correspondence to what is in reality, whether or not it agrees with one's belief.

§٣٢ والأمانةُ: حفظُ جميعِ الجوارحِ الظاهرةِ والباطنةِ مِنَ التلبُّسِ بمَنْهِيٍّ عنهُ نهْيَ تحريمٍ أو كراهةٍ.

والخيانةُ: عدمُ حفظِهما مِنْ ذلكَ.

§32 Trustworthiness (*amānah*) is protecting all external and internal faculties from engaging in anything prohibited or reprehensible.

Treachery (*khiyānah*) is failing to protect them from such things.

§٣٣ وباللّٰهِ تعالى التوفيقُ.

§33 And success is only through Allah (exalted is He). ❧

AL-SANŪSĪ'S
SHARḤ AL-MUQADDIMĀT

شرح المقدمات

Commentary on
The Prolegomena
to Islamic Theology

AUTHOR'S INTRODUCTION

مقدّمة المؤلف

بسم اللّٰه الرحمن الرحيم، وبه نستعين

In the name of Allah the All-Merciful, the Ever-Merciful; in Him we seek assistance

§٠ قال الشيخ الفقيه الإمام العالم الولي الصالح؛ أبو عبد اللّٰه محمّد بن يوسف السنوسيّ الحسنيّ رحمه اللّٰه ونفعنا به:

§0 The shaykh, jurist, imām, scholar, saintly ally of Allah, Abū ʿAbd Allāh Muḥammad ibn Yūsuf al-Sanūsī al-Ḥasanī (may Allah have mercy on him and benefit us through him), said:

الحمد لله ربّ العالمين، والصلاة والسلام على سيّدنا محمّد خاتم النبيّين وإمام المرسلين، ورضي اللّٰه تعالى عن آله وصحبه أجمعين.

Praise be to Allah, Lord of the worlds, and blessings and peace be upon our master Muḥammad, the Seal of the Prophets and the Leader of the Messengers. And may Allah (exalted is He) be pleased with all his family and companions.

وبعد:

To proceed:

فهذه كلمات قصدت بها شـرح ما وضعته من المقدّمات على سـبيل الاختصار، ومن اللّه سبحانه أسأل التوفيق للحقّ والصواب في الأقوال والأفعال فهو المولى الكريم القادر الذي يخلق ما يشاء ويختار.

With these words, I intended to explain – briefly – the prolegomena I had set forth. From Allah (glory be to Him), I ask for success in attaining truth and correctness in words and deeds, for He is the Noble Master, the Powerful who creates what He wills and chooses.

THE FIRST PROLEGOMENON

ON THE JUDGEMENTS

المقدّمة الأولى في الأحكام

§١ الحكمُ: إثباتُ أمرٍ أو نفْيُهُ.

§1 A judgement (*ḥukm*) is the affirmation or negation of a matter.

§١-٠ يعني: أن من أدرك أمرًا من الأمور:

§1.0 Meaning: That whoever apprehends a matter among matters:

فإمّا أن يتصوّر معناه فقط ولم يحكم بثبوته ولا نفيه، فهذا الإدراك يُسَمّى في الاصطلاح: تصوّرًا؛ كإدراكنا مثلًا أنّ معنى الحدوث: الوجود بعد عدم، ولم نثبته لأمر ولا نفيناه عنه.

(1) Either the meaning alone is conceived, without affirming or denying its establishment (*thubūt*). This apprehension is termed – technically – *conception* (*taṣawwur*).

For example: our apprehensions that the meaning of origination (*ḥudūth*) is existence after nonexistence, without affirming it of a thing or denying it thereof.

وإمّا أن يتصوّر مع ذلك ثبوت ذلك المعنى لأمر أو نفيه عنه، فهذا الإدراك يُسَمّى في الاصطلاح: تصديقًا، ويُسَمّى أيضًا: حكمًا؛ كإثباتنا الحدوث مثلًا -بعد تصوّرنا لمعناه- للعوالم؛ وهي ما سوى

المولـى تبـارك وتعالى، فنقـول: العوالم حادثـة، أو نفيناه عمّن وجب قدمه؛ وهو مولانا تبارك وتعالى، فنقول: مولانا جلّ وعزّ ليس بحادث.

(2) Or it may be that, along with that, the affirmation (*thubūt*) of that meaning for a thing – or its negation from it – is conceived. This cognition is termed, in technical usage, *assent* (*taṣdīq*), and is also called *judgement* (*ḥukm*).

For example: our affirming origination (*ḥudūth*) – after conceiving its meaning – of the *worlds* (*ʿāwālim*, which are all that is other than the Exalted Lord), so that we say: "The worlds are originated"; or our negating it from the One whose pre-eternity is necessary, namely our Exalted Lord, so that we say: "Our Lord (majestic and mighty) is not originated."

فإثبات أمر لأمر أو نفيه عنه هو المُسَمّى حكمًا، وبالله تعالى التوفيق.

Thus, affirming something of a thing or negating it from it is what is termed *judgement* (*ḥukm*). And success is from Allah (exalted is He).

§٢ وينقسمُ إلى ثلاثةِ أقسامٍ: شرعيٍّ، وعاديٍّ، وعقليٍّ.

§2 It divides into three divisions: legal, customary, and rational.

§٢-٠ يعنـي: أنّ الحكـم الـذي هو إثبات أمر أو نفيه يتنوّع إلى ثلاثة أقسـام؛ بمعنى: الأنواع؛ وهي الثلاثة المذكورة؛ لأنّ الثبوت أو النفي اللذين في الحكم: إمّا أن يسندا إلى الشرع بحيث لا يمكن أن يعلما إلّا منه، أو لا، والثاني إمّا أن يكتفي العقل في إدراكه من غير احتياج إلى تكرّر واختبار، أو لا.

§2.0 Meaning: That the judgement (which is the affirmation or negation of a matter) is divided into three divisions – that is, kinds – which are the three mentioned.

For the affirmation or negation in the judgement is either ascribed to the divine legislation (*sharʿ*), such that it cannot be known except through it, or not. The second – if not ascribed to the divine legislation – is either such that the intellect suffices in apprehending it without the need for repetition and testing, or not.

فالأوّل: الشرعيّ: كقولنا في الإثبات: الصلوات الخمس واجبة، وقولنا في النفي: صوم يوم عاشوراء ليس بواجب.

§2.1 The first is the *legal judgement* (*sharʿī*). For example: our statement in affirmation, "The five prayers are obligatory," and our statement in negation, "Fasting on the day of ʿĀshūrāʾ is not obligatory."

والثاني: العقليّ: كقولنا في الإثبات: العشرة زوج، وقولنا في النفي: السبعة ليست بزوج، وقولنا في النفي أيضًا: الضدّان لا يجتمعان.

The second is the *rational judgement* (*ʿaqlī*). For example: our statement in affirmation, "Ten is even," and our statement in negation, "Seven is not even," and our statement also in negation, "Contraries do not coexist."

والثالث: العاديّ: كقولنا في الإثبات: شراب السكنجبين مسكّن للصفراء، وقولنا في النفي: الفطير من الخبز ليس بسريع الانهضام.

The third is the *customary judgement* (*ʿādī*). For example: our statement in affirmation, "Syrup of oxymel is a sedative for bile," and our statement in negation, "Unleavened bread is not easily digestible."

ثمّ ينقسم هذا العاديّ إلى قسمين:

١. عاديّ قوليّ: كرفع الفاعل، ونصب المفعول، ونحو ذلك من الأحكام اللغويّة أو النحويّة.

٢. وعاديّ فعليّ: كالمثالين المذكورين.

Then this customary judgement (*ʿādī*) is divided into two divisions:

1. *verbal customary* (*ʿādī qawlī*) – such as the nominative of the agent, the accusative of the object, and the like among linguistic or grammatical rulings; and
2. *actual customary* (*ʿādī fiʿlī*) – such as the two aforementioned examples.

وكلّ واحد من هذه الأقسام الثلاثة - وهي الشرعيّ والعقليّ والعاديّ - ينقسم إلى قسمين: ضروريّ ونظريّ.

فالضروريّ: ما يدرك ثبوته أو نفيه بلا تأمّل.

والنظريّ: ما لا يدرك عادة إلّا بالتأمّل.

§2.2 Each of these three divisions – the legal, the rational, and the customary – is divided into two divisions: the immediate, and the speculative.

The *immediate* (*ḍarūrī*) is that whose affirmation (*thubūt*) or negation is apprehended without speculation.

The *speculative* (*naẓarī*) is that which is not usually apprehended except through contemplation.

فمثال الحكم الشرعيّ الضروريّ: حكمنا بأنّ الصلاة واجبة، والزنا محرّم، ونحو ذلك.

An example of an immediate legal judgement (*ḥukm sharʿī ḍarūrī*) is our judgement that prayer is obligatory, fornication is forbidden, and the like.

ومثال الحكم الشرعيّ النظريّ: حكمنا بأنّ اقتضاء الطعام من ثمن الطعام لا يجوز، وأنّ الزعفران ليس بربويّ.

An example of a speculative legal judgement (*ḥukm sharʿī naẓarī*) is our judgement that stipulating food in exchange for the price of food is impermissible, and that saffron is not subject to ribā.

ومثـال الحكـم العقلـيّ الضـروريّ: حكمنـا بأنّ النفـي والثبـوت لا يجتمعان.

An example of an immediate rational judgement (*ḥukm ʿaqlī ḍarūrī*) is our judgement that affirmation and negation do not coexist.

ومثال الحكم العقليّ النظريّ: حكمنا بأنّ الواحد ربع عشر الأربعين.

An example of a speculative rational judgement (*ḥukm ʿaqlī naẓarī*) is our judgement that one is a quarter of a tenth of forty.

ومثـال الحكـم العاديّ الضروريّ: حكمنا بأنّ النار محرقة، وأنّ الثوب ساتر، ونحو ذلك.

An example of an immediate customary judgement (*ḥukm ʿādī ḍarūrī*) is our judgement that fire burns, that a garment covers, and the like.

ومثال الحكم العاديّ النظريّ: ما تقدّم من مثالَي السكنجبين والخبز الفطير، وأكثر أحكام أهل الطبّ عاديّة نظريّة.

An example of a speculative customary judgement (*ḥukm ʿādī naẓarī*) is the pair of examples mentioned earlier – oxymel and unleavened bread. Most of the judgements of physicians are customary and speculative.

وفائدة معرفة الضروريّ والنظريّ في الحكم الشـرعيّ: معرفة ما يوجب إنـكاره الكفـر ومـا لا يوجب؛ فإنّ مَن أنكر مـا علم من الدين ضرورةً فهـو كافـر، بخلاف من أنكر الخفيّ الـذي لا يعلمه إلّا القليل؛ فإنّه لا يحكم عليه بالكفر عند كثير من المحقّقين، وباللّٰه تعالى التوفيق.

§2.3 The benefit of knowing the immediate (*ḍarūrī*) and the speculative (*naẓarī*) in the legal judgement is to distinguish what renders its denial disbelief from what does not. For whoever denies what is necessarily known of the religion is an unbeliever, unlike one who denies what is obscure and known only to a few – for such a person, disbelief is not judged according to many verifiers. And success is from Allah (exalted is He).

§٣ فالشـرعيُّ: خطابُ اللّهِ تعالى المتعلّقِ بأفعـالِ المكلّفينَ بالطلبِ أوِ الإباحةِ، أو الوضعِ لهما.

§3 The legal [judgement] is the address of Allah (exalted is He) related to the actions of morally responsible individuals, whether in the form of a demand, permission, or stipulation concerning either of them.

§٣-٠ قوله: (خطاب) كالجنس في الحدّ.

§3.0 His statement, "address" (*khiṭāb*) is like the genus[2] in the definition.

وحقيقة الخطاب: الكلام الذي يقصد به من هو أهل للفهم.

The reality of *address* (*khiṭāb*) is speech intended for one who is qualified for understanding.

واختلف: هل من شرط التسمية به وجود المخاطب أم لا؟

وعلـى ذلـك جرى الخلاف في كلام اللّه تعالى: هل يُسَـمّى في الأزل خطابًا قبل وجود المخاطبين أم لا؟

There is a disagreement: is the presence of the addressee a condition for naming with it, or not?

Accordingly, the disagreement concerns the speech of Allah, exalted is He: Is it called *address* (*khiṭāb*) in past-eternity before the existence of those addressed, or not?

2 A genus (*jins*) is the universal predicated of many things differing in realities, in answer to "What is it?" – such as *animal* in relation to *human*.

والمراد بالخطاب هنا: المخاطَب به؛ من إطلاق المصدر على اسم المفعول.

§3.1 What is meant by "address" (*khiṭāb*) here is that which is addressed – an instance of using the verbal noun to denote the object acted upon (that is, the passive participle).

وإضافة الخطاب إلى اللّٰه تبارك وتعالى يخرج خطاب غيره؛ كالملوك والآباء والأمّهات والمشايخ.

وبالجملة: يخرج بهذا القيد خطاب من سوى اللّٰه تعالى؛ من الملائكة والإنس والجنّ، فلا يُسَمّى خطاب هؤلاء كلّهم حكمًا شرعيًّا، وإنّما يُسَمّى خطاب الرسل بالتكاليف حكمًا شرعيًّا؛ لأنّهم مبلّغون عن اللّٰه تعالى، معصومون في تبليغهم من الكذب عمدًا وسهوًا.

Attributing the address to Allah (blessed and exalted is He) excludes the address of others – such as kings, fathers, mothers, and elders.

In sum: by this qualification, the address of any other than Allah (exalted is He) is excluded – such as the angels, humans, and jinn – so the address of all these is not called a legal ruling. Rather, only the address of the messengers concerning obligations is called a legal ruling, because they are transmitters on behalf of Allah (exalted is He) and are infallible in their transmission from both intentional and unintentional falsehood.

وقوله: (المتعلّق بأفعال المكلّفين) يخرج أربعة أشياء:

الأوّل: خطابه تعالى المتعلّق بذاته العليّة: نحو: ﴿لَا إِلَهَ إِلَّا اللَّهُ﴾ [الصافات: ٣٥].

الثانـي: الخطاب المتعلّق بفعله: نحو: ﴿اللَّهُ خَالِقُ كُلِّ شَـيْءٍ﴾ [الرعد: ١٦].

الثالـث: الخطـاب المتعلّـق بالجمـادات: نحـو: ﴿وَيَـوْمَ نُسَـيِّرُ الْجِبالَ﴾ [الكهف: ٤٧].

الرابع: الخطاب المتعلّق بذوات المكلّفين: نحو: ﴿ولقد خلقناكم ثمّ صورناكم﴾ (الأعراف: ١١].

His statement, "that pertains to the acts of morally responsible individuals," excludes four things:

First: His (exalted is He) address pertaining to His sublime essence (*dhāt*) – such as: "There is no god but Allah."[3]

Second: The address pertaining to His act – such as: "Allah is the Creator of all things."[4]

Third: The address pertaining to inanimate objects – such as: "And [mention] the Day We shall cause the mountains to move."[5]

Fourth: The address pertaining to the essences (*dhawāt*) of the morally responsible – such as His saying, "And We certainly created you, then We fashioned you."[6]

والمراد بفعل المكلّف: ما يصدر منه؛ ليشمل القول والنيّة.

والمكلّـف: هـو البالغ العاقل، ومـن هنا يعلم: أنّ الصبيّ لا يتعلّق حكـم، هكـذا قيل، وانظر هذا مع مـا ذكر في الأصول من الخلاف في الأمر بالأمر بالشيء: هل هو أمر بذلك الشيء أم لا؟

فإن قيـل: ليـس أمرًا.. فبقي الصبيان لم يأمزهـم الشـرع، فالمتعلّق بهم ليس حكم الشرع، بل حكم أوليائهـم.

3 al-Ṣāffāt: 37:35.
4 al-Ra'd: 13:16.
5 al-Kahf: 18:47.
6 al-A'rāf: 7:11.

وإن قلنـا: إنّـه أمـر بـه.. فالأقـرب أنّ الصبيان مكلّفون من الشـرع بمثل هذا الأمر.

§3.2 What is meant by "the act of the morally responsible individual" is that which issues from him, so as to include speech and intention.

The legally responsible individual (*mukallaf*) is one who has reached maturity and possesses intellect. From this, it is understood that no ruling pertains to a child – so it has been stated.

Consider this alongside what is mentioned in the principles regarding the disagreement over the command to command something: is it itself a command of that thing, or not? If it is said that it is not a command, then children remain unaddressed by the divine legislation. Thus, what pertains to them is not a ruling of the divine legislation, but rather a ruling of their guardians. But if we say it is a command concerning it, then the closer view is that children are charged by the divine legislation with such a command.

وإذا كان النـدب تكليفًـا فـي حقّ البالغين على قـول مع أنّه لا يلحق بتركه عقوبة شرعيّة لا في الدنيا ولا في الآخرة.. فأمر الصبيان بالصلاة أقرب لأنّ يكون تكليفًا؛ لاستحقاقهم بتركها عقوبة الشرع في الدنيا، هذا فيمَن بلغ منهم عشـر سـنين، ومن لم يبلغها كان طلب الصلاة منه كالمندوب في حقّ من بلغ؛ وهو تكليف على قول، اللّهمّ إلّا أن يوجد إجماع على أنّ البلوغ شرط التكليف، فانظر ذلك.

If recommendation (*nadb*) is considered a legal obligation (*taklīf*) for those who have reached legal majority – according to one opinion – despite its omission not entailing legal punishment in this world or the hereafter, then commanding children to perform prayer is even closer to being a legal obligation, since they are liable to legal punishment in this world for omitting it.

This applies to those who have reached the age of ten. As for those who have not, the request for prayer from them is like recommendation for one who has reached legal majority – and that is a legal obligation according to one opinion, unless there is consensus (*ijmāʿ*) that legal majority is a condition for legal obligation. So consider this.

قولـه: (بالطلـب، أو الإباحـة، أو الوضـع لهمـا) المجـرور الـذي هو (بالطلـب) أحسـن مـا فيـه أن يتعلّـق بقوله: (خطـاب)، وفيه وصف المصـدر قبـل إعمالـه، إلّا أنّـه يسـهّله أنّ المجرور يعمـل فيه العامل الضعيـف والقـويّ، وأيضًا: فالمصدر هنا لم يبق على حقيقته، وإنّما المراد به: المخاطب به، على ما سبق.

His statement, "by command, or permissibility, or stipulated for them": the genitive phrase – namely "by command" – is best construed as connected to His statement, "address." In this, the verbal noun is being described before being put to use. This is facilitated by the fact that both weak and strong agents may govern a genitive. Moreover, the verbal noun here no longer retains its literal meaning (*ḥaqīqah*); rather, what is meant by it is that which is addressed, as previously mentioned.

قولـه: (أو الوضـع لهما) معطوف على الإباحـة؛ أي: تعلّق الخطاب بالأفعال: إمّا بأنّ يطلب فيها طلبًا، أو بأنّ يبيحها، أو بأنّ يضع سببًا وشبهه لها.

His statement, "or the stipulation for both," is conjoined to "permissibility"; that is, the address pertains to actions either by requesting them, by permitting them, or by designating a cause or something similar for them.

وتخصيص هذا النوع من الأحكام باسم الوضع محض اصطلاح، وإلّا فالأحكام كلّها -أعني: المتعلّقات بالأفعال التنجيزيّة- بوضع الشرع، لا مجال للعقل ولا للعادة في شيء منها.

The designation of this type of rulings by the name "stipulative" (*waḍʿ*) is purely terminological; otherwise, all rulings – namely, those pertaining to actualised actions – are stipulative on the part of the Lawgiver. There is no scope for the intellect or for customary practice in any of them.

§٤ ويَدْخُلُ في الطلبِ أربعةٌ: الإيجابُ، والندبُ، والتحريمُ، والكراهةُ.

§4 Four [legal judgements] are included under demand:
1. obligation (*ījāb*),
2. recommendation (*nadb*),
3. prohibition (*taḥrīm*), and
4. reprehensibility (*karāhah*).

فالإيجابُ: وهو طلبُ الفعلِ طلبًا جازمًا؛ كالإيمانِ باللّهِ ورُسُـلِهِ، وكقواعدِ الإسلامِ الخمسِ.

***Obligation* (*ījāb*) is the request to perform an act with decisiveness – such as belief in Allah and His Messengers, and the five pillars of Islam.**

والندبُ: وهو طلبُ الفعلِ طلبًا غيرَ جازمٍ؛ كصلاةِ الفجرِ ونحوِها.

***Recommendation* (*nadb*) is the request to perform an act without decisiveness – such as praying the Fajr Prayer.**

والتحريمُ: وهو طلبُ الكفِّ عنِ الفعلِ طلبًا جازمًا؛ كشـربِ الخمرِ والزنا ونحوِهما.

***Prohibition* (*taḥrīm*) is the request to abstain from an act with decisiveness – such as drinking wine, fornication, and the like.**

والكراهةُ: وهي طلبُ الكفِّ عنِ الفعلِ طلبًا غيرِ جازمٍ؛ كقراءةِ القرآنِ في الركوعِ والسجودِ مثلًا.

***Reprehensibility* (*karāhah*) is the request to abstain from an act without decisiveness – such as reciting the Qurʾān during bowing and prostration.**

وأمَّا الإباحةُ: فهي إذنُ الشرعِ في الفعلِ والتركِ معًا مِنْ غيرِ ترجيحِ لأحدِهما على الآخرِ؛ كالنكاحِ والبيعِ ونحوِهما.

As for *permissibility* (*ibāḥah*), it is the divine legislation authorising both performing and foregoing an act – without either being preferred over the other – such as marriage, trade, and the like.

§٤-٠ لا إشكال في دخول الأربعة الأحكام في الطلب؛ لأنّ الطلب: إمّا طلب فعل أو طلب ترك، وكلّ واحد منهما: إمّا جازم أو غير جازم، فالمجموع أربعة؛ من ضرب اثنين في اثنين.

§4.0 There is no problem in the inclusion of the four rulings under the category of demand; for demand is either a demand for an act or a demand for omission, and each of the two is either decisive or non-decisive. The total is four, by multiplying two by two.

وقولنا في حدّ الإيجاب: (طلب) جنس في الحدّ.

Our statement in the definition of obligation, "a demand," is the genus in the definition.

وقولنا: (الفعل) فصل يخرج التحريم والكراهة؛ لأنّهما طلب كفّ عن فعل، لا طلب فعل.

Our statement, "action," is the differentia[7] that excludes prohibition and disapproval, for both are a demand to refrain from an action, not a demand to perform one.

وقولنا: (طلبًا جازمًا) يخرج الندب؛ لأنّه طلب للفعل من غير جزم في الطلب؛ بألا يؤذن في الترك، بل هو قد سمح له في الترك، ولا يخفى عليك معرفة ما يحترز بالقيود عنه في سائر الحدود.

Our statement, "a decisive request," excludes recommendation (*nadb*), for it is a request to perform an act without decisiveness, since omission is not prohibited – rather, it is permitted. You are no doubt aware of what is excluded by such qualifications in all other definitions.

واعلم: أنّ مذهب جمهور الأصوليّين: أنّ الأحكام التكليفيّة -وهي التي يخاطب بها المكلّفون- خمسة: الإباحة والأربعة الداخلة في الطلب.

Know that the position of the majority of the scholars of *uṣūl* is that the prescriptive rulings (*aḥkām taklīfiyyah*) – which are those addressed to morally responsible agents – are five: permissibility, and the four that fall under the category of request.

وزاد السبكيّ سادسًا؛ وهو خلاف الأولى؛ لأنّ النهي غير الجازم عنده إن تعلّق بالكفّ عن فعل بدلالة المطابقة؛ كالنفي المتعلّق بالقراءة في الركوع مثلًا.. فهو الكراهة، وإن تعلّق بالكفّ عن الفعل بدلالة الالتزام؛ كدلالة طلب المندوب بدلالة الالتزام على النهي عن ضدّه.. فهو خلاف الأولى؛ كطلب قيام الليل؛ فإنّه يدلّ بالالتزام على النهي عن ضدّه؛ كنوم الليل كلّه، فيطلق على النوم أنّه خلاف

7 A differentia (*faṣl*) is the universal predicated of a thing in answer to "Which species is it?" – such as *rational* in relation to *human*.

الأولى، ولا يطلق عليه أنّه مكروه. وتبع السبكيّ في زيادة هذا القسم السادس إمامَ الحرمين، قال: (والإمام أوّل من علمناه ذكره)، قال العراقيّ: (بل نقله الإمام عن غيره فقال: إنّه ممّا أحدثه المتأخّرون).

Al-Subkī added a sixth: that which is contrary to what is preferable (*khilāf al-awlā*). This is because, in his view, a non-decisive prohibition, if it pertains to refraining from an act by way of denotation (*dalālat al-muṭābaqah*) – such as a negation related to recitation during bowing – is considered reprehensibility (*karāhah*). But if it pertains to refraining from an act by way of implicature (*dalālat al-iltizām*) – such as the implied prohibition of a contrary action entailed by the request to perform a recommended act – then it is considered something contrary to what is preferable. For example, the request to perform night prayer implies, by implicature, a prohibition of its contrary – such as sleeping the entire night. Thus, sleep is described as contrary to what is preferable, but it is not described as reprehensible (*makrūh*).

In adding this sixth category, al-Subkī followed Imām al-Ḥaramayn. He [al-Subkī] said: "The Imām is the first whom we know to have mentioned it." Al-ʿIrāqī responded: "Rather, the Imām transmitted it from someone else, saying that it is among the things introduced by the later scholars."

§٥ وأمّا الوضعُ لهما: فهو عبارةٌ عن نصبِ الشارعِ أمارةً على حكمٍ مِنْ تلكَ الأحكامِ الخمسةِ.

§5 As for their being stipulated (*waḍʿ*), it refers to the Lawgiver placing an indicator for one of those five judgements.

§٥-٠ يعني: أنّ الحكم الوضعيّ: عبارة عن جعل الشارع أمرًا من الأمور أمارةً على حكم من تلك الأحكام الخمسة، سواء كان ذلك المجعول أمارةً من أفعال المكلّفين؛ كجعل السرقة سببًا للقطع، أو

ليس من أفعالهم؛ كجعل زوال الشمس سببًا لإيجاب صلاة الظهر مثلًا.

§5.0 Meaning: The stipulative ruling (*ḥukm waḍʿī*) is the Lawgiver's designation of a given matter as a sign for one of the five rulings – whether that designated sign is an act of a morally responsible agent – such as making theft a cause for amputation; or not – such as making the sun's passing the zenith a cause for the obligation of the Ẓuhr prayer, for example.

وقوله: (نصب الشارع أمارةً) أشار بلفظ (أمارة) إلى أن أحكام اللّٰه تعالى ليست تابعةً للأسباب والشروط والموانع، بل هذه الأمور أمارات على الأحكام، نعرفها نحن منها لخفائها علينا، وليس شيء منها باعثًا لمولانا جلّ وعزّ على حكم من الأحكام كما زعم من ضلّ وابتدع.

His statement, "the Lawgiver has appointed a sign," by the word "sign" (*amārah*), indicates that the rulings of Allah (exalted is He) do not follow from causes, conditions, or impediments. Rather, these matters are signs (*amārāt*) of the rulings – by which we come to know them, due to their being hidden from us. None of these is an impelling cause for our Master (majestic and mighty is He) to issue any ruling, as claimed by those who have gone astray and innovated.

§٦ وهي: السببُ، والشرطُ، والمانعُ.

§6 They are: cause, condition, and impediment.

§٦-٠ الضمير يعود على الأمارة، ووجه انحصار الأمارة في هذه الثلاثة: أنّ ما يجعله الشرع أمارةً على حكم من الأحكام:

١. إمّا أن يجعل كلّ واحد من وجوده وعدمه أمارةً ودليلًا.

٢. أو يجعل عدمه فقط أمارةً.

٣. أو يجعل وجوده فقط أمارةً.

فالأوّل: السبب، والثاني: الشرط، والثالث: المانع.

§6.0 The pronoun refers to the sign (*amārah*), and the reason for restricting the *amārah* to these three is that whatever the divine legislation designates as a sign for a ruling among the rulings must fall under one of them. Either it makes:

1. both the existence and nonexistence of a thing a sign and proof (*dalīl*);
2. only its nonexistence a sign; or
3. only its existence a sign.

The first is the cause, the second the condition, and the third the impediment.

§٧ فالسببُ: ما يلزمُ مِنْ وجودِهِ الوجودُ، ومِن عدمِهِ العدمُ لذاتِهِ؛ كزوالِ الشمسِ لوجوبِ الظهرِ مثلًا.

§7 A cause (*sabab*) is that (*mā*) whose existence entails existence, and whose nonexistence entails nonexistence – by its very essence. Such as the sun's passing the zenith for the obligation of the Ẓuhr prayer, for instance.

§٧-٠ قوله: (ما) كالجنس.

§7.0 His statement, "*mā*" is like the genus.

وقوله: (يلزم من وجوده الوجود) فصل يخرج الشرط والمانع.

His statement, "whose existence entails existence," is a clause that excludes the condition and the impediment.

وقوله: (ومن عدمه العدم) يخرج الدليل على الحكم من الكتاب أو السنّة أو الإجماع أو القياس، فإنّ الدليل يلزم طرده؛ أي: يلزم من

وجـوده الوجـود، ولا يلزم عكسـه؛ أي: لا يلزم من عدمـه العدم، أمّا السبب فإنّه يلزم طرده وعكسه.

His statement, "and whose nonexistence, nonexistence," excludes the evidences for a ruling derived from the Book, the Sunnah, consensus, or analogical reasoning (*qiyās*). For evidence entails the ruling when present – that is, the ruling follows from its presence – but the converse does not hold: the ruling does not cease to exist simply because the evidence is absent. As for the cause (*sabab*), both forward entailment and its converse apply – the ruling follows from its presence, and its absence follows from its absence.

وقوله: (لذاته) يدخل السبب الذي لم يلزم من وجوده الوجود لمقارنته انتفاء شرط؛ كالعقل والبلوغ، أو وجود مانع لوجود المسبّب؛ كالحيض الذي يقارن دخول الوقت ونحوه، فإنّ السبب في ذاته يقتضي وجود المسبّب، وإنّما انتفى المسبّب لما عرض له من وجود المانع أو نفي الشرط.

His statement, "by its very essence," includes the cause from which the effect does not follow due to the accompanying absence of a condition – such as intellect or maturity; or the presence of an impediment to the effect – such as menstruation coinciding with the entry of the prayer time and the like. For the cause, in its essence, entails the existence of the effect; the effect is absent only due to the presence of an impediment or the absence of a condition.

ويدخـل أيضًـا في هذا القيد: السـبب الذي لم يلـزم من عدمه العدم لمقارنـة عدمـه وجود سـبب آخر؛ كوجود البول المقـارن لعدم الغائط الذي هو أحد أسباب وجوب الطهارة.

Also included under this qualification is a cause whose nonexistence does not entail nonexistence due to its absence coinciding with the presence of another cause. For example: the presence of urine coinciding with the absence of faeces, which is one of the causes of the obligation of purification.

§٨ والشرطُ: ما يلزمُ مِنْ عدمِهِ العدمُ، ولا يلزمُ مِنْ وجودِهِ وجودٌ ولا عدمٌ لذاتِهِ؛ كتمامِ الحولِ لوجوبِ الزكاةِ.

§8 A condition (*sharṭ*) is that whose nonexistence entails nonexistence, while its presence entails neither existence nor nonexistence – by its very essence. For example: the completion of a lunar year for the obligation of Zakāh.

§٨-٠ الشرط في اللغة: هو العلامة، ومنه: أشراط الساعة؛ أي: علاماتها. وأمّا في الاصطلاح: فمعناه ما ذكر، وهو ينقسم إلى: شرط عقليّ، وشرط عاديّ، وشرط شرعيّ.

§8.0 A condition (*sharṭ*), in language, is a sign – as in: the portents (*ashrāṭ*) of the Hour, meaning its signs.

In technical usage, its meaning is as mentioned. It is divided into rational condition, customary condition, and legal condition.

مثال الشرط العقليّ: الحياة للإدراك؛ فإنّه يلزم من عدم الحياة عدم الإدراك، ولا يلزم من وجود الحياة وجود الإدراك ولا عدمه؛ لأنّه قد توجد الحياة ويكون معها غيبة بنوم أو إغماء أو جنون، حتى لا يدرك الحيّ مع هذه الآفات شيئًا أصلًا.

An example of the rational condition (*sharṭ ʿaqlī*) is life as a condition for perception, for the nonexistence of life entails the nonexistence of perception, while the existence of life does not entail either the existence or nonexistence of perception. This is because life may exist alongside sleep, fainting, or madness – such that the living being, afflicted by these states, perceives nothing whatsoever.

ومثـال الشـرط العـاديّ: النطفة في الرحم للـولادة؛ فإنّه يلزم من نفي النطفـة فـي الرحم نفي الـولادة، ولا يلزم من وجـود النطفة في الرحم وجـود ولادة ولا عدمهـا؛ لأنّـه بعد أن توجد فـي الرحم قد يكون اللّٰه تعالى منها ولادة وقد لا يكون.

An example of a customary condition (*sharṭ ʿādī*) is the presence of the seed (*nuṭfah*) in the womb for birth, for the absence of semen in the womb entails the absence of birth, but its presence does not entail either the existence or nonexistence of birth – for once it is present in the womb, Allah (exalted is He) may bring about birth from it, or He may not.

ومثال الشـرط الشرعيّ: الطهارة لصحّة الصلاة، وتمام الحول لوجوب الـزكاة في العين والماشـية مثلًا؛ فإنّـه يلزم من نفي الطهارة مع القدرة على تحصيلها عدم صحّة الصلاة، ولا يلزم من حصول الطهارة صحّة الصلاة ولا عدمها؛ لإمكان فسادها بعد حصول الطهارة باختلال ركن مـن أركانهـا ونحو ذلك. وكـذا يلزم من عدم تمام الحول عدم وجوب الـزكاة في العين والماشـية، ولا يلزم مـن حصول تمام الحول وجوب الـزكاة فيهمـا؛ لتوقّفـه على سـبب؛ وهو ملك النصاب ملـكًا كاملًا، وزيادة مجيء الساعي في الماشية إن جرت العادة بمجيئه، ونفي مانع الدين في العين دون الماشية، ونفي مانع الرقّ والكفر فيهما.

An example of a legal condition is purification for the validity of prayer and the completion of a lunar year for the obligation of Zakāh on cash and livestock, for instance. For the absence of purification – while one is able to obtain it – entails the invalidity of the prayer. However, the attainment of purification does not entail either the validity or invalidity of the prayer, due to the possibility of its corruption after purification through the disruption of one of its pillars or the like.

Likewise, the absence of a full year entails the non-obligation of Zakāh on cash and livestock. However, the completion of the year does not entail the obligation of Zakāh on either of them, for it is dependent on a cause: namely, full ownership of the *niṣāb* (minimum zakātable amount) – along with the arrival of the collector in the case of livestock, if his arrival is customary; the absence of the impediment of debt in the case of cash but not livestock; and the absence of the impediments of slavery and disbelief in both.

وقولنا: (لذاته) راجع للجملة الأخيرة، وهي قولنا: (ولا يلزم من وجوده وجود ولا عدم) لأنّ وجود الشرط هو الذي قد يتّفق أن يصحبه وجود مانع، فيلزم فيه عدم المشروط حينئذٍ، لكن لا بالنظر إلى ذات الشرط، بل بالنظر إلى ذات المانع.

Our statement, "by its very essence" (*li-dhātihi*), refers back to the final clause – namely, our saying, "while its presence entails neither existence nor nonexistence" – because the existence of the condition may happen to coincide with the existence of an impediment, in which case the nonexistence of the conditioned would follow. However, this is not due to the essence of the condition, but rather due to the essence of the impediment.

وقد يصحب وجوده وجود السبب ونفي المانع، فيلزم حينئذٍ من وجوده وجود المشروط؛ كما لو صاحب تمام الحول وجود السبب؛ وهو ملك النصاب ملكًا كاملًا، ونفي المانع الذي هو الدين، فيلزم حينئذٍ وجوب الزكاة، لكن لم تجب بالنظر إلى ذات الشرط الذي هو تمام الحول، وإنّما وجبت بسبب ما قارنه من وجود سبب الزكاة ونفي مانعها، ولو صاحب تمام الحول وجود المانع الذي هو الدين مثلًا..

لـزم معـه عدم الزكاة، لكن ليس بالنظر إليه لزم عدمها، بل بالنظر إلى المانع الذي هو الدين.

Its existence may coincide with the existence of the cause and the absence of the impediment – such that the conditioned follows from the presence of the condition. This occurs, for example, when the completion of the year coincides with the presence of the cause – namely, full ownership of the *niṣāb* (minimum zakātable amount) – and the absence of the impediment, which is debt. In that case, Zakāh becomes obligatory. However, it is not obligatory by virtue of the condition itself – that is, the completion of the year – but rather due to what accompanies it: the presence of the cause of Zakāh and the absence of its impediment.

If, however, the completion of the year coincides with the presence of the impediment – such as debt – then Zakāh is not obligatory. But this is not due to the condition itself, but rather due to the impediment, which is debt.

وأمّـا الجملـة الأولى -وهي قولنا: (ما يلزم مـن عدمه العدم)- فمعناها لازم للشـرط على كلّ حال، فلو قيّدناه بذات الشـرط لأوهم أنّه قد لا يلزم من عدم الشـرط عدم المشـروط؛ لمصاحبة عدمه أمرًا يقتضي ذلك، وذلك باطل، وبالله تعالى التوفيق.

As for the first phrase – namely, our statement, "that whose absence entails nonexistence" – its meaning is that the absence of the conditioned necessarily follows from the absence of the condition in every case. Were we to restrict this to the essence (*dhāt*) of the condition, it would suggest that the absence of the condition might not entail the absence of the conditioned, due to that absence being accompanied by something that necessitates it – and that is false. And success is from Allah (exalted is He).

§٩ والمانـعُ: مـا يلزمُ مِنْ وجودِهِ العـدمُ ولا يلزمُ مِنْ عدمِهِ وجودٌ ولا عدمٌ لذاتِهِ؛ كالحيضِ لوجوبِ الصلاةِ.

§9 An impediment (*māniʿ*) is that whose existence entails non-existence, while its nonexistence entails neither existence nor nonexistence – by its very essence. For example: menstruation as an impediment to the obligation of prayer.

§٩-٠ المانع من الشيء على ضربين:

أحدهما: أن يمنع لمنافاته لسببه.

الثاني: أن يمنع منه لمنافاته له في نفسه.

§9.0 The impediment of a thing is of two kinds:

The first: That which prevents it due to opposition to its cause.

The second: That which prevents it due to opposition to the thing itself.

مثـال الأوّل: الديـن فـي زكاة العين؛ فإنّه يمنع مـن وجوبها؛ لمنافاته لسببها الذي هو الملك الكامل للنصاب، ومثله الرقّ؛ فإن كلّ واحد من الدين والرقّ مانع من كمال التصرّف في المال، فلم يثبت معهما الغنى بذلك المال الذي هو حكمه وجوب الزكاة فيه؛ كما قال النبيّ صلّى اللّه عليه وسلّم: «خذها من أغنيائهم، وردّها على فقرائهم».

An example of the first is debt in the case of Zakāh on tangible property – for it prevents the obligation due to its incompatibility with the cause, which is full ownership of the *niṣāb*. Likewise is slavery – for both debt and slavery are impediments to complete disposal over wealth. Thus, such wealth does not constitute affluence, whose ruling is that Zakāh is obligatory upon it – just as the Prophet (may Allah bless him and give him peace) said, "Take it from their affluent ones, and return it to their poor."[8]

8 al-Bukhārī, no. 4347; Muslim, no. 19.

ومثال الثاني: الكفر مثلًا بالنسبة إلى صحّة الصلاة؛ فإنّه مانع من صحّتها لا لمنافاته لسببها من دخول الوقت، بل لمنافاته لها في نفسها؛ إذ لا يمكن مع الكفر التقرّب بها إلى المولى تبارك وتعالى، وهذا معنى قول الأصوليّين: (المانع ينقسم: إلى مانع السبب، وإلى مانع الحكم).

An example of the second is disbelief (*kufr*) in relation to the validity of prayer – for it is an impediment to its validity, not due to opposition to its cause (the entrance of the prayer time), but due to its intrinsic incompatibility with prayer itself. For it is not possible, along with disbelief, to draw near to the Master (blessed and exalted is He) through it.

This is the meaning of the jurists' statement, "An impediment is divided into an impediment to the cause and an impediment to the ruling."

وقولنا أيضًا في حدّ المانع: (لذاته) راجع للجملة الأخيرة؛ وهي قولنا: (ولا يلزم من عدمه وجود ولا عدم) لأنّ عدم المانع أيضًا هو الذي يتّفق أن يصحبه وجود السبب والشرط، فيلزم حينئذٍ من عدمه الوجود، لكن ليس ذات عدمه هي التي اقتضت الوجود، بل الذي اقتضاه اجتماع السبب مع الشرط عند عدم ذلك المانع، وقد يصحب عدم المانع عدم السبب أو عدم الشرط، فيلزم حينئذٍ العدم، لكن ليس لذات عدم المانع، بل لمصاحبة عدم السبب أو عدم الشرط.

Our statement in the definition of the impediment (*māniʿ*), "by its very essence," pertains to the final clause – namely, our statement, "while its nonexistence entails neither existence nor nonexistence." For the absence of the impediment may coincide with the presence of both the cause and the condition, in which case existence follows.

However, it is not its absence in itself that necessitated existence, but rather the conjunction of the cause and the condition at the time of the impediment's absence.

Likewise, the absence of the impediment may coincide with the absence of the cause or the condition, in which case nonexistence follows – but not due to the absence of the impediment in itself, rather due to the absence of the cause or the condition.

وأمّا الجملة الأولى -وهي قولنا: (ما يلزم من وجوده العدم)- فمعناها لازم للمانع على كلّ حال.

As for the first sentence – namely, our statement, "that whose existence entails nonexistence" – its meaning necessarily applies to the impediment in all cases.

واختلف الأصوليّون: إذا قارن وجود المانع عدم السبب؛ كأن يقارن الحيض مثلًا عدم دخول الوقت.. هل يعلّل عدم الحكم بوجود ذلك المانع وإن انتفى أيضًا لعدم السبب؛ لأنّ الأمارات أدلّة تعدّدها، أو لا يصحّ تعليل العدم به إلّا حيث يوجد السبب المقتضي للحكم؛ إذ الذي يتبادر من معنى المانع أنّ المقتضي للحكم موجود، لكن انتفى الحكم لوجود المانع؟ وهذا رأي الفخر، والأوّل مختار ابن الحاجب وجماعة، وهو الذي يؤخذ من حدّنا للمانع؛ لأنّ قولنا: (يلزم من وجوده العدم) شامل لما إذا وجد المقتضي أو فقد.

وبالجملة: فقد جعلناه ملزومًا للعدم في كِلا الحالين، وهذا هو عين القول الأوّل، وبالله تعالى التوفيق.

The scholars of the principles of jurisprudence (*uṣūlīs*) differed:

(1) If the existence of an impediment (*māni'*) coincides with the nonexistence of the cause – such as menstruation coinciding with the nonarrival of the prayer time – does one attribute the

nonexistence of the ruling to the existence of that impediment, even though it too is absent due to the nonexistence of the cause, because the indicators are evidences whose multiplicity is admissible?

(2) Or is it invalid to attribute the nonexistence to it except in the case where the cause that necessitates the ruling is present – since what is immediately understood from the meaning of "impediment" is that the necessitating cause of the ruling is present, but the ruling is negated due to the existence of the impediment?

This [latter one] is the view of Fakhr al-Dīn, while the first view is the choice of Ibn al-Ḥājib and a group, and it is the one that follows from our definition of the impediment; for our statement, "its existence entails nonexistence," includes both the case when the necessitating cause is present and when it is absent.

In sum: we have made it entail nonexistence in both cases – and this is precisely the first view. And with Allah (exalted is He) lies success.

§١٠ وأمّا الحكمُ العاديُّ: فهو عبارةٌ عن إثباتِ الربطِ بينَ أمرٍ وأمرٍ وجودًا أو عدمًا بواسطةِ التكرُّرِ، معَ صحّةِ التخلُّفِ، وعدمِ تأثيرِ أحدِهما في الآخرِ ألبتَّةَ.

§10 As for the customary judgement (*ḥukm ʿādī*), it refers to affirming a correlation between two matters – whether in existence or nonexistence – based on repetition, while allowing for exceptions, and with no causal influence whatsoever between them.

§١٠-٠ يعني: أنّ الحكم العاديّ: هو إثبات الربط بين وجود أمر أو عدمه، وبين وجود أمر آخر أو عدمه.

§10.0 Meaning: The customary judgement is the affirmation of a connection between the existence or nonexistence of one thing and the existence or nonexistence of another.

فقولنـا: (وجـودًا أو عدمًا) راجع لكلّ واحد من الأمرين، لا لأحدهما فقط؛ إذ لو كان كذلك لَما دخل تحت هذا الكلام جميع الأقسـام الأربعة الآتية.

Our statement, "whether in existence or nonexistence," pertains to each of the two matters, not to one of them alone; for if it were so, then not all four of the following divisions would fall under this statement.

واحتـرز بقوله: (بواسـطة التكـرّر) من الربط بين أمرين عقلًا أو شـرعًا؛ كالربـط العقلـيّ بين قيام العلـم بمحلّ وبين كون ذلك المحلّ عالمًا، وكالربط الشرعيّ الذي بين زوال الشمسيّ ووجوب صلاة الظهر مثلًا، فهذان الربطان لا يُسَمّى واحد منهما عاديًّا؛ لعدم توقّفه على تكرّر.

He excluded by his statement, "based on repetition," the connection between two things established by the intellect or the divine legislation – such as the rational connection between the subsistence of knowledge (*'ilm*) in a subject and that subject being a knower, and such as the legal connection between the sun's passing the zenith and the obligation of the Ẓuhr prayer, for example. These two connections are not called customary, because they do not depend on repetition.

وأمّا قولنا: (مع صحّة التخلّف، وعدم تأثير أحدهما في الآخر ألبتّة) فلـم نذكره لبيان حقيقة الحكـم العاديّ، بل للتنبيه على تحقيق علم ودفع جهالة ابتلي بها الأكثر في الأحكام العاديّة؛ حتى توهّموا أنّه لا معنـى للربـط الذي حصل في الحكـم العاديّ إلّا ربط اللزوم الذي لا يمكـن معـه انفكاك؛ كاللزوم العقلـيّ، أو ربط التأثير من أحدهما في الآخـر، فنبّهنـا بهـذه الجملة على أنّ الربط الـذي حصل في الحكم

العاديّ إنّما هو ربط اقتران ودلالة جعليّة، لا ربط لزوم عقليّ، ولا ربط تأثير من أحدهما في الآخر.

As for our statement, "while allowing for exceptions, and with no causal influence whatsoever between them," we did not include it to define the essence of a customary judgement, but rather to highlight a precise understanding and to correct a common misunderstanding that afflicts most people concerning such judgements: they assume that the link in a customary judgement must be one of necessary concomitance – from which separation is impossible, like rational necessity – or one of causal influence from one thing upon the other.

So we clarified by this phrase that the connection in a customary judgement is merely one of concomitance and assigned indication – not one of rational necessity, nor of causal efficacy between the two.

فأشرنا إلى عدم الربط فيه بطريق اللزوم الذي يشبه اللزوم العقليّ بقولنا: (مع صحّة التخلّف) وفيه تنبيه على جهالة من فهم أنّ الربط في العاديّات بطريق اللزوم الذي لا يصحّ معه التخلّف، فأنكر بسبب هذه الجهالة البعث، وإحياء الموتى في القبر، والخلود في النار مع استمرار الحياة؛ لأنّ ذلك كلّه عندهم على خلاف العادة المستمرّة في الشاهد، والربط المتقرّر فيها لا يصحّ فيه التخلّف عندهم! وأشرنا إلى عدم الربط فيه بطريق التأثير بقولنا: (وعدم تأثير أحدهما في الآخر ألبتّة).

Thus, we indicated the absence of connection by way of rational necessity (*luzūm 'aqlī*) through our statement, "while allowing for exceptions." This serves as a clarification against the misunderstanding of those who believed that the connection in customary phenomena is one of necessary concomitance that admits no exception. Due to this error, they went so far as to deny the resurrection, the revivification of the dead in the grave, and eternal damnation in the Fire alongside the continuation of life – because, in their view, all of that contradicts the continuous custom observable in the sensible world, and the established link therein allows for no exception.

And we indicated the absence of any causal connection by our statement, "and with no causal influence whatsoever between them."

وقد يقال: إن ذكر هذين القيدين في تعريفنا الحكم العاديّ إنّما هو لإفادة معرفته؛ بناءً على أنّ الجهل بصفة حقيقة وإثبات ضدّها لتلك الحقيقة.. موجب للجهل بها، وهو مذهب أبي عمران الفاسيّ رضي اللّه تعالى عنه في المسألة المشهورة بالخلاف؛ وهي الجهل بصفات المولى تبارك وتعالى وإثبات ضدّها له ممّا لا يليق به جلّ وعلا؛ كإثبات الجسميّة له والجهة ونحو ذلك ممّا هو مستحيل عليه تبارك وتعالى.. هل يصدق على معتقد ذلك أنّه جاهل بالمولى تبارك وتعالى أم لا؟

It may be said: the mention of these two qualifications in our definition of customary judgement is only to achieve cognisance of it – on the basis that ignorance of a property in its reality, along with affirming its contrary, entails ignorance of that reality. This is the view of Abū ʿImrān al-Fāsī (may Allah – exalted is He – be pleased with him) concerning the well-known disputed issue: Whether ignorance of the attributes of the Lord (blessed and exalted is He), along with affirming their contraries of Him – such as affirming corporeality, spatial direction, and the like, all of which are impossible for Him (majestic is He) – entails that such a person is ignorant of the Lord (exalted is He) or not.

والأظهـر: أنّـه جاهـل بـه جلّ وعلا كمـا اختار أبو عمـران رحمه اللّه تعالـى، والجهـل بـه تعالى كفر، فعلى هذا: مـن جهل صفة الحكم العـاديّ بأنّـه ربط اقتران جعليّ يصحّ فيـه التخلّف، واعتقد لجهله أنّ الربـط فيـه ربط تأثير أو ربط لزوم لا يمكن فيه التخلّف.. فإنّه يصدق عليـه أنّـه جاهـل بالحكم العـاديّ بناءً على هـذا القـول الأظهر؛ أنّ الجهـل بالصفـة جهـل بالموصوف، وإسـقاط هذين القيديـن إذا من تعريف الحكم العاديّ.. قد يخل بمعرفته، وباللّه تعالى التوفيق.

The more apparent view is that such a person is ignorant of Allah (majestic and exalted is He), as held by Abū ʿImrān (may Allah (exalted is He) have mercy on him). And ignorance of Allah is disbelief.

Accordingly, whoever is ignorant of the attribute of the customary judgement (*ḥukm ʿādī*) – namely, that it is a conventional correlation in which exception is possible – and, due to his ignorance, believes that the correlation is one of causal efficacy or necessary entailment that admits no exception, then such a person is to be considered ignorant of the customary judgement. This follows from the more apparent view: that ignorance of the attribute entails ignorance of the one described.

Omitting these two qualifiers from the definition of the customary judgement may therefore impair its understanding. And success is from Allah (exalted is He).

§١١ وأقسامُهُ أربعةٌ:

١. ربطُ وجودٍ بوجودٍ: كربطِ وجودِ الشبعِ بوجودِ الأكلِ.

٢. وربطُ عدمٍ بعدمٍ: كربطِ عدمِ الشبعِ بعدمِ الأكلِ.

٣. وربطُ وجودٍ بعدمٍ: كربطِ وجودِ الجوعِ بعدمِ الأكلِ.

٤. وربطُ عدمٍ بوجودٍ: كربطِ عدمِ الجوعِ بوجودِ الأكلِ.

§11 It has four categories:

1. **Correlating existence with existence – such as the correlation of satiety with the existence of eating.**
2. **Correlating nonexistence with nonexistence – such as the correlation of the nonexistence of satiety with the nonexistence of eating.**
3. **Correlating existence with nonexistence – such as the correlation of hunger with the nonexistence of eating.**
4. **Correlating nonexistence with existence – such as the correlation of the nonexistence of hunger with the existence of eating.**

§١١-٠ قد عرفت أنّ الربط بين أمرين في الحكم العاديّ يصحّ في وجود كلّ واحد منهما وعدمه، فلزم انقسامه -أي: الربط- إلى أربعة أقسام؛ من ضرب اثنين -وهما وجود أحد الأمرين وعدمه- في اثنين؛ وهما وجود الأمر الآخر وعدمه.

§11.0 You have already seen that the correlation between two things in a customary judgement applies whether each exists or not. Therefore, the correlation – that is, the relation – must be divided into four types, by considering both the existence and nonexistence of each of the two things.

فإذا كان أحد الأمرين سببًا عاديًّا للآخر.. ارتبط وجوده بوجوده، وعدمه بعدمه.

وإذا كان أحد الأمرين شرطًا عاديًّا للآخر.. ارتبط عدمه بعدمه، ولا يرتبط وجوده بوجود الآخر ولا عدمه.

وإذا كان أحد الأمرين مانعًا عاديًّا من وجود الآخر.. ارتبط وجود المانع بعدم الآخر، ولا يرتبط عدمه بعدم الآخر ولا وجوده.

For if one of the two matters is a customary cause for the other, then the existence of the cause is correlated with the existence of the effect, and its nonexistence with the effect's nonexistence.

And if one of the two matters is a customary condition for the other, then its nonexistence is correlated with the nonexistence of the other, while its existence is not correlated with either the existence or the nonexistence of the other.

And if one of the two matters is a customary impediment to the existence of the other, then the existence of the impediment is correlated with the nonexistence of the other, while its nonexistence is not correlated with either the existence or the nonexistence of the other.

فإن قلت: مقتضى ما ذكرتم أن تكون الأقسام ثلاثة:

١. ارتباط وجود بوجود، وذلك في السبب العاديّ.

٢. وارتباط عدم بعدم، وذلك في السبب أيضًا وفي الشرط.

٣. وارتباط عدم بوجود، وذلك في المانع العاديّ.

وبقي ارتباط وجود بعدم، فإنّه لا مقتضى له من هذه الثلاثة، والربط العاديّ منحصر فيها، فمن أين جاءكم هذا القسم الرابع؟.

Should you say: The implication of what you have mentioned is that the divisions should be three:

1. the correlation of existence with existence – and that applies to the customary cause;
2. the correlation of nonexistence with nonexistence – which applies to the cause as well as to the condition; and
3. the correlation of nonexistence with existence – which pertains to the customary impediment.

The correlation of existence with nonexistence remains – and none of these three entail it, while customary correlations are confined to them. So where has this fourth category come from?

قلت: المقتضي لهذا القسم الرابع -وهو ارتباط وجود بعدم- السبب والشرط العاديّان؛ وذلك أنّك قد عرفت أنّ عدم السبب يقتضي عدم المسبّب، وعدم الشرط يقتضي عدم المشروط، ومن لازم اقتضاء عدم السبب لعدم المسبّب اقتضاء عدمه لوجود نقيض المسبّب، فلزم ارتباط وجود نقيض المسبّب لعدم السبب، وافهم مثل هذا في اقتضاء عدم الشرط لوجود نقيض المشروط، فيكون وجود نقيض المشروط مرتبطًا بعدم الشرط.

I reply: What necessitates this fourth category – namely, the correlation of existence with nonexistence – are the customary cause and the customary condition. You have already understood that the absence of the cause entails the absence of the effect, and the absence of the condition entails the absence of the conditioned.

Now, since the absence of the cause entails the absence of the effect, it also entails the existence of the negation of the effect. Thus, the existence of the negation of the effect is correlated with the absence of the cause. Understand likewise that the absence of the condition entails the existence of the negation of the conditioned – so that the existence of the negation of the conditioned is correlated with the absence of the condition.

مثال السبب العاديّ: أكل الطعام المقتات بالنسبة إلى الشبع. ومثال الشرط العاديّ: السلامة من الشهوة الكلبيّة بالنسبة إلى الشبع أيضًا. ومثال المانع العاديّ له: الشهوة الكلبيّة.

An example of a customary cause is the consumption of nourishing food in relation to satiety.

An example of a customary condition is the absence of canine appetite, also in relation to satiety.

And an example of a customary impediment is canine appetite itself.

والأمثلة التي ذكرناها في الأصل راجعة للسبب العاديّ؛ وهو أكل الطعام المقتات باعتبار وجوده أو نقيضه بالنسبة إلى وجود المسبّب وهو الشبع أو ضدّه أو نقيضهما، وبالله تعالى التوفيق.

The examples we mentioned in the main text revert to the customary cause – namely, the consumption of nourishing food – considered in terms of its existence or its negation, in relation to the existence of the effect (satiety), its contrary, or the negation of either. And with Allah (exalted is He) lies success.

§١٢ وأمّا الحكمُ العقليُّ: فهو إثباتُ أمرٍ أو نفْيُهُ مِنْ غيرِ توقُّفٍ على تكرُّرٍ ولا وضعِ واضعٍ.

§12 As for the rational judgement (*ḥukm ʿaqlī*), it is the affirmation or negation of a matter without reliance on repetition or the stipulation of a stipulator.

§١٢-٠ إنّما أضيف هذا الحكم إلى العقل وإن كانت الأحكام كلّها لا تدرك إلّا بالعقل؛ لأنّ مجرّد العقل بدون فكرة أو معها كاف في إدراك هذا الحكم.

§12.0 The reason this judgement is ascribed to the intellect – even though all judgements are not apprehended except by the intellect – is that the intellect alone, whether with or without reflection, suffices for apprehending this type of judgement.

فقوله: (إثبات أمر) مثاله: الواحد نصف الاثنين.

His statement, "affirmation of a matter": an example is: one is half of two.

وقوله: (أو نفيه) مثاله: الثلاثة ليست نصفًا للأربعة.

His statement, "or its negation": an example is: three is not a half of four.

وهذا القيد -وهو: (إثبات أمر أو نفيه)- جنس للحدّ.

And this qualifier – "affirmation or negation of a matter" – constitutes the genus of the definition.

وقوله: (من غير توقّف على تكرّر) فصل أخرج الحكم العاديّ؛ كقولنا: شراب السكنجبين يسكن الصفراء؛ فإنّ هذا الحكم لم يثبت له إلّا بواسطة التكرّر والتجربة، حتى عرف أنّه ليس باتّفاقي.

His statement, "without reliance on repetition," is the differentia that excludes the customary judgement – such as our saying, "The syrup of oxymel soothes bile." For this judgement is only established through repetition and experience, until it becomes known that it is not merely coincidental.

§١٢-١ فإن قلت: ها نحن نثبت هذا الحكم للسكنجبين تقليدًا للأطّباء وإن لم يتكرّر عندنا ولا جربناه.

§12.1 Should you say: Here we affirm this judgement concerning oxymel in imitation of the physicians, even though it has not recurred for us nor have we tested it.

قلت: إنّما أثبتنا فيه هذا الحكم بواسطة التجربة التي صدقنا فيها الأطّباء، وليس من شرط التكرّر والتجربة في الحكم العاديّ أن يكونا من كلّ أحد، بل هو المستند لثبوت الحكم العاديّ وإن حصل من البعض الموثوق بتجربته.

I reply: We have affirmed this judgement based on experience, relying on the physicians in that regard. It is not a condition for repetition and experience in the case of customary judgement that they be personally observed by every individual. Rather, they serve as the basis for establishing the customary judgement, even if confirmed only by some whose experience is trustworthy.

قوله: (ولا وضع واضع) فصل آخر أخرج به الحكم الشرعيّ.

His statement, "[n]or the stipulation of a stipulator" is another qualification by which he excludes the legal ruling.

فإن قلت: كيف يصحّ أن يقال في الحكم الشرعيّ: إنّه حصل بالوضع والجعل، وهو خطاب اللّٰه تعالى وكلامه القديم، والقديم ليس بموضوع ولا مجعول؟

§12.2 Should you say: How is it valid to assert, regarding the legal ruling, that it came about through stipulation (*waḍʿ*) and enactment (*jaʿl*), while it is the address of Allah (exalted is He) and His eternal speech – and the eternal is neither stipulated nor enacted?

قلت: المراد بالحكم الشرعيّ هنا: التعلّق التنجيزيّ لخطاب اللّٰه تعالى القديم المتعلّق بأفعال المكلّفين بعد وجودهم وتوفر شرائط التكليف فيهم، وهذا التعلّق ليس بقديم، والقديم إنّما هو كلام اللّٰه تعالى وتعلّقه العقليّ الصلاحيّ بأفعال المكلّفين في الأزل، وإطلاق الحكم الشرعيّ على التعلّق التنجيزيّ الحادث.. مشهور عند الفقهاء والأصوليّين، وباللّٰه تعالى التوفيق.

I say: What is meant here by the legal ruling is the temporal executive link (*taʿalluq tanjīzī ḥādith*) of Allah's eternal address to the acts of morally responsible agents, after their coming into existence and the fulfilment of the conditions of moral responsibility. This link is not eternal; rather, what is eternal is Allah's speech (exalted is He) and its eternal aptitudinal link (*taʿalluq ṣalāḥī qadīm*) to the acts of morally responsible agents in past-eternity.

The application of the term "legal ruling" to this temporal executive link is well known among jurists and scholars of the principles of jurisprudence. And success is from Allah (exalted is He).

§١٣ وأقسامُهُ ثلاثةٌ: الوجوبُ، والاستحالةُ، والجوازُ.

§13 Its categories are three: necessity, impossibility, possibility.

§١٣-٠ لا بدّ من حذف مضاف في هذا الكلام، تقديره: إثبات الوجوب، وإثبات الاستحالة، وإثبات الجواز، ولك أن تحذف المضاف إليه في لفظ (أقسامه) ويكون التقدير: وأقسام متعلّقه، وإنّما احتجنا إلى هذا الحذف لأنّ الحكم العقليّ ليس هو نفس هذه الثلاثة المذكورة، فلا تكون أقسامًا له؛ لأنّ من شرط القسمة صدق اسم المقسوم على كلّ واحد من أقسامه، ولا يصدق على الوجوب أو الاستحالة أو الجواز اسم الحكم، وإنّما يصدق عليها أنّها محكوم بها، وقرينة الحذف جليّة.

§13.0 It is necessary to supply a missing genitive in this statement, the intended meaning being: the affirmation of necessity, the affirmation of impossibility, and the affirmation of possibility.

Alternatively, one may elide the genitive in the phrase "its divisions," so that it means: the divisions of its object.

This elision is necessary because rational judgement (*ḥukm ʿaqlī*) is not itself identical with the three mentioned items, and therefore they cannot be its actual divisions. For a condition of division is that the name of the whole applies to each of its parts – and the term "judgement" (*ḥukm*) does not apply to necessity, impossibility, or possibility themselves, but only to their being objects of judgement. The context clearly indicates the elision.

ووجه انحصار الحكم العقليّ في هذه الثلاثة: أن كلّ ما يحكم به العقل:

١. إمّا أن يقبل الثبوت والانتفاء جميعًا.
٢. أو يقبل الثبوت فقط.
٣. أو يقبل الانتفاء فقط. فالأوّل: هو الجائز، والثاني: هو الواجب، والثالث: هو المستحيل.

The reason for restricting rational judgement to these three is that everything about which the intellect passes judgement admits of:

1. both affirmation (*thubūt*) and negation,
2. affirmation only, or
3. negation only.

The first is the possible.
The second is the necessary.
The third is the impossible.

§١٤ فالواجبُ: ما لا يُتصوَّرُ في العقلِ عدمُهُ؛ إمَّا ضرورةً؛ كالتحيُّزِ للجِرْمِ، وإمَّا نظرًا؛ كوجوبِ القِدَمِ لمولانا جلَّ وعزَّ.

§14 The necessary (*wājib*) is that which the intellect cannot conceive as nonexistent. It is either immediate (*ḍarūrī*) – such as a body occupying space; or speculative (*naẓarī*) – such as the necessity of pre-eternity for our Lord (majestic and mighty is He).

§١٤-٠ يعني: أنّ حقيقة الواجب العقليّ: هو ما لا يتصوّر في العقل عدمه؛ أي: لا يدرك في العقل عدمه:

§14.0 Meaning: The reality of the rationally necessary (*wājib ʿaqlī*) is that which the intellect cannot conceive as nonexistent – that is, the intellect does not apprehend its nonexistence:

إمّا ضرورةً؛ أي: ابتداءً بلا تأمّل؛ كالتحيّز للجرم؛ وهو أخذه قدر ذاته من الفراغ، فإنّ ثبوت هذا المعنى له لا يتصوّر في العقل ضرورة نفيه، ونظير هذا في الوجوب الضروريّ: كون الاثنين أكثر من الواحد.

(1) Either immediately – that is, apprehended without preparation or reflection – such as spatial delimitation (*taḥayyuz*) for a body (*jirm*), which is its occupying a volume commensurate with itself within space. For the affirmation of this meaning for the body cannot be conceived by the intellect as negated.

An analogous case of immediate (*ḍarūrī*) necessity is the fact that two is greater than one.

وإمّا نظرًا؛ أي: بعد التأمّل؛ كثبوت القدم لمولانا تبارك وتعالى، فإنّه لا يتصوّر في العقل نفيه عنه جلّ وعلا، لكن بعد التأمّل فيما يترتّب على نفيه من المستحيلات؛ كالدور، والتسلسل، وتعدّد الآلهة، وتخصيص كلّ واحد منهم بنوع من الممكنات بلا مخصّص، ونظير هذا في الوجوب النظريّ: كون الواحد ربع عشر الأربعين.

(2) Or speculative (*naẓarī*) – that is, after reflection – such as the establishment (*thubūt*) of pre-eternity for our Master (blessed and exalted is He). For the intellect cannot conceive its negation from Him (majestic and sublime is He), except after reflecting on the impossibilities that follow from such negation – such as circularity (*dawr*), infinite regress (*tasalsul*), the multiplicity of deities, and the specification of each with a kind of contingent being without a specifier.

An analogous case of speculative necessity (*wujūb naẓarī*) is the fact that one is a quarter of a tenth of forty.

وهذا الواجب المعرّف هو الواجب الذاتيّ.

And this necessary, as defined, is what is called the *necessary by its very essence* (*wājib li-dhātih*).

وأمّا الواجب العرضيّ -وهو ما يجب لتعلّق إرادة اللّه تعالى به؛ كتعذيب أبي جهل-: فإنّه بالنظر إلى ذاته جائز يصحّ في العقل وجوده وعدمه، وبالنظر إلى ما أخبر به الصادق المصدوق صلوات اللّه وسلامه عليه من إرادة اللّه تعالى لعذابه.. هو واجب لا يتصوّر في العقل عدمه.

As for the *adventitiously necessary* (*wājib ʿaraḍī*) – that is, what becomes necessary due to the linking of the will of Allah (exalted is He) to it, such as the torment of Abū Jahl – it is, considered in itself, possible (*jāʾiz*), such that the intellect deems both its existence and nonexistence conceivable. But when considered in light of what the truthful, trustworthy one – Allah's blessings and peace be upon him – has informed us of, namely Allah's will for his torment, then it is necessary (*wājib*), such that its nonexistence is inconceivable to the intellect.

وإنّما لم يحتج إلى تقييد الواجب بالذاتيّ؛ لأنّه عند الإطلاق لا يحمل إلّا على الذاتيّ، ولا يحمل على العرضيّ إلّا بالتقييد، وباللّه تعالى التوفيق.

The reason there is no need to qualify the necessary (*wājib*) as "by its very essence" (*dhātī*) is that, when unqualified, it is understood only as the necessary by its very essence, and it is not taken to mean the adventitiously necessary (*ʿaraḍī*) except with qualification. And success is from Allah (exalted is He).

§١٥ والمستحيلُ: ما لا يُتصوَّرُ في العقلِ وجودُهُ؛ إمَّا ضرورةً؛ كتعرِّي الجِرْمِ عنِ الحركةِ والسكونِ معًا، وإمَّا نظرًا؛ كالشريكِ لمولانا جلَّ وعزَّ.

§15 The impossible (*mustaḥīl*) is that which the intellect cannot conceive as existent. It is either immediate – such as a body being devoid of both motion and rest; or speculative – such as a partner for our Lord (majestic and mighty is He).

§١٥-٠ هذا أيضًا هو المستحيل الذاتيّ.

§15.0 This, too, is the impossible by its very essence (*mumtaniʿ li-dhātih*).

وأمّا المستحيل لعارض منفصل عنه: فهو من قبيل الجائز. كاستحالة إيمان أبي لهب لما عرض له من إرادة اللّٰه تعالى لعدمه.

As for that which is impossible due to an extrinsic adventitious factor, it belongs to the category of the possible (*jāʾiz*) – such as the impossibility of the faith of Abū Lahab, due to Allah's willing its non-occurrence.

ونظير تعرّي الجرم عن الحركة والسكون -أي: تجرّده عنهما معًا- في كونه مستحيلًا ضرورةً؛ أي: ابتداءً بلا تأمّل: كون الاثنين مثلًا ربع الأربعة، أو نصف الثمانية، أو نحو ذلك من المستحيلات الضروريّة، ونظير الشريك في كونه مستحيلًا بالنظر؛ أي: بعد التأمّل: كون الواحد نصف عشر الأربعين.

An analogous case to a body being devoid of both motion and rest – that is, stripped of both – in its being immediately impossible (that is, from the outset, without reflection), is the case of two being, for example, a quarter of four, or half of eight, or similar cases of immediate impossibilities.

And analogous to the case of a partner being speculatively impossible – that is, after reflection – is the case of one being half of a tenth of forty.

§١٦ والجائزُ: ما يصحُّ في العقلِ وجودُهُ وعدمُهُ؛ إمَّا ضرورةً؛ كالحركةِ لنا، وإمَّا نظرًا؛ كتعذيبِ المطيعِ وإثابةِ العاصي.

§16 The possible (*jāʾiz*) is that which the intellect deems both existence and nonexistence conceivable. It is either immediate – such

as our motion – or speculative – such as punishing the obedient and rewarding the disobedient.

§١٦-٠ الجائز: لفظ مشترك يطلق ويراد به هذا الذي ذكرنا هنا؛ وهو ما لا يترتّب على تقدير وجوده ولا على تقدير عدمه محال لذاته، وهذا معنى قولنا: (يصحّ في العقل وجوده وعدمه) أي: لا يلزم من هذين التقديرين فيه محال لذاته.

§16.0 "Possible" (*jā'iz*) is an equivocal term (*lafẓ mushtarak*);[9] what is meant by it here is that whose existence or nonexistence does not, in either case, entail an impossibility by its very essence. This is the meaning of our statement, "the intellect deems both existence and nonexistence conceivable" – that is, neither assumption entails an essential impossibility.

ويدخل فيه ثلاثة أقسام:

الأوّل: الجائز المقطوع بوجوده: كاتّصاف الجرم المطلق بخصوص البياض أو خصوص الحركة ونحوهما، وكالبعث والثواب والعقاب ونحو ذلك.

الثاني: الجائز المقطوع بعدمه: كإيمان أبي لهب وأبي جهل، ودخول الكافر الجنّة، ونحو ذلك.

الثالث: المحتمل للوجود والعدم: كقبول الطاعة منا، وفوزنا بحسن الخاتمة، والسلامة من عذاب الآخرة، ونحو ذلك.

It comprises three categories:

First: the possible (*jā'iz*) whose existence is decisively established – such as the attribution of an absolute body to a specific

9 An equivocal term (*mushtarak*) is one assigned to two or more meanings by convention, without being transferred from one of them to the other.

whiteness or motion, and the like; and such as resurrection, reward, and punishment.

Second: the possible whose nonexistence is decisively established – such as the faith of Abū Lahab and Abū Jahl, or the entry of the disbeliever into Paradise, and the like.

Third: that which may either exist or not exist – such as our acceptance of obedience, our attainment of a good end, and safety from the punishment of the Hereafter, and the like.

وإنّما زدنا التقييد بالذات في قولنا: (لا يترتّب على تقدير وجوده ولا على تقدير عدمه محال لذاته) أي: بالنظر إلى ذات ذلك الجائز؛ أي: حقيقته؛ ليدخل فيه القسمان الأوّلان؛ وهما المقطوع بوجوده، والمقطوع بعدمه، فإنّ كلّ واحد منهما بالنظر إلى ذاته لا يلزم محال في وجوده ولا عدمه؛ فإنّ الثواب والعقاب مثلًا بالنظر إلى حقيقتهما لا يلزم في وجودهما ولا عدمهما محال، ولو نظرنا إلى ما تعلّق بهما من إخبار اللّه تعالى ورسله عليهم الصلاة والسلام بوجودهما.. لترتّب حينئذٍ على عدمهما محال؛ وهو الكذب والخلف في خبر من يستحيل عليه ذلك، ونحو ذلك البعث وغيره من الجائزات التي أخبر الصادق المصدّق بوقوعها.

We have added the qualification "by its very essence" in our statement – "does not, in either case, entail an impossibility by its very essence" – that is, in view of the essence (*dhāt*) of that possible, meaning its true reality (*ḥaqīqah*) – in order to include the first two categories – namely: that whose existence is decisively established and that whose nonexistence is decisively established.

For each of these, when considered by its very essence, no impossibility follows from either its existence or its nonexistence. For example, reward and punishment – when considered in view of their very essences – do not entail impossibility whether they exist or not.

However, if we consider what they are linked to – namely, the report of Allah (exalted is He) and His messengers (peace be upon them) affirming their existence – then their nonexistence would entail an impossibility: namely, falsehood and failure in the report of one for whom such is impossible. The same applies to resurrection and other possible things whose occurrence has been affirmed by the truthful one,[10] whose truthfulness is guaranteed.

وكذا دخول الكافر الجنّة؛ فإن نظرنا إلى حقيقته في نفسه.. لم يلزم من وجوده ولا عدمه محال، ولو نظرنا إلى ما عرض له من إخبار اللَّه تعالى ورسله عليهم الصلاة والسلام بأنّه لا يكون له دخول الجنّة أبدًا.. لترتّب حينئذٍ على تقدير وجوده محال؛ وهو كذب من لا يجور عليه الكذب عقلًا.

Likewise, the entry of the disbeliever into Paradise: if we consider its reality in itself, then neither its existence nor its nonexistence entails impossibility. But if we consider what is connected to it from the report of Allah (exalted is He) and His messengers (peace be upon them) – that he will never enter Paradise – then, in that case, the supposition of its existence would entail an impossibility: namely, the falsehood of one for whom falsehood is rationally impossible.

ويطلق الجائز أيضًا ويراد به: المحتمل المشكوك في وجوده وعدمه، فيكون على هذا خاصًّا بالقسم الثالث.

The term *possible* (*jā'iz*) is also used to mean that which is potential and doubted in both its existence and nonexistence. In this usage, it is specific to the third category.

10 (Tr:) Namely: the Prophet (may Allah bless him and give him peace).

ويطلق الجائز أيضًا ويراد به: ما أذن الشرع في فعله وتركه، فيكون مرادفًا للمباح؛ كالبيع والنكاح ونحوهما، أو ما أذن الشرع في فعله وإن لم يأذن في تركو.. فيكون على هذا أعمّ من المباح؛ لأنّه حينئذٍ يصدق على الواجب والمندوب.

§16.1 The term *permissible* (*jā'iz*) is also used to mean:

(1) That which the Law has permitted to be done or omitted, in which case it is synonymous with the permissible (*mubāḥ*) – such as sale, marriage, and the like.

(2) Or it may refer to that which the Law has permitted to be done, even if it has not permitted its omission. In this case, it is broader than the permissible (*mubāḥ*), for it would then apply to the obligatory (*wājib*) and the recommended (*mandūb*).

وبالجملة: فالجائز الذي هو أحد أقسام الحكم العقليّ إنّما يريدون به المعنى الأوّل؛ وهو ما لا يترتّب على تقدير وجوده ولا على تقدير عدمه بالنظر إلى ذاته.. محال، وليس بمعنى المحتمل المشكوك فيه، ولا بمعنى المأذون فيه شرعًا، ولا بمعنى المباح.

In sum: the possible (*jā'iz*), which is one of the divisions of rational judgement, is intended in its first sense – namely, that whose existence or nonexistence, when considered by essence, entails no impossibility. It is not meant in the sense of what is potential and doubted, nor what is permitted by divine legislation, nor what is classified as permissible (*mubāḥ*).

ويطلق أيضًا على الجائز الذي هو أحد أقسام الحكم العقليّ: الممكن، فالممكن والجائز العقليّ في اصطلاح المتكلّمين مترادفان، والممكن الخاصّ عند أهل المنطق هو المرادف للجائز العقليّ، وأمّا الممكن

العـامّ عندهـم: فهو ما لا يمتنـع وقوعه، فيدخل فيـه الواجب والجائز العقليّان، ولا يخرج منه إلّا المستحيل العقليّ.

The term *rationally possible* (*jā'iz 'aqlī*), which is one of the divisions of rational judgement, is also applied to the contingent (*mumkin*). Thus, in the terminology of the theologians (*mutakallimūn*), the contingent (*mumkin*) and the rationally possible (*jā'iz 'aqlī*) are synonymous.

The specific contingent (*mumkin khāṣṣ*), according to the logicians, is equivalent to the rationally possible. As for the general contingent (*mumkin 'āmm*) in their usage: it is that whose occurrence is not impossible – and thus it includes both the necessary (*wājib*) and the rationally possible (*jā'iz 'aqlī*), and excludes only the rationally impossible (*mustaḥīl 'amalī*).

وقولنا في مثل الجائز الضروريّ: (كالحركة لنا) معناه: أنّ الجائز أيضًا على قسمين:

Our statement regarding the immediately apprehended possible – such as "motion for us" – means that the possible (*jā'iz*) is also of two kinds:

(١) جائز تدرك صحّة وجوده وعدمه ضرورةً؛ أي: بلا تأمّل؛ كاتّصافنا - معشـر الأجـرام - بخصـوص الحركـة؛ فإنّا بالمشـاهدة نعلم صحّة وجودها وعدمها للجرم.

(1) A possible whose existence and nonexistence are apprehended immediately – that is, without reflection – such as our being characterised, as corporeal beings, by the specific attribute of motion. For we know through direct observation that motion may exist or not exist in a body.

(٢) وجائـز لا يـدرك إلّا بالتأمّـل؛ كتعذيـب مَن أطـاع اللّٰه تعالى ولم يعصـه قـطْ، فإنّ هذا فـي الابتداء قد ينكر العقل جـوازه، بل يتوهّمه مستحيلًا كما توهّمته المعتزلة، وأمّا بعد النظر في وحدانيّة اللّٰه تعالى وانفـراده بخلـق جميع الممكنات وإرادتها بلا واسـطة، خيرًا كانت أو شرًّا؛ وأنّ الأفعال كلّها بالنسبة إليه تعالى سواء، لا نفع له تبارك وتعالى فـي طاعـة، ولا ضـرر ولا نقص يلحقه جلّ وعـزّ بكفر كافر أو معصية عـاص، ولا حجـر عليـه ولا حكـم لأحـد عليه.. فنعلـم حينئذٍ على القطع أنّ ما رتّبه سبحانه وتعالى على الكفر من العذاب الأليم، وعلى الطاعة من النعيم المقيم، لو عكس تعالى في ذلك، أو لم يرتّب جلّ وعلا عليهما شيئًا أصلًا.. لم يلزم عن ذلك بالنظر إلى حقيقة الطاعة والكفر والمعصية نقص ولا محال أصلًا، وباللّٰه تعالى التوفيق.

(2) A possible that is not apprehended except through speculation – such as the punishment of one who obeyed Allah (exalted is He) and never disobeyed Him. At first, the intellect may reject the possibility of this, even mistakenly judging it to be impossible, as the Mu'tazilah erroneously imagined. But after reflecting on the oneness of Allah (exalted is He), His exclusivity in creating all possible things and willing them without intermediary – whether good or evil – and that all acts, in relation to Him, are alike; that no benefit reaches Him from obedience, nor any harm or imperfection from disbelief or disobedience; that He is subject to no constraint, and none may pass judgement over Him, we then know with certainty that what He (exalted is He) has assigned to disbelief with painful punishment, and to obedience with everlasting bliss – were He to reverse that, or to assign nothing at all to either – nothing impossible or deficient would follow from that, in view of the realities of obedience, disbelief, and disobedience.

And success is from Allah (exalted is He).

THE SECOND PROLEGOMENON
ON THE DOCTRINES CONCERNING THE VOLITIONAL ACTS OF LIVING CREATURES

المقدّمة الثانية في المذاهب في أفعال الحيوان الاختياريّة

§١٧ والمذاهـبُ في الأفعالِ ثلاثةٌ: مذهـبُ الجبريَّةِ، ومذهبُ القدريَّةِ، ومذهبُ أهلِ السنَّةِ.

فمذهـبُ الجبريَّـةِ: وجودُ الأفعـالِ كلِّها بالقدرةِ الأزليَّـةِ فقطْ مِنْ غيرِ مُقارَنَةٍ لقدرةٍ حادثةٍ.

ومذهـبُ القدريَّـةِ: وجـودُ الأفعـالِ الاختياريَّـةِ بالقـدرةِ الحادثةِ فقطْ مباشرةً أو تَوَلُّدًا.

ومذهبُ أهلِ السنَّةِ: وجودُ الأفعالِ كلِّها بالقدرةِ الأزليِّ فقطْ معَ مُقارَنَةِ الأفعالِ الاختياريَّةِ لقدرةٍ حادثةٍ لا تأثيرَ لها لا مُباشَرَةً ولا تَوَلُّدًا.

§17 The doctrines concerning volitional acts are three: the doctrine of the Jabariyyah, the Qadariyyah, and the People of the Sunnah.

The doctrine of the Jabariyyah is that all actions exist through the past-eternal capability alone – without concurrence with any originated capability.

The doctrine of the Qadariyyah is that volitional acts exist through an originated capability alone – whether directly or through causal generation (*tawallud*).

The doctrine of the People of the Sunnah is that all actions exist through the past-eternal capability alone – with voluntary acts occurring in concurrence with an originated capability that has no effect, neither directly nor through causal generation.

§١٧-٠ يعني بالأفعال: أفعال الحيوانات عاقلة أو غير عاقلة.

§17.0 By "acts," he means the acts of living creatures, whether rational or non-rational.

فجعل الجبريّة جميعها اضطرارًا؛ كحركة الارتعاش، ليس للحيوان قدرة تتعلّق بها.

§17.1 The Jabriyyah held that all acts are acts of compulsion – like the motion of trembling – to which the living creature's capability does not apply.

وجعل القدريّة الاختياريّة منها -وهو ما لا يحسّ فيه الإلجاء إلى الفعل- مخترعًا للحيوان بالقدرة التي خلق اللّه تعالى له على سبيل الاستقلال، وليس للمولى تبارك وتعالى فيها اختراع عندهم، وإنّما الذي يوجده سبحانه وتعالى فيهم ما لا يتيسّر منها عليهم؛ كالألوان والطعوم والروائح وحركة الارتعاش ونحو ذلك.

§17.2 The Qadariyyah hold that voluntary acts – those in which there is no perceived compulsion toward the act – are brought into being by the living creature through the capability (*qudrah*) that Allah (exalted is He) created for it, independently. According to them, the Master (blessed and exalted is He) does not originate such acts. Rather, what He (exalted is He) brings into being in them are those acts that are not within their capacity – such as colours, tastes, scents, tremulous motion, and the like.

ثمّ قالوا: إنّ الحيوان في اختراعه لأفعاله الاختياريّة على ضربين.

ما وجد منها في محلّ قوّته: كحركاته وسكناته، وقيامه وقعوده، ومشيه وجريه؛ فهو مخترع له مباشرة.

وما وجد منها خارجًا عن محلّ قوته: كتحريك الحجر والسهم، والضرب بالسيف والرمح، والقتل والجرح ونحو ذلك؛ فهو مخترعه تولّدًا؛ أي: بواسطة اختراعه لحركات في محلّ قوته.

Then they said: The living creature, in its origination of voluntary acts, is divided into two types.

Whatever among them occurs within the substrate of his capability – such as his motions and stillness, his standing and sitting, his walking and running – is directly originated by him.

And whatever of these occurs outside the substrate of his capability – such as moving a stone or an arrow, striking with a sword or a spear, killing, wounding, and the like – is originated by him through causal generation; that is, by means of his originating motions within the substrate of his capability (*quwwah*).

ويختلف أثر التولّد عندهم باختلاف قوّة العصب والأعضاء وضعفها، ولهذا كانت حقيقة التولّد عندهم: وجود حادث عن مقدور بالقدرة الحادثة، فحركة الحجر مثلًا متولّد عندهم؛ لأنّه حادث نشأ عن شيء مقدور بالقدرة الحادثة؛ وهو حركة اليد والاعتماد بها مثلًا.

The effect of causal generation (*tawallud*), according to them, varies depending on the strength or weakness of the nerves and organs.

Thus, the reality of generation, according to them, is the occurrence of an originated event arising from something possible through an originated capability (*qudrah ḥādithah*).

For example, the movement of a stone is, in their view, a generated act – because it is an originated event that arose from something possible through an originated capability: namely, the movement of the hand and the force applied by it.

ومذهب أهل السنّة والحقّ مجانب لِكِلا المذهبين الفاسدين، وقد جمع بفضل اللّه بين الحقيقة والشريعة، وسلّم بتوفيق اللّه تعالى من بدعة الفريقين؛ لأنّهم جانبوا الجبريّة؛ بتقسيمهم الأفعال إلى قسمين: اختياريّة واضطراريّة، وأنّ الأولى مقدورة للعباد؛ بمعنى: أن لهم قدرة حادثة تقارن تلك الأفعال الاختياريّة وتتعلّق بها من غير تأثير، وهذه الأفعال هي التي في وسع المكلّف عادةً، وبها وقع التكليف على حسب ما دلّ عليه الشرع؛ قال جلّ من قائل: ﴿لَا يُكَلِّفُ اللَّهُ نَفْسًا إِلَّا وُسْعَهَا﴾ [البقرة: ٢٨٦] أي: إلّا ما تسعه طاقتها بحسب الظاهر والعادة، وأمّا بحسب ما في نفس الأمر.. فليس في وسعها فعل من الأفعال.

§17.3 The doctrine of the Sunnis and the adherents of truth diverges from both of the two corrupt schools. By the grace of Allah, it unites reality and divine law, and by the enabling grace of Allah (exalted is He), it has been protected from the innovations of both factions.

They opposed the Jabriyyah by dividing acts into two categories: volitional (*ikhtiyāriyyah*) and compulsory (*iḍṭirāriyyah*).

They held that the former are within the capability of human beings, in the sense that they possess an originated capability (*qudrah ḥādithah*) that coincides with those volitional acts and links to them – but without exerting any effect. These acts are those ordinarily within the capacity of the morally responsible agent, and upon them legal responsibility is assigned, in accordance with what the divine legislation indicates.

Allah (exalted is He) said: "Allah does not burden a soul beyond its capacity"[11] – meaning: beyond what its power bears according

11 al-Baqarah: 2:286.

to outward appearance and customary estimation. As for what lies in reality, it is not within its capacity to perform any act whatsoever.

وجانبوا أيضًا القدريّة؛ لأنّهم لم يجعلوا لتلك القدرة الحادثة التي يخلق اللّـه تعالـى في الحيوانات.. تأثيرًا ألبتّـة في أثر ما عمومًا، بل الحيوان عندهم وقوته الحادثة ومقدور تلك القوّة.. جميع ذلك مخلوق لمولانا تبارك وتعالى بلا واسـطة ولا شـريك أصلًا، حسب ما دلّ عليه برهان الوحدانيّـة ووجوب عموم قدرته جـلّ وعلا وإرادته لجميع الممكنات، وعليه دلّ الكتاب والسنّة وإجماع السلف الصالح قبل ظهور البدع.

They also opposed the Qadariyyah, for they did not assign to that originated capability – which Allah (exalted is He) creates in living creatures – any effect whatsoever in producing outcomes of any kind. Rather, the living creature itself, its originated capability, and the object of that capability – all of it is created by our Master (blessed and exalted is He), without any intermediary or partner whatsoever.

This accords with what is established by the proof of divine oneness, and the necessity of the universality of His capability (glorious and exalted is He) and His Will over all possible things. This is what is indicated by the Book, the Sunnah, and the consensus of the righteous predecessors (*al-salaf al-ṣāliḥ*) before the appearance of innovation.

والحاصل: أنّ العبد الصحيح القويّ القادر عند أهل الحقّ مجبور في قالب مختار.

مجبور من حيث إنّه لا أثر له ألبتّة في أثر ما عمومًا، وإنّما هو وعاء وظـرف للحـوادث والأعراض، يخلق المولى تبارك وتعالى فيه ما شـاء منها وكيف شاء، لا حجر عليه تعالى ولا معين، ولا وكيل ولا وزير.

ومختار من حيث إنّ عادة مولانا جلّ وعزّ لما جرت معه بعدم دوام موالاة الفعل عليه، لا سيّما حال خلقه جلّ وعزّ فيه كراهة للفعل، وإنّما يمدّه تبارك وتعالى بالفعل في بعض الأوقات على حسب الحاجة، وخصوصًا حال خلقه تبارك وتعالى له عزمًا وتصميمًا على الفعل.. صار العبد بهذه العادة العجيبة الدالّة على سعة قدرة من لا يشغله شأن عن شأن، وتنفذ إرادته في كلّ ممكن، ووسع علمه كلّ معلوم.. مختارًا متمكّنًا من الفعل والترك بحسب الظاهر، لا يحسّ إلجاء إلى ما يحبّ فعله، ولا إكراهًا على ما يكره وجوده.

The upshot is that the sound, strong, and capable servant, according to the people of truth, is compelled in the mould of a volitional agent.

He is compelled inasmuch as he has no effect whatsoever on any outcome in general; rather, he is a vessel and receptacle for events and accidents, within which the Lord (blessed and exalted is He) creates whatever He wills, however He wills. There is no restriction upon Him, no assistant, no agent, and no minister.

And he is a volitional agent (*mukhtār*) inasmuch as the custom of our Master (majestic and exalted is He) has proceeded in such a way that He does not continually sustain the flow of action within him – especially in cases where He has created within him an aversion to the act. Rather, He supports him in acting at certain times, according to need, and particularly when He creates within him a firm resolve and determination to act.

Thus, through this wondrous custom – which points to the vastness of the capability of the One whom no affair distracts from another, whose will is effective in every possible thing, and whose Knowledge encompasses all that is known – the servant becomes, by outward appearance, a volitional agent, capable of both acting and refraining. He does not feel compelled toward what he wishes to do, nor coerced into what he wishes to avoid.

فسبحان المولى الملك القهّار اللطيف، الذي لطف بعض قهره حتى عزب عن إدراك كثير من العقول فضلًا عن الأوهام، فاعتقدت لجهلها بباطن الأمر، وكفرانها نعمة كسـوة المولى جلّ وعزّ لقهره بثياب يسـرّه وطـرده آلام جبـره .. أنّهـا قد خرجت في بعـض تصفاتها عن قبضة تدبيره، وعموم قدرته وإرادته.

So transcendent is the Master – the Sovereign, the Subduer, the Subtle – who has softened some of His overpowering to the point that it escaped the grasp of many intellects, let alone imaginations. And so, due to their ignorance of the inner reality of the matter, and their ingratitude for the favour of the Master (majestic and exalted is He) – who cloaked His subjugation in garments of ease and drove away the pain of compulsion – they came to believe that, in some of its aspects, it had slipped beyond the grip of His governance, and beyond the universality of His capability and will.

ما اقتصرنا عليه في النقل عن أهل السنّة؛ من أنّ القدرة التي للحيوان لا تأثير لها في الأفعال، لا مباشرةً ولا تولّدًا.. هو المعروف المشهور عنهم، ولا يصحّ عقلًا ولا شرعًا خلافه.

§17.4 What we have limited ourselves to reporting from the Sunnis – namely, that the capability possessed by the living creature has no effect on actions, neither directly nor through causal generation – is the view widely known and transmitted from them. It is not valid to oppose it, either rationally or in divine legislation.

وبعض مَن أولع بنقل الغثّ والسـمين من الأقوال ينقل هنا أقوالًا أخر ينسبها أيضًا لأهل السنّة.

Some of those preoccupied with transmitting both the worthless and the valuable indiscriminately also report other statements here, which they likewise attribute to the Sunnis.

فمنهـا: مـا نقل عن القاضي أبي بكر الباقلانيّ رضي اللّٰه تعالى عنه: أنّ القدرة الحادثة تؤثّر في أخصّ وصف الفعل؛ ككونه صلاةً أو غصبًا أو زنًـا أو نحـو ذلك، لا في وجود أصل الفعل، هكذا مثل التفتازانيّ الأخصّ في «شرح المقاصد الدينيّة» له.

Among them is what has been transmitted from Qāḍī Abū Bakr al-Bāqillānī (may Allah – exalted is He – be pleased with him): that the originated capability has effect upon the most specific description of the act – such as its being a prayer, or an act of usurpation, or fornication, or the like – but not upon the fundamental existence of the act itself. This is how al-Taftāzānī illustrated the most specific description in his *Sharḥ al-Maqāṣid al-Dīniyyah.*

ونقـل عـن الأسـتاذ أبي إسـحاق: مثلـه، إلّا أنّه لمّـا كان يقول بنفي الأحـوال عبّـر عن أخصّ وصف الفعل بالوجه والاعتبار؛ فقال: القدرة الحادثة تؤثّر في وجه واعتباره.

Something similar was transmitted from al-Ustadh Abū Isḥāq – except that, since he denied the reality of notional states (*aḥwāl*),[12] he expressed what others referred to as "the most specific description" of the act by the terms "aspect" (*wajh*) and "notional consideration" (*i'tibār*). Thus, he said: the originated capability has effect upon an aspect and a notional consideration of the act.

ومنها: ما نقل عن إمام الحرمين في آخر أمره: أنّ القدرة الحادثة تؤثّر في وجود الفعل على وفق مشيئة المولى تبارك وتعالى.

12 (Tr:) That is, a third ontological category for what is neither existent nor nonexistent.

Among them is what has been transmitted from Imām al-Ḥaramayn toward the end of his life: that the originated capability has causal effect upon the existence of the act – in accordance with the will of the Master (blessed and exalted is He).

ولا يخفى فساد هذه الأقوال ومصادمتها للعقل والشرع، وقد أشبعنا الكلام في ردّها في «شرحنا على عقيدتنا الكبرى»، و «شرحنا على عقيدتنا الوسطى».

The invalidity of these statements, and their contradiction to both reason and divine legislation, is not hidden. We have thoroughly addressed their refutation in our commentaries on our *Kubrā* and *Wusṭā* doctrinal texts.

والواجب تنزيه هؤلاء الأئمّة عن اعتقاد ظاهر ما نقل عنهم؛ لأنّ الموجود في كتبهم الكلاميّة إنّما هو ضدّ هذا المنقول عنهم؛ وهو تعميم قدرة اللّه تعالى وإرادته لجميع الممكنات، ونقلوا إجماع السلف الصالح على ذلك.

It is obligatory to absolve these imams of affirming the apparent meaning of what has been transmitted from them – for what is found in their theological works is in fact the opposite of what has been reported: namely, the universal extension of Allah's capability and will to all possible things. And they transmitted the consensus of the righteous predecessors (*al-salaf al-ṣāliḥ*) on this.

وقد نقل القاضي رحمه اللّه تعالى الإجماع في مواضع من كتبه على كفر من نسب الاختراع لغير اللّه تعالى، ونقل أيضًا إجماع الأمّة على كفر من لم يقل بعموم صفات الباري تبارك وتعالى.

The Qāḍī – may Allah (exalted is He) have mercy on him – transmitted the consensus in several places in his works regarding the disbelief of one who attributes origination to other than Allah (exalted is He). He also transmitted the consensus of the Ummah on the disbelief of one who does not affirm the universality of the attributes of the Creator (blessed and exalted is He).

ويجب تأويل ما صدر عنهم إن صحّ النقل به أنّه إنّما قالوه على سبيل الجدل في مناظرة الخصوم من المبتدعة، وإلزامهم على مقتضى أصولهم الفاسدة أقوالًا فاسدةً لم يقولوا بها؛ ليظهروا لهم أنّهم لم يبنوا فيما يقولون على أساس صحيح، وإنّما يبنون أقوالهم على أساس فاسد، فمهما بنوا عليه قولًا رمته رياح الجدل، وألزمتهم أن يجدّدوا على ذلك الأساس الفاسد بناءً آخر فاسدًا لا ثبات له، ويوافقون على عدم استقراره، لكن ألزموا أن يبنوه لاقتضاء أساسهم الفاسد إيّاه، وهذا ظاهر، وبالله تعالى التوفيق.

It is necessary to reinterpret what has been transmitted from them – if the transmission is sound – as having been said only by way of disputation during debate with opponents from among the innovators, and as obligating those opponents, based on their own corrupt premises, to accept corrupt statements that the Imāms themselves did not uphold.

This was done to show them that their claims rest on no sound foundation, but rather on a corrupt one – such that whatever they construct upon it collapses under the force of debate. They are then forced, by the demands of that corrupt foundation, to construct yet another unstable structure, which they themselves acknowledge to be unsound – though they are obliged to build it by the logic of their own position. This is evident. And success is from Allah (exalted is He).

§١٨ وأمّا الكسبُ: فهو عبارةٌ عن تعلُّقِ القدرةِ الحادثةِ بالمقدورِ في محلِّها مِنْ غيرِ تأثيرٍ.

§18 As for acquisition (*kasb*), it refers to the originated capability's connection to an object of capability (*maqdūr*) in its substrate – without any effect.

§١٨-٠ اعلم أنّه لمّا ثبت بالعقل والنقل وجوب انفراد المولى تبارك وتعالى باختراع جميع الكائنات عمومًا بلا واسطة، وأطلق في الشرع أنّ العبد مكتسب للحسنات والسيّئات، وأنّ الشرع إنّما يكلّفه ويثيبه ويعاقبه بما كسبه أو نشأ عن كسبه وإن لم يكن كسبًا له.. احتيج من أجل هذا كلّه إلى بيان معنى الكسب الذي هو محلّ التكليف الشرعيّ؛ وهو الذي جعل للمكلّف أمارةً على الثواب والعقاب، والمدح والذمّ الشرعيّين؛ فإنّ بعض مَن لا علم عنده بحقيقة توحيد اللّٰه تعالى يفسّر معنى الكسب بكون القدرة الحادثة لها تأثير ما في الأفعال.

§18.0 Know that since it has been established by both reason and transmission that the Lord (blessed and exalted is He) must be solely the one who originates all existents universally, without any intermediary, and since the Law has unreservedly declared that the servant acquires good and evil deeds, and that the Law only obligates, rewards, and punishes him for what he has acquired or for what has arisen from his acquisition – even if it is not, strictly speaking, something he has acquired – there arose, on account of all this, a need to clarify the meaning of acquisition (*kasb*), which is the locus of legal obligation: it is that which has been designated for the legally responsible agent as a sign of reward and punishment, and of legal praise and blame. For some who have no knowledge of the reality of Allah's oneness (*tawḥīd*) interpret the meaning of acquisition as the originated capability's having some effect upon acts.

وبالجملة: فلغير العارفين في تفسير الكسب خبط كثير، وعبارات مختلفة موهمة نشأت عن جهل وعدم تحقيق لباب الوحدانيّة ومقاصد الشرع، والذي يعوّل عليه في تفسيره، ولا يصحّ غيره؛ إذ هو الجاري على القواعد العقليّة، وعلى السنّة وإجماع السلف.. ما فسّرناه به؛ وهو أنّه عبارة عن تعلّق القدرة الحادثة بالمقدور في محلّها من غير تأثير.

In sum: those lacking true understanding have fallen into much confusion in interpreting acquisition (*kasb*), and have employed various misleading expressions – all of which arise from ignorance and a failure to grasp the essence of divine oneness and the aims of the divine legislation.

The interpretation to be relied upon – to the exclusion of all others, for it alone accords with rational principles, the Sunnah, and the consensus of the early generations – is the one we have explained: that acquisition (*kasb*) is the linking of the originated capability to the object of capability (*maqdūr*) in its substrate – without any effect.

واحترزنا بقولنا: (الحادثة) من تعلّق القدرة الأزليّة، فلا يقال فيه: كسب، بل هو اختراع.

By our statement "the originated," we excluded the linkage of the past-eternal capability – so acquisition (*kasb*) is not said of it, but rather: origination (*ikhtirāʿ*).

واحترزنا بقولنا: (بالمقدور في محلّها) أي: في محلّ القدرة.. من الفعل الذي خرج عن محلّ القدرة؛ كالرمي بالحجر، والضرب بالسيف والرمح، والقتل والجرح، ونحو ذلك، فهذه الأفعال حادثة غير مكتسبة

للعبد؛ لأنّها خارجة عن محلّ قدرته، إلّا أنّها لمّا كانت مخلوقةً عند كسبه عادةً.. جرى فيها التكليف والثواب والعقاب.

We excluded by our statement, "with the object of capability in its substrate" – that is, within the substrate of capability – those acts that fall outside the substrate of capability, such as the throwing of a stone, striking with a sword or spear, killing, wounding, and the like. These acts are originated but not acquired by the servant, because they lie outside the substrate of his capability.

However, since they are created concomitantly with his acquisition (*kasb*) by customary practice, legal responsibility, reward, and punishment apply to them.

واحترزنا بقولنا: (من غير تأثير) ممّا يعتقده القدريّة مجوس هذه الأمّة؛ مـن أنّ تعلّـق القدرة الحادثة بالأفعال إنّما هـو تعلّق اختراع وتأثير، لا تعلّق اقتران ودلالةً على الأفعال، وبالله تعالى التوفيق.

We excluded, by our statement "without any effect," what the Qadariyyah – the Zoroastrians of this Ummah[13] – hold: namely, that the link of originated capability to acts is a link of origination and effectuation, not a link of concomitance and indication of acts. And with Allah (exalted is He) lies success.

13 This alludes to the hadith: "Every nation has its Magians, and the Magians of this nation are those who deny divine decree. If they fall ill, do not visit them; if they die, do not attend their funerals. They are the partisans of the Dajjāl, and Allah will gather them with him." From Ḥudhayfa: Aḥmad, no. 23503; Abū Dāwūd, no. 4692; and al-Bayhaqī, no. 20659; also al-Bazzār, no. 2937. See Jalāl al-Dīn al-Suyūṭī, *Jāmiʿ al-aḥādīth*, ed. ʿAlī Jumʿa et al., 13 vols. (n.p., n.d.), no. 18602.

THE THIRD PROLEGOMENON

ON THE TYPES OF POLYTHEISM

المقدّمة الثالثة في أنواع الشرك

§١٩ أنواعُ الشركِ ستةٌ:

١. شركُ استقلالٍ: وهو إثباتُ إلهينِ مستقلينِ؛ كشركِ المجوسِ.

٢. وشركُ تبعيضٍ: وهو تركيبُ الإلهِ مِنْ آلهةٍ؛ كشركِ النصارى.

٣. وشركُ تقريبٍ: وهو عبادةُ غيرِ اللّهِ تعالى ليقرّبَ إلى اللّهِ تعالى زُلْفَى؛ كشركِ متقدِّمي الجاهليَّةِ.

٤. وشركُ تقليدٍ: وهو عبادةُ غيرِ اللّهِ تعالى تبعًا للغيرِ؛ كشركِ متأخِّري الجاهليَّةِ.

٥. وشركُ أسبابٍ: وهو إسنادُ التأثيرِ للأسبابِ العاديَّةِ؛ كشركِ الفلاسفةِ والطبائعيِّينَ ومَنْ تبعَهم على ذلكَ.

٦. وشركُ الأغراضِ: وهو العملُ لغيرِ اللّهِ تعالى.

§19 The varieties of *shirk* (associating partners with Allah) are six.

1. *Shirk* of Independence: this refers to affirming two independent deities – such as the *shirk* of the Majūs [the Zoroastrians].
2. *Shirk* of Division: this refers to composing the deity from multiple deities – such as the *shirk* of the Christians.
3. *Shirk* of Approximation: this refers to the worship of other than Allah (exalted is He) as a means of drawing nearer to Him – such as the *shirk* of the early pre-Islamic Arabs.

4. **_Shirk_ of Imitation: this refers to the worship of other than Allah (exalted is He) in imitation of others – such as the _shirk_ of the later pre-Islamic Arabs.**
5. **_Shirk_ of Causes: this refers to attributing causal influence to customary causes – such as the _shirk_ of the philosophers, the naturalists, and those who follow them in that.**
6. **_Shirk_ of Purposes: this refers to performing acts for other than Allah (exalted is He).**

§١٩-١ أمّـا المجوسـن: فالحامـل لهم على الشـرك الـذي انتحلوه: اعتقادهـم أنّ فعـل الخير يجب أن يكون له باعث يباين الباعث على فعـل الشـرّ، وإذا تباينا لم يمكـن أن يجتمعا في ذات واحدة، فوجب التعدّد في ذات الإله، فلزم إثبات إلهين مسـتقلّين؛ أحدهما يسـتقلّ بفعل الخير، ويُسَـمّى عندهم: (هرمز)، والآخر يسـتقلّ بفعل الشـرّ، ويُسَمّى عندهم: (أزدان).

§19.1 As for the Magians (*Majūs*), what led them to the polytheism they adopted was their belief that doing good must have a motive distinct from the motive for doing evil. And if the two motives are distinct, they cannot coexist within a single essence (*dhāt*).

Therefore, multiplicity in the essence of the deity becomes necessary – entailing the affirmation of two independent gods: one independently responsible for doing good, whom they call Hormuz; and the other independently responsible for doing evil, whom they call Azdān.

وأيضًا: ففاعل الخير يُسَمّى خيرًا، وفاعل الشرّ يُسَمّى شريرًا، والوصفان متباينـان لا يمكـن اجتماعهما في موصوف واحـد، فوجب أن يكون موصوفهمـا اثنيـن. ويلزمهـم على مقتضـى هذا النظر الفاسـد الذي نظروه: إثبات إله ثالث؛ ليفعل من الممكنات ما ليس بخير ولا شرّ،

وإن نفوا هذا القسم من الممكنات وحصروها في قسمين -وهما الخير والشرّ- فهم مباهتون وجاحدون لما قطع بوجوده.

Also: the doer of good is called "good," and the doer of evil is called "evil"; and the two descriptors are mutually exclusive and cannot be combined in a single subject. Therefore, their subjects must be two.

It follows from this corrupt speculation (*naẓar*) which they have employed that they must affirm a third deity to bring into being, from among the contingents (*mumkināt*), that which is neither good nor evil. If they deny this category of contingents and restrict them to two categories – namely, good and evil – then they are acting with obstinacy and repudiating what is definitively known to exist.

وأيضًا: فيلزمهم في الشاهد أنّ الفاعل من المخلوقات للخير لا يمكن أن يكون فاعلًا للشرّ، وفاعل الشرّ لا يمكن أن يكون فاعلًا للخير، والمشاهدة تقتضي بطلان ذلك.

Also: it would follow for them, in the observable realm, that a created agent who does good could not do evil, and one who does evil could not do good – whereas observation affirms the falsity of that.

وأيضًا: يلزم على قولهم حدوث الإلهين، وافتقارهما إلى ثالث يخصّص كلّ واحد منهما بما اختصّ به من باعث الخير أو باعث الشرّ.

Also: their assertion entails the origination of the two gods and their dependence upon a third that specifies each of them with his respective instigator – of good or of evil.

وأيضًا: يلزم بين الإلهين المفروضين التمانع عند إرادة أحدهما اختراع الخير في محلّ وإرادة الآخر اختراع الشرّ فيه في زمن واحد.

Also: mutual hindrance necessarily follows between the two posited deities when one of them wills to originate good in a substrate and the other wills to originate evil therein at the same time.

ومن عرف وجوب تنزه المولى العظيم تبارك وتعالى عن الأغراض والاتّصاف بالباعث على الفعل، وتنزّهه عن سريان كمال أو نقص من الأفعال إلى ذاته العليّة.. اتّضح له هوس هؤلاء الكفرة المجوس فيما اعتقدوه.

Whoever understands the necessity of the Exalted Lord (blessed and exalted is He) being transcendent above purposes and above being characterised by any instigator of action, and His transcendence above any perfection or deficiency from actions passing into His sublime Essence (*dhāt*), the delusion of these disbelieving Magians in what they have believed becomes clear to him.

§١٩-٢ وأمّا النصارى أهلكهم اللّه تعالى: فإنّهم لما رأوا توقّف الفعل في الشاهد -نبات الزرع ووجود الثمار ونحوهما- على تعدّد المؤثّر.. قالوا تعالى اللّه عن قولهم: الإله مركّب من ثلاثة أقانيم: وهي أقنوم الوجود، وأقنوم العلم، وأقنوم الحياة، وحكموا عليها بأنّها آلهة ثلاثة مع أنّها صفات!

§19.2 As for the Christians (may Allah destroy them), when they observed that action in the sensible realm – such as the growth of crops, the appearance of fruits, and the like – depends on a multiplicity of agents, they said (exalted is Allah above what they say!) that the deity is composed of three hypostases (*aqānīm*): the hypostasis of existence, the hypostasis of knowledge, and the hypostasis of life.

They judged these to be three gods – even though they are attributes!

ثمّ قالوا مع ذلك: إنّما مجموع الثلاثة إله واحد! فجمعوا بين نقيضين: وحـدة وكثـرة، وجعلوا الذات تتركب من مجرّد أحوال لا وجود لها، أو وجوه واعتبارات لا توجد إلّا في الأذهان، وذلك غير معقول لعاقل.

They then said, on top of that: the totality of the three is but one God! Thus they combined two contradictories – unity and multiplicity – and made the essence (*dhāt*) composed of mere notional states (*aḥwāl*) that have no existence, or of existences and notional constructs (*iʿtibārāt*) that exist only in minds. That is inconceivable to any rational person.

ثمّ زعموا أيضًا: أنّ أقنوم العلم منها - ويُسَمّى الكلمة - اتّحد بناسوت عيسى؛ أي: جسـده، فكان إلهًا بسـبب ذلك. واختلفـوا في معنى اتّحاد الكلمة به.

They also claimed that the hypostasis of knowledge – which they call the Word – united with the human nature of ʿĪsā, that is, his body; and thus he became a god on account of that. They differed concerning the meaning of the union of the Word with him:

فمنهـم مـن فسّـره بقيام الكلمة به كمـا يقوم العـرض بالجوهر: وهذا يوجـب مفارقتـه لـذات الجوهـر الـذي هو عندهـم مجمـوع الأقانيم الثلاثة، وهم يقولون: اتّحد اللاهوت بناسوت عيسى عليه السلام من غيـر أن يفـارق ذات الجوهر، ومـن المعلوم ضرورةً: أنّ المعنى الواحد لا يقوم بذاتين.

Some among them interpreted it as the subsistence of the Word in ʿĪsā, just as an accident subsists in a substance. But this entails its separation from the essence of the substance – which, according to them, is the composite of the three hypostases.

Yet they claim that the Divinity (*lāhūt*) united with the humanity of ʿĪsā (peace be upon him) without separating from the essence of the substance. However, it is necessarily known that a single meaning cannot subsist in two essences (*dhātayn*).

ومنهم مَن فسّر هذا الاتّحاد بالاختلاط والمزج: كاختلاط الخمر مع الماء ونحوهما من المائعات، وكيف يعقل الاختلاط الحسّيّ الذي هو من صفات الأجسام في الكلمة التي هي معنى من المعاني، بل هي حال عندهم وخاصّيّة للذات الأزليّة؟!

Some among them interpreted this union as a blending – like the mixing of wine with water and other liquids. But how can one conceive of sensory blending, which is among the attributes of bodies, in the case of the Word, which is a meaning from among meanings – indeed, a state (*ḥāl*), according to them, and a property of the past-eternal essence (*dhāt*)?!

ومنهم مَن فسّر الاتّحاد بالانطباع: كانطباع صورة النقش في الشمع، ومعلوم أن نقش ذلك الشيء لم يحصل فيما طبع فيه، وإنّما يحصل فيه مثاله.

Some among them interpreted union (*ittiḥād*) as impression (*inṭibā'*): like the impression of an engraved image upon wax. But it is known that the engraving itself does not occur in the thing impressed upon; rather, what occurs therein is its likeness.

فانظر إلى هذا المذهب الركيك ما أخسّه وأرذله! وهو مذهب غير معقول، والنصارى أخسّ الفرق كلّها وأرذلها أفهاما، وإدراك الحقائق على مثلهم عسير.

So consider this feeble doctrine – how base and vile it is! It is unintelligible, and the Christians are the basest and vilest of all sects in understanding – and grasping realities is difficult for the likes of them.

§١٩-٣ قال الإمام الفخر: (ناظرت بعض أحبارهم، فوجدته في غاية البعد من المعقول، فعلمته قاعدةً واحدةً من المعقول لأناظره بها؛ وهي أنّ الدليل يلزم من وجوده وجود المدلول، ولا يلزم من عدم الدليل عدم المدلول؛ كحدوث العالم مثلاً؛ فإنّه دليل على وجود مولانا جلّ وعزّ، فيلزم من وجود الحدوث وجود مدلوله الذي هو وجود مولانا جلّ وعزّ، ولا يلزم من عدم الدليل -الذي هو الحدوث- عدم مدلوله الذي هو وجود مولانا تبارك وتعالى؛ فإنّه كان الحدوث منفيًّا في الأزل، ووجود مولانا جلّ وعزّ واجب في الأزل وواجب فيما لا يزال.

§19.3 Imām al-Fakhr said: "I debated one of their priests and found him extremely far from rationality, so I taught him a single principle of rational discourse (*maʿqūl*) by which to debate him – namely, that the existence of a proof (*dalīl*) entails the existence of that which it proves (*madlūl*), but the absence of the proof does not entail the absence of the thing proved.

"For example, the origination of the world (*ḥudūth al-ʿālam*) is a proof of the existence of our Lord (majestic and exalted is He). Thus, from the existence of origination follows the existence of its signified – the existence of our Lord (majestic and exalted is He). But from the absence of the proof – which is origination – it does not follow that the signified, namely the existence of our Lord (blessed and exalted is He), is absent. For origination was negated in past-eternity, while the existence of our Lord (majestic and exalted is He) was necessary (*wājib*) in past-eternity and remains necessary everlastingly.

فعسر عليه فهم هذه القاعدة، فلم أزل معه حتى فهمها وسلّم لزوم صدقها، فقلت له حينئذٍ: لم خصّصتم اتّحاد أقنوم العلم بناسوت عيسى عليه السلام حتى جعلتموه إلها؟

"He found it difficult to understand this principle, so I remained with him until he understood it and conceded the necessity of its truth.

"I then said to him: 'Why did you single out the union of the hypostasis of knowledge with the human nature of 'Īsā (peace be upon him) as the basis for declaring him to be a god?'

فقال لي: خصّصنا به الاتّحاد لما ظهر على يديه من إحياء الموتى ونحوه ممّا لا يقع إلّا من الإله.

"He said to me: 'We singled out union (*ittiḥād*) for him due to what appeared at his hands – such as the raising of the dead and the like – which occurs only from God.'

فقلت له: يلزمكم أن تقولوا بألوهيّة موسى عليه السلام؛ لما ظهر على يديه من إحياء العصا ثعبانًا عظيمًا، وفلق البحر أطوادًا، ونحو ذلك ممّا يقطع أنّه ليس من فعل المخلوق ألبتّة.

"So I said to him: 'Then you are compelled to affirm the divinity of Mūsā (peace be upon him) on account of what appeared at his hands – such as the transformation of the staff into a great serpent, the splitting of the sea into towering masses, and the like – all of which is decisively not the act of any created being whatsoever.'

فأراد أن ينكر، فقلت له: قد سلّمت أنّه يلزم من وجود الدليل وجود المدلول، ودليل ألوهيّة عيسى عليه السلام على زعمكم موجود في موسى عليه السلام، فيلزم أن يكون إلهًا مثله؛ لاستحالة وجود الدليل بدون المدلول.

"He wished to deny it, so I said to him: 'You have conceded that the existence of the proof entails the existence of that which it proves, and – according to your claim – the proof of the divinity of 'Īsā (peace be upon him) is present in Mūsā (peace be upon him).

"'It therefore follows that he too would be a god, for the existence of a proof without that which it proves is impossible.'

ثـمّ قلـت له: هـل يجوز أن نكـون نحن وهـذه الحيوانـات المحتقرة كالخنافس ونحوها آلهة؟

"Then I said to him: 'Is it permissible that we – and these despicable living creatures, such as beetles and the like – be gods?'

فقال: لا أجوّز ذلك؛ لعدم دليل الألوهيّة فيها.

"He said: 'I do not allow that, due to the absence of any proof of divinity in them.'

فقلـت لـه: كيـف وقـد سـلّمت أنّـه لا يلـزم من عـدم الدليـل عدم المدلـول؟! فلعلّهـا تكون آلهـةً في نفس الأمر علـى مقتضى أصلكم ولم يظهر لكم بعد دليل ألوهيّتها؟! ﴿فَبُهِتَ الَّذِي كَفَرَ وَاللَّهُ لاَ يَهْدِي الْقَوْمَ الظَّالِمِينَ﴾ [البقرة: ٢٥٨].

"So I said to him: 'How can that be, when you have conceded that the absence of evidence does not entail the absence of that which is signified? It may well be that they are gods in reality, by the standard of your own principle – and the evidence for their divinity has simply not yet appeared to you!'

"So the disbeliever was confounded; and Allah does not guide the wrongdoing people."[14]

§١٩-٤ وأمّـا شـرك التقريب الذي دان به متقدّمـو الجاهليّة: الحاملة لهم على ذلك: تسـويل الشـيطان لهم؛ أن وسوس لهم: إن عبادتكم للمولـى العظيـم على مـا أنتم عليه من غاية الضعـف والدناءة والعجز والمهانة، وترككم التقرّب إليه بعبادة من هو أعلى منكم عنده وأشرف

14 al-Baqarah: 2:258.

وأقوى؛ كالملائكة والشمس والقمر والنجوم والنار ونحوها.. سوء أدب عظيم.

§19.4 As for the *shirk* of approximation (*shirk al-taqrīb*) to which the early pagans of the Age of Ignorance adhered: what led them to this was the enticement of Satan, who whispered to them: "Your worship of the great Lord while you are in a state of utter weakness, baseness, incapacity, and humiliation – and your failure to draw near to Him by worshipping those who are, in His sight, higher, nobler, and stronger, such as the angels, the sun, the moon, the stars, the fire, and the like – is a grave impropriety."

ألا ترى في الشاهد: أن تخطّي الأدنى الحقير جدًّا خدمة الحاكم والقائد والمزوار والوزير ونحوهم ممّن هو شريف عند الملك؛ إلى مباشرة خدمة الملك ابتداءً.. سوء أدب على الملك؛ لما فيه من تجاسر الحقير على القرب منه، وعدم مراعاة هيبته وعظمته بالتوسّل إليه من بعد بمن يمكنه التوصّل إلى خدمته من أعوانه وخواصّ مماليكه؟!

Do you not see, in observable cases, that for someone extremely lowly and insignificant to bypass serving the ruler's commander, chamberlain, minister, and the like – those honoured in the king's sight – and to proceed directly to serving the king himself from the outset, is a breach of decorum toward the king? For it entails the audacity of the insignificant in drawing near to him, and a failure to observe his awe and majesty by seeking access to him from a distance through those among his aides and chosen retainers who can facilitate service to him.

§١٩-٥ ثمّ لمّا رأى بعضهم غيبة من اختار عبادته وخدمته عنه؛ إمّا دائمًا؛ كالملائكة عليهم الصلاة والسلام، أو في بعض الأوقات؛

كالشمس والقمر والنجوم وعيسى عليه السلام.. صنعوا الأصنام أمثلة لِما غاب عنهم من معبوداتهم، ولازموا عبادتها، والتقرّب إليها بالذبح والأموال، ونيّتهم التقرّب بذلك لِما جعلت مثالًا له، والقصد من الجميع أن يتقرّبوا إلى المولى العظيم تبارك وتعالى!

§19.5 Then, when some of them observed the absence of those whom they had chosen for worship and service – whether continually – such as the angels (peace be upon them); or at certain times – such as the sun, the moon, the stars, and ʿĪsā (peace be upon him) – they fashioned idols as representations of those they worshipped who were absent from them.

They remained committed to worshipping these idols and drawing near to them through sacrificial offerings and wealth, intending thereby to draw near to those for whom the idols had been made as likenesses.

The aim of all of this was to draw near to the Exalted Master (blessed and exalted is He)!

ولا خفاء في ضلالتهم، وتلاعب الشيطان اللعين بعقولهم، نسأل الله تعالى السلامة والعافية بمنّه.

Their misguidance is plain, and the accursed devil's tampering with their minds is evident.

We ask Allah (exalted is He) for safety and well-being by His grace.

ولو تنبّهوا أدنى تنبّه لعلموا استواء جميع العوالم؛ علويها وسفليها، مظلمها ومضئها، قويها وضعيفها.. في العجز والافتقار العامّ اللازم إلى المولى العظيم جلّ وعلا، وهو سبحانه المباشر لجميعها بالخلق والإمداد بالأعراض، ويخصّ ما شاء منها بما شاء من شرف أو ضدّه، وليس له منها معين ولا وزير ولا وكيل ولا واسطة أصلًا، وليس شيء

منهـا يغيب عن علمه وتدبيره وسـمعه وبصـره، ولا يقدر أحد منها أن يقرب نفسـه -فكيف بغيره؟!- إلى نعمة، أو يبعدها عن نقمة؛ إلّا أن يتفضّل المولى العظيم بذلك على من يشـاء بمحض الفضل والكرم، من غير غرض ولا وجوب ولا استحقاق.

Had they been even slightly attentive, they would have recognised the sameness of all the worlds – the higher and the lower, the dark and the luminous, the strong and the weak – in their universal incapacity and absolute need before the Supreme Lord (majestic and exalted is He).

He (glorified be He) directly brings them all into being and sustains them by supplying their transient states (*aʿrāḍ*), and He singles out whomever He wills among them with whatever He wills of honour or its contrary.

He has no helper, no minister, no agent, and no intermediary whatsoever from among them. Nothing of them escapes His knowledge, governance, hearing, or sight. None of them has the power to draw itself – let alone another – near to a blessing or to distance itself from a punishment, except that the Supreme Lord bestows that upon whomever He wills, purely out of grace and generosity, without motive, obligation, or entitlement.

وعبادتـه جـلّ وعلا وخدمته ومعصيته تبـارك وتعالى إنّما هي أفعال من أفعالـه المخترعـة لـه في ذوات عبيده، ليس لـه حاجة في طاعتها ولا غرض، ولا ينال من إيجادها كمالًا كما لا ينال من خلقه لأضدادها نقصًـا، سـبحانه عليها ما شـاء من ثـواب وعقاب، فـضلًا وعدلًا، لا لقضاء حقّ في الثواب، ولا لإشفاء غيظ في العقاب.

His worship (majestic and exalted is He), His service, and even disobedience to Him (blessed and exalted is He) are but acts from among His own acts, originated by Him in the essences (*dhawāt*) of His servants. He has no need for their obedience, nor any purpose in it; nor does He attain by bringing them into being any perfection – just as He incurs no deficiency by creating their contraries.

Exalted is He. He dispenses upon them whatever He wills of reward and punishment – as grace or as justice – not in fulfilment of any due right in reward, nor to relieve any rage in punishment.

§١٩-٦ فيلزم من هذا كلّه عجز العقول عن إدراك أحكامه الشرعيّة من جهة فكرتها وقياساتها؛ إذ لا مثل له تبارك وتعالى لا شاهدًا ولا غائبًا يقــاس عليــه، وإنّما تدرك أمارة الثواب والعقاب، وما يباح وما لا يباح، وحقائــق ذلــك وكيفياته وأوقاته.. مــن جهة المولى العظيم فقط؛ بمن بعثــه من رســله الكرام، الذيــن أيّدهم بأدلّة صدقهم في كلّ ما يبلغون عنه، وعصمهم بفضله في جميع أقوالهم وأفعالهم واعتقاداتهم من كلّ ما ينهى سبحانه عنه نهي تحريم أو كراهة.

§19.6 It follows from all this that the intellect is incapable of comprehending His revealed rulings through its own conceptualisations and analogical reasoning; for there is nothing like Him (blessed and exalted is He) – neither in the visible nor the invisible realm – by which He could be analogised.

Rather, only the indicators of reward and punishment, what is permitted and what is forbidden, and the realities of these matters – their nature, how they take place, and their appointed times – are known from the Exalted Lord alone, through His noble messengers: those whom He sent and supported with proofs of their truthfulness in all they convey from Him, and whom He protected, by His grace, in all their statements, actions, and beliefs from everything He (glorified is He) prohibits, whether by way of prohibition or disapproval.

وقـد أطبقت رسـل المولى تبارك وتعالى وأجمعـوا كلّهم، من لدن آدم عليـه الـسلام إلى خاتم النبيّين وسـيّد المرسـلين نبيّنـا ومولانا محمّد صلّى اللّه عليه وسـلّم.. على أنّ اللّه سـبحانه كلّف عبيده بتوحيده، وحـرم عليهـم التشـريك في ألوهيّتـه وعبادته، وبلغوا عـن المولى تبارك وتعالـى أنّ مَـن ابتلي بهذا المحرّم؛ وهو الشـرك في الألوهيّة والعبادة، ومـات علـى ذلـك.. فهو محروم مـن جميع نعم الآخـرة، مخلّد في العذاب العظيم إلى غير نهاية.

The messengers of the Lord (blessed and exalted is He) unanimously concurred – from Ādam (peace be upon him) to the Seal of the Prophets and Master of the Messengers, our Prophet and our Master Muḥammad (may Allah bless him and grant him peace) – that Allah (glorified is He) has charged His servants with affirming His oneness, and has forbidden them from associating others with Him in His divinity and worship.

They conveyed from the Lord (blessed and exalted is He) that whoever is afflicted with this forbidden matter – namely, *shirk* in divinity and worship – and dies upon that, is deprived of all the blessings of the Hereafter and will abide eternally in the great torment, without end.

وإذا نظـرت إلـى شـبهة هؤلاء الذين أشـركوا بالتقريـب.. وجدتها غير مقتضيـة للشـرك، وإنّمـا تقتضي مجـرّد التقرّب إلى الملـك بمَن هو شريف عنده إن علم أنّ الملك يأذن في ذلك ويحبّه.

And if you examine the specious argument (*shubhah*) of those who committed *shirk* of approximation, you will find that it does not entail *shirk*; rather, it merely entails seeking nearness to the king through one who is noble in his sight – if it is known that the king permits and loves that.

§١٩-٧ وقد جاء الشرع بالتوسّل إلى المولى تبارك وتعالى، والتشفّع إلى نيل كرمه بأنبيائه ورسله وملائكته وأوليائه، لا سيّما أشرف خلقه الشفيع المشفّع عنده؛ سيّدنا ونبيّنا ومولانا محمّد صلّى اللّٰه عليه وسلّم، ولم تقتض تلك الشبهة أن يشرك مع الملك غيره من خواصّ عبيده، فيجعلون ملوكًا مثله، ويخاطبون بالملك مثل خطابه، ويخدمون على صفة خدمته، ومن علم منه الملوك ذلك أهلكوه هو وشريكه إن رضي بتلك الشركة.

§19.7 The divine legislation has sanctioned seeking means (*tawassul*) to the Exalted Lord, and seeking His bounty through intercession by His prophets, messengers, angels, and saints – especially the noblest of His creation, the intercessor whose intercession is accepted by Him: our master, our prophet, and our patron Muḥammad (may Allah bless him and grant him peace).

Nor does that specious argument (*shubhah*) entail associating others (*shirk*) with the Sovereign in His sovereignty – such that they are made kings like Him, addressed with the same titles of sovereignty, or served in the manner of His service. Any king who perceives such a thing from someone would destroy both him and his associate, if the latter approved of that partnership.

فقد استبان لك: هوسهم واختلال عقولهم في هذا الشرك من كلّ وجه، نعوذ بوجه مولانا الكريم من كلّ شكّ وشرك ونفاق وسيئ أخلاق إلى الممات؛ بجاه نبيّه وأشرف خلقه، سيّدنا محمّد صلّى اللّٰه عليه وسلّم.

It has thus become clear to you: their delusion and intellectual disarray in this *shirk*, in every respect. We seek refuge in the Countenance of our Noble Lord from every doubt, *shirk*, hypocrisy, and vile trait until death – by the rank of His Prophet, the noblest of His creation, our master Muḥammad (may Allah bless him and grant him peace).

§١٩-٨ وأمّا شـرك التقليد: فسـببه غلبة الهـوى، والحمق، والتعصّب للآباء والأجداد في متابعتهم على الباطل وأسباب الهلاك في العاجل والآجـل، ولـو تأمّلوا أدنى تأمّل لقاسـوا هذا الحمـق الموجب للهلاك الـذي وقـع فيه آباؤهم وأجدادهم؛ من الشـرك باللّـه تعالى في ألوهيّته وعبادته، وتكذيبهم رسـله عليهم الصلاة والسلام بعد شـهادة المولى العظيـم تبـارك وتعالـى لهـم بالصـدق.. على ما لـو ابتلي بـه آباؤهم وأجدادهم بالحمق العرفيّ، وذهبوا بسبب حمقهم الى شواهي الجبال ليلقوا أنفسهم منها، جاهلين بما يترتّب لهم على ذلك من الهلاك!

§19.8 As for *shirk* of imitation: its cause is the dominance of caprice, foolishness, and fanaticism for forefathers and ancestors – in following them upon falsehood and the causes of destruction in both this world and the next.

Had they possessed the least capacity for reflection, they would have weighed this ruinous foolishness into which their forefathers and ancestors had fallen – by associating others with Allah (exalted is He) in His divinity and worship, and by denying His messengers (peace be upon them) after the Mighty Lord (blessed and exalted is He) had borne witness to their truthfulness – against the case of their forefathers being afflicted with ordinary foolishness and, due to it, hurling themselves from mountain cliffs, ignorant of the destruction that would befall them as a result!

ولا خفاء أنّهم لا يقلّدونهم في هذا الأمر، ولا يتابعونهم على أسباب هـذا الهلاك الناشـئ عن اختلال العقل، بـل إن أدركوهم وقدروا على ردّهـم عمـا ابتلـوا به بالرفـق أو بالعنف ولـو بالرباط أو القتـال.. فعلوا مجهودهم في ذلك، وإن فاتوهم بإهلاك أنفسـهم ورميها من شـواهق

الجبـال.. لـم يقلّدوهم في ذلـك، وهربوا من حمقهـم وأفعالهم غاية الهـروب، وتبـرّؤوا من متابعتهم غاية التبرّؤ، ورأوا أنّ التعصّب للأحمق بمتابعته في الحمق وأفعاله.. هو غاية الحمق.

It is clear that they would never imitate them in such a case, nor follow them in the causes of this destruction resulting from intellectual disarray. Rather, if they reached them and were able to turn them back from what they had been afflicted with – whether through gentleness, force, restraint, or even combat – they would exert their utmost effort to do so.

And if their forefathers had already destroyed themselves by throwing themselves from mountain cliffs, they would not imitate them in that. They would flee from their madness and deeds with total aversion, renounce following them altogether, and judge that fanaticism for a fool – by following him in his foolishness and actions – is the very height of foolishness.

ولا شكّ أنّ هذا الحمق العرفيّ ليس بأكثر من الحمق الأوّل العقليّ، بـل هـذا الحمـق العقليّ واللّه أعلم أعلى من هـذا الحمق العرفيّ بما لا نهايـة لـه، ومـا ينـشأ عنه من الـهلاك الدنيويّ والأخرويّ لا نسـبة بينه وبين الهلاك الناشـئ عن الحمق العرفيّ، فما بالهم قلّدوا آباءهم وأجدادهم في هذا الحمق الأقوى، وتعصّبوا لهم وهم لا يقلّدونهم في ذلك الحمق الأضعف جدًّا بالنسبة إلى الأوّل؟!

There is no doubt that this customary folly is no greater than the original intellectual folly. Rather, this intellectual folly – and Allah knows best – is far graver than the customary folly, by an immeasurable degree. The worldly and otherworldly destruction that results from it is incomparable to the destruction that arises from customary folly.

So why do they imitate their fathers and forefathers in this more severe folly, and show fanaticism on their behalf – while they do not imitate them in that much lesser folly by comparison?

§١٩-٩ فإن قلت: إنّما قلّدوهم في ذلك الحمق العقليّ لأنّهم لم يستبن لهم أنّه حمق، بخلاف هذا الحمق العرفيّ.

§19.9 Should you say: They imitated them in that rational folly because it was not clear to them that it was folly – whereas this conventional folly is clear.

فالجواب: أنّه سبحانه قد تفضّل ببعث رسول صادقي نبّههم على سفه عقول آبائهم، وما ارتكبوا في ذلك من الضلال وأسباب الهلاك المؤبّد، وشرح لهم ذلك شرحًا لا يبقى معه ريب ولا شبهة، فلم يصغوا إليه، ولا تأمّلوا في كلامه، مع معرفتهم بأنّه واحد منهم، مشهور بالأمانة والصدق ورزانة العقل، بعيد من أسباب التّهم كلّها، وأنّه لم يحمله على ذلك حامل دنيويّ، ولم يقصد إلّا نصحهم وإنقاذهم من المعاطب التي وقع فيها آباؤهم، ثمّ تابعوهم على ذلك بلا تأمّل أصلًا.

The answer is that He (exalted is He) graciously sent a truthful Messenger who alerted them to the folly of their forefathers' intellects and to the misguidance and causes of eternal perdition they had committed. He explained this to them with an explanation that left no doubt or specious argument (*shubhah*). Yet they did not listen to him, nor did they reflect upon his words – despite knowing that he was one of them, well known for trustworthiness, truthfulness, and sound intellect, far removed from all causes of suspicion, and that no worldly motive impelled him to do so. He sought nothing but to advise them and to save them from the perils into which their forefathers had fallen – yet they followed them in that, without any preparation or speculation whatsoever.

فقد استبان لك أيضًا بهذا: هوس المقلّدين في الشرك، واختلال عقولهم في تقليدهم لذوي الضلال والاختلال، مثل هوس من قلّدوه واختلاله.

It has thus become clear to you as well: the mania of the imitators in committing *shirk*, and their intellectual derangement in imitating those given to misguidance and confusion – a mania and derangement like that of those they imitate.

نسأله سبحانه أن يحسن علينا بحسن الخاتمة في عافية بلا محنة، بجاه الشفيع المشفّع عنده، سيّدنا ومولانا محمّد صلّى اللّه عليه وسلّم.

We ask Him (glorified is He) to grant us a good ending in well-being without tribulation, by the rank of the intercessor whose intercession is accepted with Him, our master and patron Muḥammad (may Allah bless him and grant him peace).

§١٩-١٠ وأمّا شرك الأسباب العاديّة: فسببه عمى البصيرة، والاغترار بما ظهر للحسّ من اقتران حادث بحادث، ودورانه معه وجودًا وعدمًا على ما شاء المولى تبارك وتعالى؛ كدوران طبخ الطعام مع قربه من النار مثلًا، وستر العورة مع لبس الثوب مثلًا، ونحو ذلك ممّا لا ينحصر، فاعتقد الناظر في ذلك إذا كان أعمى البصيرة أنّ ذلك السبب العاديّ هو الذي أثر في وجود ما اقترن معه، وأنّه ليس من فعل المولى تبارك وتعالى.

§19.10 As for *shirk* of customary causes: its origin lies in the blindness of inner perception and in being beguiled by what is manifest to the senses – namely, the conjunction of one contingent event with another, and their coincidence in coming to be and ceasing to be, according to the will of the Lord (blessed and exalted is He).

As in the case of cooking food occurring alongside its nearness to fire, or the covering of nakedness alongside the wearing of clothing, and so on – cases too numerous to list – the observer, if blind in inner perception, assumes that the customary cause is what brings about what accompanies it, and that it is not from the Act of the Lord (blessed and exalted is He).

وهـذا كاغتـرار فقير أحمـق أعمى البصيرة جرت عادتـه أنّه مهما جاء لباب من أبواب دار الملك جعل في يده عند وقوفه على ذلك الباب مـا يأكل أو ما يشـرب أو ما يلبـس أو نحو ذلك ممّا يحتاج إليه، فلم يشكّ لحمقه وعمى بصره لعدم مشاهدة من ألقى في يده ذلك.. أنّ تلك الأبواب هي التي تعطيه أغراضه بطبعها أو بقوّة فيها، فامتلأ قلبه بحبّها، وأكثر بلسانه الثناء عليها، وأنشد القصائد في مدحها، ونسي ذكر الملك وفضله وانفراده بالعطاء، وليس له في قلبه كبير موقع.

This is like the delusion of a foolish pauper, blind in insight, whose habit has been that whenever he comes to a door among the doors of the king's palace, there is placed in his hand, as he stands at that door, something to eat, or drink, or wear, or the like of what he needs. Due to his foolishness and blindness of sight, and his failure to perceive the one who placed that thing in his hand, he does not doubt that these doors themselves, by their nature or by some power within them, are what grant him his needs.

Thus, his heart becomes filled with love for them. He frequently praises them with his tongue, composes odes in their praise, and forgets the king, his bounty, and his exclusive bestowal of gifts – and the king holds no real place in his heart.

وفي معنى شرك الأسباب العاديّة: شرك القدريّة فيما اعتقدوه من تأثير القدرة التي خلقها اللّٰه تعالى للحيوانات فيما يقارنها من الأفعال، وقد تقدّم بيان هوسهم.

Related to *shirk* of customary causes is the *shirk* of the Qadariyyah, in their belief that the capability created by Allah (exalted is He) in living creatures produces the acts that accompany it. Their delusion has already been explained.

§١٩-١١ وأمّا شرك الأغراض: فهو العمل المأمور به من واجب ومندوب، وترك محرّم ومكروه؛ لغير امتثال أمر مولانا جلّ وعزّ، بل لمجرّد نيل مدح من بعض عبيده، أو حبّ منه له، أو رئاسته عنده، أو ظفر بمال من قبله، أو صرف مذمّة يخافها منه، ونحو ذلك: العمل لمجرّد الظفر بالحور والقصور، ونعيم الجنان والسلامة من النيران.

§19.11 As for *shirk* of purposes: it is the performance of a commanded act – whether obligatory or recommended – and the avoidance of a prohibited or disliked act, not out of compliance with the command of our Master (majestic and exalted is He), but rather for the sake of obtaining praise from some of His servants, or out of love from them, or for status in their eyes, or to attain wealth from them, or to avert blame feared from them, and the like – such as acting for the sake of attaining houris and palaces, enjoying the bliss of Paradise, or securing safety from the Fire.

والسبب الحامل على ذلك: نسيان توحيد المولى تبارك وتعالى، حتى توهّم العامل لهذه الأغراض إمكان حصول نفع أو دفع ضرّ من غيره تبارك وتعالى، فتوهّم أنّ الخلق يقدرون على النفع والضرّ، حتى راعاهم في طاعته، وتوهّم أيضًا أنّ طاعته تؤثّر في استجلاب نفع أو دفع ضرّ دنيا أو أخرى، فجعلها سببًا لذلك.

The motive behind that is the forgetting of the oneness of the Master (blessed and exalted is He), such that the one acting upon these aims imagined that benefit could be obtained or harm repelled from other than Him (blessed and exalted is He). He assumed that creation possesses the capacity to benefit and harm, and so he took them into account in his obedience. He further imagined that obedience itself has an effect in procuring benefit or averting harm – whether in this world or the next – and thus made it a cause for that.

ولو أحضر في ذهنه انفراد المولى جلّ وعزّ بخلق جميع الكائنات بلا واسطة ولا أثر لكلّ ما سواه عمومًا، ومن جملة ذلك طاعته.. لَما قصد بطاعته إن وفّق لها إلّا مجرّد الامتثال لأمر مولانا جلّ وعزّ، ثمّ يطمع عندها بما وعد به المولى جلّ وعزّ من الخير معها بمحض الفضل من غير وجوب ولا استحقاق، فالمراد بالعمل في كلامنا: العمل المطلوب شرعًا؛ إذ هو الذي يحرم فيه الرياء.

If he were to bring to mind that the Master (majestic and exalted is He) alone creates all existents – without intermediary and without any effect from anything else whatsoever – including obedience itself, then, if he were granted success in obeying, he would intend nothing in it but compliance with the command of our Master (majestic and exalted is He).

Thereafter, he would hope for what the Master (majestic and exalted is He) has promised of good in connection with it, purely out of grace – without obligation or entitlement.

What is meant by "action" in our discourse is the action that is required by divine legislation, for it is this in which ostentation is forbidden.

§٢٠ وحكمُ الأربعةِ الأوَّلِ: الكفرُ بالإجماعِ، وحكمُ السادسِ: المعصيةُ مِنْ غيرِ كفرٍ بإجماعٍ، وحكمُ الخامسِ: التفصيلُ؛ فمَنْ قالَ في الأسبابِ

العاديَّـةِ: إنَّهـا تُؤَثِّرُ بطبعِها.. فقد حُكِيَ الإجمـاعُ على كُفْرِهِ، ومَنْ قالَ: إنَّهـا تُؤَثِّـرُ بقُـوَّةٍ أودعَها اللَّهُ تعالى فيها.. فهو فاسـقٌ مبتـدعٌ، وفي كُفْرِهِ قولانِ.

§20 The judgement of the first four is disbelief, by consensus.

[The judgement of] the sixth is disobedience without disbelief, also by consensus.

The judgement of the fifth is detailed: if someone claims that customary causes affect by their nature, consensus has been reported on his disbelief. But if he claims they affect through a power Allah (exalted is He) placed in them, then he is a transgressing innovator – and there are two opinions regarding his disbelief.

§٢٠-٠ مـراده بالأربعة الأوّل: كفر الاسـتقلال، وكفر التبعيض، وكفر التقريب، وكفر التقليد، ولم يجعل الشرع التأويل ولا التقليد في الكفر الصريح عذرًا لصاحبه؛ لإمكان معرفة الخطأ فيه بأدنى نظر.

§20.0 What he means by the four is:

1. Disbelief of independence (*kufr al-istiqlāl*).
2. Disbelief of division (*kufr al-tabʿīḍ*).
3. Disbelief of approximation (*kufr al-taqrīb*).
4. Disbelief of imitation (*kufr al-taqlīd*).

The divine legislation has not accepted either interpretation or imitation as an excuse for one guilty of explicit disbelief, because the error in such views can be recognised with the slightest speculation (*naẓar*).

§٢٠-١ وإنّمـا اختلفـوا فيمَن قال قولًا يلزم عنـه النقص أو الكفر لزومًا خفيًّـا لـم يشـعر به قائله؛ كالقول بالجهة في حـقّ اللَّه تعالى، وإنكار صفـات المعانـي دون المعنويّة، وإضافـة الأفعـال الاختياريّة إلى قدر الحيوانات على سبيل الاستقلال، وإثبات تشبيه أو نعت بجارحة، أو

نفي صفة كمال على طريق التأويل والاجتهاد المخطئ المفضي إلى الهوى والبدعة، فهذا النوع ممّا اختلف السلف والخلف في تكفير قائله ومعتقده.

§20.1 They only differed concerning one who uttered a statement from which deficiency or disbelief follows as a hidden entailment, of which the speaker was unaware – such as asserting direction with respect to Allah (exalted is He); denying the entitative attributes (*ṣifāt al-maʿānī*) while affirming the derivative attributes (*ṣifāt maʿnawiyyah*); attributing volitional acts to the capabilities of living creatures independently; affirming anthropomorphism or a description involving a bodily organ; or negating an attribute of Perfection by way of erroneous interpretation and fallible reasoning that leads to caprice and innovation.

This category is one over which the early and later generations differed regarding whether its proponent and adherent is to be declared a disbeliever.

فقال القاضي عياض: (وأكثر أقوال السلف تكفيرهم).

ثمّ ذكر: أنّ مِن الفقهاء والمتكلّمين مَن صوّب التكفير الذي قال به الجمهور من السلف، ومِنهم مَن أباه ولم ير إخراجهم من سواد المؤمنين، وهو قول أكثر الفقهاء والمتكلّمين.

Qāḍī ʿIyāḍ said: "Most of the statements of the predecessors were that they are to be declared disbelievers."

Then he mentioned that among the jurists and theologians are those who affirmed the position of declaring them disbelievers, which was the view of the majority of the early generations (*salaf*); and among them are those who rejected that view and did not consider them deserving of removal from the general ranks of the believers. This is the position of most jurists and theologians.

وقال: (هم فسّاق عصاة ضلال، ونورّثهم من المسلمين، ونحكم لهم بأحكامهم، ولهذا قال سحنون: لا إعادة على مَن صلّى خلفهم، قال: وهو قول جميع أصحاب مالك؛ منهم المغيرة وابن كنانة وأشهب، قال: لأنّه مسلم، وذنبه لم يخرجه من الإسلام.

He said:

> They are transgressors, sinners, and those who have gone astray. Yet we treat them as Muslims in matters of inheritance, and apply to them the rulings that pertain to Muslims."
>
> For this reason, Saḥnūn said: "There is no need to repeat the prayer performed behind them."
>
> He said: "This is the view of all the companions of Mālik – among them al-Mughīrah, Ibn Kinānah, and Ashhab."
>
> He said: "For he is a Muslim, and his sin has not expelled him from Islam."

واضطرب آخرون في ذلك، ووقفوا عن القول بالتكفير أو ضدّه، واختلاف قولي مالك في ذلك، وتوقّفه عن إعادة الصلاة خلفهم.. منه.

> Others were unsettled in this matter and withheld judgement on whether to declare them disbelievers or not. The divergence of Mālik's two statements on this – and his hesitation regarding the obligation to repeat the prayer performed behind them – reflects this.

وإلى نحو هذا ذهب القاضي أبو بكر إمام أهل التحقيق والحقّ، وقال: إنّها من المُعوِصات؛ إذ القوم لم يصرّحوا بالكفر، وإنّما قالوا قولًا يؤدّي إليه.

To this view inclined Qāḍī Abū Bakr, the Imām of the people of verification and truth. He said: It is among the thorny questions, for the group did not explicitly profess disbelief; rather, they uttered a statement from which disbelief follows as a consequence.

واضطـرب قولـه في المسألـة على نحو اضطـراب إمامه مالك بن أنس، حتى قال في بعض كلامه: إنّهم على رأي من كفرهم بالتأويل لا تحـلّ مناكحتهـم، ولا أكل ذبائحهـم، ولا الـصلاة علـى ميّتهـم، ويختلف في مواريثهم على الخلاف في ميراث المرتدّ.

His view on the matter was unsettled, similar to the fluctuation of his imām, Mālik ibn Anas, to the extent that he said, in some of his statements, that according to the view of those who declared them disbelievers on the basis of interpretive grounds (*ta'wīl*), it is not lawful to marry them, nor to eat their slaughtered animals, nor to perform the funeral prayer over their dead; and there is disagreement regarding their inheritance, mirroring the disagreement over the inheritance of apostates.

وقـال أيضًـا: نورّث ميّتهـم ورثتهم من المسـلمين، ولا نورّثهم هم من المسلمين.

He also said: We allot the inheritance of their deceased to their heirs from among the Muslims, but we do not allot inheritance to them from the Muslims.

وأكثر ميله إلى ترك التكفير بالمآل.

And his greater inclination was toward refraining from declaring someone a disbeliever based on the downstream implications of their statements (*bi-l-ma'āl*).

وكذلك اضطرب فيه قول شيخه الشيخ أبي الحسن الأشعريّ، وأكثر قوله ترك التكفير، وأنّ الكفر خصلة واحدة؛ وهو الجهل بوجود البارئ تعالى.

Likewise, the position of his teacher, Shaykh Abū al-Ḥasan al-Ash'arī, fluctuated on this matter. The greater part of his view leaned toward refraining from declaring others disbelievers, and that disbelief consists of a single matter: ignorance of the existence of the Creator (exalted is He).

وقال مرّة: مَن اعتقد أنّ اللّٰه تعالى جسم، أو المسيح، أو بعض من يلقاه في الطريق.. فليس بعارف به، وهو كافر.

He once said: Whoever believes that Allah (exalted is He) is a body (*jism*), or that He is the Messiah, or that He is someone encountered on the road – such a person does not know Him and is a disbeliever.

وإلى مثل هذا ذهب أبو المعالي رحمه اللّٰه تعالى في أجوبته لأبي محمّد عبد الحقّ، وكان سأله عن المسألة، واعتذر له بأنّ الغلط فيها يصعب؛ لأنّ إدخال الكافر في الملّة وإخراج المسلم منها.. أمر عظيم في الدين.

Abū al-Ma'ālī (may Allah (exalted is He) have mercy on him) held a similar view in his responses to Abū Maḥammad 'Abd al-Ḥaqq, who had asked him about the issue. He expressed his reservation by saying that error in this matter is difficult to avoid, for admitting a disbeliever into the religion or expelling a Muslim from it is a grave matter in the religion.

وقال غيرهما من المحقّقين: الذي يجب الاحتراز منه التكفير في أهل التأويل؛ فإنّ استباحة دماء المسلمين الموحّدين خطر، والخطأ في ترك ألف كافر أهون من الخطأ في سفك محجمة من دم مسلم واحد.

And other verifying scholars have said: What must be guarded against is declaring the people of interpretation (*ta'wīl*) to be disbelievers, for deeming the blood of monotheistic Muslims licit is a grave danger. The error of withholding judgement from a thousand disbelievers is less severe than the error of shedding a single cupping's worth of blood from one Muslim.

وقد قال عليه الصلاة والسلام: «فإذا قالوها» يعني: الشهادة «عصموا مني دماءهم وأموالهم إلّا بحقّها، وحسابهم على اللّه»، والعصمة مقطوع بها مع الشهادة، ولا ترتفع ولا يستباح خلافها إلّا بقاطع، ولا قاطع من شرع، ولا قياس عليه، وألفاظ الأحاديث الواردة في الباب معرضة للتأويل).

The Prophet (peace and blessings be upon him) said: "When they say it" – meaning the testimony – "they have protected from me their blood and their wealth, except with due cause, and their reckoning is with Allah."[15]

Legal protection is definitively established with the testimony, and it is not nullified, nor is its violation permitted, except by definitive proof. And no such proof exists in the divine legislation, nor is there any valid analogy based upon it. As for the wordings of the ḥadīths transmitted in this chapter – they are open to interpretation.[16]

ثمّ قال القاضي بعد هذا: (والصواب: ترك إكفارهم، والإعراض عن الحتم عليهم بالخسران، وإجراء حكم الإسلام عليهم؛ في قصاصهم، ووراثاتهم، ومناحاتهم، ودياتهم، والصلاة عليهم، ودفنهم في مقابر المسلمين، وسائر معاملاتهم، للكنهم يغلظ عليهم بوجيع الأدب وشديد الزجر والهجر، حتى يرجعوا عن بدعتهم.

15 al-Suyūṭī, *Jāmi' al-aḥādīth*, no. 5391 (Muslim, no. 21; Ibn Ḥibbān, no. 174).
16 Qāḍī 'Iyāḍ, *Al-Shifā*, 839–41.

Then the Qāḍī said after this:

> The correct view is to refrain from declaring them unbelievers, to avoid asserting their perdition as definitive, and to apply the rulings of Islam to them – in matters of retribution, inheritance, marital dealings, blood money, the funeral prayer over them, burial in Muslim cemeteries, and all other dealings. However, they are to be subjected to severe disciplinary measures, stern rebuke, and shunning, until they abandon their innovation.

وهـذه كانت سـيرة الصـدر الأوّل فيهـم، وقد كان نـشأ على زمان الصحابة وبعدهـم في التابعين من قال بهذه الأقوال؛ من القدريّة ورأي الخـوارج والاعتـزال، فما أزاحوا لهم قبرًا، ولا قطعوا لأحد منهم ميراثًا، لكنّهـم هجروهـم، وأدّبوهـم بالضرب والنفي والقتل على قدر أحوالهـم؛ لأنّهم فسّاق ضلال عصاة أصحاب كبائر عند المحقّقين وأهل السنّة ممّن لم يقل بكفرهم منهم، خلافًا لمَن رأى غير ذلك انتهى.

> And this was the conduct of the earliest generation toward such people. Indeed, during the time of the Companions and thereafter among the Followers, there arose those who espoused these doctrines – such as the Qadariyyah, those who held the views of the Khārijites, and the Muʿtazilah. Yet they neither denied them burial places nor cut off inheritance from any of them. Rather, they shunned them and disciplined them according to their respective conditions – whether by beating, banishment, or execution.
>
> This was because, according to the verifiers and the People of the Sunnah who did not declare them disbelievers, they were transgressors, misguided sinners, and people of major sins – contrary to the view of those who held otherwise.[17]

End.

---

17 Qāḍī ʿIyāḍ, *Al-Shifā*, 860.

وبالجملة: فالذي أجمع عليه أهل الحقّ: أنّ الصواب والحقّ في العقليّات واحد، والمخطئ فيه آثم عاص فاسق، ثمّ اختلفوا في التكفير على حسب ما سبق.

In sum: what the adherents of truth have unanimously agreed upon is that there is a single correct position in rational matters (*'aqliyyāt*), and that whoever errs in them is sinful, disobedient, and transgressing. They then differed regarding whether such a person is to be declared a disbeliever, as detailed above.

وقد ذهب العنبريّ من المبتدعة إلى تصويب أقوال المجتهدين في أصول الدين فيما كان عرضة للتأويل، وفارق في ذلك إجماع الأمّة.

Al-'Anbarī, one of the innovators, held the view that the statements of the *mujtahids* in the principles of religion are correct in matters open to interpretation, thereby departing from the consensus of the Ummah.

قال القاضي في «الشفا»: (وقد حكى القاضي أبو بكر الباقلانيّ مثل قول عبيد الله -يعني: العنبريّ- عن داود الأصبهانيّ، قال: وحكى قوم عنهما أنّهما قالا ذلك في كلّ مَن علم الله من حاله استفراغ الوسع في طلب الحقّ من أهل ملّتنا أو من غيرهم، وقال نحو هذا الجاحظ وثمامة؛ في أنّ كثيرًا من العامّة والنساء والبله ومقلّدة النصارى واليهود وغيرهم.. لا حجّة لله عليهم؛ إذ لم تكن لهم طباع يمكن معها الاستدلال.

Qāḍī 'Iyāḍ said in *al-Shifā'*:

> Qāḍī Abū Bakr al-Bāqillānī transmitted a view similar to that of 'Ubayd Allāh – meaning al-'Anbarī – from Dāwūd al-Aṣbahānī. He said: And some have reported from both of them that they held this view regarding everyone whom Allah knows to have

exerted their utmost effort in seeking the truth, whether from among the people of our religion or others.

Al-Jāḥiẓ and Thumāmah said something similar: that many among the common folk, women, the simple-minded, and the imitators of the Christians, Jews, and others – Allah has no conclusive proof against them, since they do not possess the faculties needed for inference.

قال: وقد نحا الغزاليّ قريبًا من هذا المَنحى في كتاب «التفرقة»، وقائل هذا كافر؛ بالإجماع على كفر مَن لم يكفّر أحدًا من النصارى واليهود، وكلّ مَن فارق دين الإسلام، أو وقف في تكفيرهم أو شكّ.

He said: al-Ghazālī adopted an approach close to this in his book *al-Tafriqah*. And whoever says this is himself a disbeliever – by the consensus that whoever does not declare any of the Christians or Jews disbelievers, or anyone who has departed from the religion of Islam, or refrains from declaring them disbelievers, or doubts their disbelief, is himself a disbeliever.

قال القاضي أبو بكر: لأنّ التوقيف والإجماع على كفرهم، فمَن وقف في ذلك فقد كذّب النصّ والتوقيف أو شكّ فيه، والتكذيب والشكّ فيه لا يقع إلّا من كافر) انتهى.

Qāḍī Abū Bakr said: Because there is revealed text and consensus regarding their disbelief, so whoever hesitates concerning that has either denied the text and the scriptural determination or doubted it – and denial or doubt concerning it occurs only from a disbeliever.[18]

End.

قلت: والذي أظنّه أنّ الغزاليّ رحمه اللّه تعالى إنّما ذكر في «التفرقة» العذر في حقّ من بعدت بلاده من بلاد المسلمين، ولم تصله دعوة

18 Qāḍī ʿIyāḍ, *Al-Shifā*, 845–6.

النبيّ صلّى اللّه عليه وسلّم أصلًا، أو وصلته على غير وجهها؛ من النساء والبله ونحوهم.

I say: What I believe is that al-Ghazālī – may Allah (exalted is He) have mercy on him – only mentioned in *al-Tafriqah* the excuse concerning those whose lands are distant from the lands of the Muslims, and to whom the Prophet's (may Allah bless him and grant him peace) call never reached, or to whom it came in an incorrect form – such as women, the dim-witted, and others like them.

وأمّا مَن قربت بلاده من بلاد المسلمين، ووصلته دعوة النبيّ صلّى اللّه عليه وسلّم على وجهها، وأمكنته معرفتها من المسلمين.. فالغزاليّ يوافق على كفره، وأنّه لا عذر له في الآخرة.

As for one whose lands are near the lands of the Muslims, to whom the Prophet's (peace be upon him) call has reached in its proper form, and it was possible for him to learn it from the Muslims – al-Ghazalı agrees that he is a disbeliever, and that he has no excuse in the Hereafter.

وعلى هذا: فقول الغزاليّ رضي اللّه تعالى عنه بعيد من أقوال أولئك المبتدعة والمخالفين لإجماع أهل الحقّ، واللّه تعالى أعلم.

Accordingly, the statement of al-Ghazālī (may Allah – exalted is He – be pleased with him) is far removed from the assertions of those innovators and dissenters from the consensus of the people of truth. And Allah (exalted is He) knows best.

§٢٠-٢ قوله: (وحكم السادس: المعصية) يعني بالسادس: شرك الأغراض؛ وهو أن يعمل عملًا من الأعمال الصالحة بنيّة الوصول به إلى غرض دنيويّ؛ وهو رياء محرّم، سواء طلب ذلك الغرض من الخلق أو من مولانا جلّ وعزّ، إلّا أن يطلب ذلك الغرض الدنيويّ ليستعين

بـه علـى طاعته تبارك وتعالـى، فلا يكون ذلك حينئذٍ رياء، وعلى هذا يحمل ما ورد في بعض الطاعات أنّها سـبب للتوسّـع في الرزق، وقد يحمل ذلك على التوسّعة المعنويّة؛ بخلق القناعة في القلب، والزهد، والغناء بالمولى تبارك وتعالى عن كلّ ما سـواه، وهذا هو الغناء الأكبر والتوسّعة الحقيقيّة.

§20.2 His statement, "And the judgement of the sixth: disobedience."

By "the sixth," he means *shirk* of purposes (*shirk al-aghrāḍ*): that is, to perform a righteous deed with the intention of using it to attain a worldly aim. This is forbidden ostentation (*riyāʾ*), whether that aim is sought from created beings or from our Master (majestic and exalted is He).

However, if that worldly aim is sought in order to seek assistance thereby in obeying Him (blessed and exalted is He), then it is not considered ostentation. On this basis is interpreted what has been reported concerning certain acts of obedience being a cause for increase in provision. This may also be understood as a spiritual expansion through the creation of contentment (*qināʿah*) in the heart, renunciation (*zuhd*), and sufficiency (*ghinā*) through the Master (blessed and exalted is He) above all else.

This is the greater sufficiency and the true expansion.

قوله: (وحكم الخامس: التفصيل) يعني بالخامس: شـرك الأسـباب؛ وهو اعتقاد تأثيرها فيما قارنها عادةً، ولا شكّ أنّ اعتقاد الناس في هذه الأسباب العاديّة على أربعة أوجه:

§20.3 His statement, "And the ruling of the fifth is detailed" – he means by the fifth: *shirk* of customary causes; that is, the belief in their effect upon what they customarily accompany. There is no doubt that people's belief regarding these customary causes falls into four categories.

(١) منهــم: مَــن يعتقــد قدمها واســتقلالها بالتأثير مــن طباعها؛ أي: حقائقها من غير جعل من اللّه تعالى، وهذا مذهب كثير من الفلاسفة والطبائعيّين، وقد حكى ابن دهاق وغيره الإجماع على كفرهم.

(1) Among them are those who believe in the pre-eternity of these causes and their independent effectuation by their own natures – that is, by their intrinsic realities – without any origination from Allah (exalted is He). This is the doctrine of many philosophers and naturalists; Ibn Dahhāq and others have reported consensus on their disbelief.

(٢) ومــن النــاس: مَــن يعتقد حدوثها وتأثيرها فيمــا قارنها، لكن ليس مــن طباعهــا، وإنّما يخلق اللّه تعالى فيها قوّةً مؤثّرةً، ولو نزعها منها لم تؤثّر، فهؤلاء مبتدعة ضلال فسّاق، وفي كفرهم من الخلاف ما سبق.

(2) Among the people are those who believe that these causes are originated and that they have an effect upon what they accompany – but not by their nature. Rather, Allah creates within them a power by which they influence, and if He were to remove it, they would have no effect.

These are innovators, astray, and transgressors; and there is a difference of opinion concerning their disbelief, as previously mentioned.

(٣) ومــن النــاس: مَــن يعتقــد حدوثها وعــدم تأثيرها فيمــا قارنها، لا بطباعهــا ولا بقــوّة جعلت فيها، لكنّه يعتقــد ملازمتها لما قارنها، وأنّه لا يصــحّ فيهــا التخلّف، وهذا الاعتقاد يؤوّل بصاحبه إلى الكفر؛ لأنّه يســتلزم إنــكار معجــزات الأنبيــاء عليهم الـصلاة والـسلام، وإنكار ما أخبــروا بــه من أحــوال الموت والقبر والآخرة؛ لأنّ ذلك كلّه من باب

خرق العوائد الذي تتخلّف فيه الأسباب العاديّة عمّا يقارنها، ولأجل اعتقاد عدم التخلّف في العاديّات أنكر الجاهليّة البعث، وقالوا: ﴿أَإِذَا كُنَّا عِظَامًا وَرُفَاتًا أَإِنَّا لَمَبْعُوثُونَ خَلْقًا جَدِيدًا﴾ [الإسراء: ٤٩].

(3) Among the people are those who believe that these causes are originated and that they have no effect upon what they accompany – neither by their nature nor by any power placed within them. However, they believe that these causes invariably accompany the effects they are joined with, and that deviation from this is impossible.

This belief leads its holder to disbelief, for it entails the denial of the miracles of the Prophets (peace be upon them), and the denial of what they reported concerning the states of death, the grave, and the Hereafter. All of that falls under the category of breaching customary norms (*kharq al-ʿādāt*), wherein ordinary causes fail to produce their usual effects.

Because of this belief in the impossibility of deviation in customary patterns, the pagans denied the resurrection, saying, "When we have become bones and dust, shall we indeed be raised up as a new creation?"[19]

(٤) ومن الناس: مَن يعتقد حدوث الأسباب العاديّة وعدم تأثيرها فيما قارنها، لا بطبعها ولا بقوّة جعلت فيها، وأنّ مولانا جلّ وعزّ جعلها أمارات ودلائل على ما شاء سبحانه من الحوادث من غير ملازمة عقليّة بينها وبين ما جعلت دليلًا عليه، فلهذا صحّ أن يخرق جلّ وعزّ العادة فيها لمَن شاء، وفي أيّ وقت شاء، وهذا الاعتقاد هو الحقّ، والقائلون به هم المؤمنون أهل السنّة، وقد تقدّم شرح الحكم العاديّ على هذا المذهب السنّيّ.

19 al-Isrāʾ: 17:49.

(4) Among the people are those who believe in the origination of customary causes and their lack of effect upon what accompanies them – neither by their nature nor by a capability placed within them – and that our Master (majestic and exalted is He) has made them signs and indicators of what He wills of occurrences, without there being any rational necessitation between them and that for which they have been made as indicators.

For this reason, it is valid that He (majestic and exalted is He) may break the custom in them for whomever He wills and whenever He wills. This belief is the truth, and those who hold it are the believers, the People of the Sunnah. The explanation of customary judgement (*ḥukm ʿādī*) according to this Sunni doctrine has already preceded.

THE FOURTH PROLEGOMENON
ON THE ROOTS
OF DISBELIEF AND INNOVATIONS

المقدّمة الرابعة في أصول الكفر والبدع

§٢١ وأصولُ الكُفْرِ والبِدَعِ سبعةٌ:

١. الإيجابُ الذاتيُّ: وهو إسنادُ الكائناتِ إلى اللَّهِ تعالى على سبيلِ التعليلِ أو الطبعِ مِنْ غيرِ اختيارٍ.

٢. والتحسينُ العقليُّ: وهو كونُ أفعالِ اللَّهِ تعالى وأحكامِهِ موقوفةً عقلًا على الأغراضِ؛ وهي: جلبُ المصالحِ، ودرءُ المفاسدِ.

٣. والتقليدُ الرديءُ: وهو مُتَابَعَةُ الغيرِ لأجلِ الحميَّةِ والتعصُّبِ مِنْ غيرِ طلبٍ للحقِّ.

٤. والربطُ العاديُّ: وهو إثباتُ التلازُمِ بينَ أمرٍ وأمرٍ وجودًا أو عدمًا بواسطةِ التكرُّرِ.

٥. والجهلُ المركَّبُ: وهو أنْ يجهلَ الحقَّ، ويجهلَ جهلَهُ بهِ.

٦. والتمسَّكُ في عقائدِ الإيمانِ بمجرَّدِ ظواهرِ الكتابِ والسنَّةِ: مِنْ غيرِ تفصيلٍ بينَ ما يستحيلُ ظاهرُهُ منْها وما لا يستحيلُ.

٧. والجهلُ بالقواعدِ العقليَّةِ: التي هي العلمُ بوجوبِ الواجباتِ، وجوازِ الجائزاتِ، واستحالةِ المستحيلَاتِ، وباللسانِ العربيِّ: الذي هو علمُ اللغةِ والإعرابِ والبيانِ.

§21 The roots of disbelief and innovation are seven.

1. **Intrinsic Necessitation (*ījāb dhātī*): this is ascribing created entities to Allah (exalted is He) by way of causality or nature, without His volition.**
2. **Rational Moral Appraisal (*taḥsīn ʿaqlī*): this is the view that Allah's actions and judgements (exalted is He) are contingent upon purposes – namely, attaining benefits and averting detriments.**
3. **Vile Imitation (*taqlīd radīʾ*): this is following others out of solidarity and fanaticism, without any pursuit of the truth.**
4. **Customary Association (*rabṭ ʿādī*): this is affirming a correlation between two matters – whether in existence or nonexistence – based on repetition.**
5. **Compound Ignorance (*jahl murakkab*): this is to be ignorant of the truth while also being ignorant of one's ignorance of it.**
6. **Adherence to Apparent Meanings (*tamassuk bi-ẓawāhir*): this is adherence in matters of belief to the mere outward meanings of the Qur'an and Sunnah – without distinction between those whose apparent meanings are impossible and those which are not.**
7. **Ignorance of Rational and Linguistic Principles: that is, ignorance of the rational principles by which one knows the necessity of what is necessary, the possibility of what is possible, and the impossibility of what is impossible – and ignorance of the Arabic language, meaning knowledge of lexicography, syntax, and rhetoric.**

§٢١-٠ يعني: أنّ اعتقاد واحد من هذه الأمور: قد ينشأ عنه كفر مجمع عليه، وقد ينشأ عنه بدعة مختلف في كفر صاحبها.

§21.0 Meaning: Belief in one of these matters may lead to disbelief over which there is consensus, or to an innovation about whose proponent there is disagreement concerning whether he is a disbeliever.

§٢١-١ أمّا الأمر الأوّل؛ وهو الإيجاب الذاتيّ؛ أي: اعتقاد أنّ الذات العليّة في وجود الممكنات لا بالاختيار، بل بطريق العلّة والطبيعة: فلا إشكال في كفر مَن يعتقد هذا؛ لأنّ من لازم هذا المذهب إنكار القدرة والإرادة الأزليّتين، ومن لازمه قدم العالم، ومن لازمه تكذيب القرآن في قوله تعالى: ﴿وَرَبُّكَ يَخْلُقُ مَا يَشَاءُ وَيَخْتَارُ﴾ [القصص: ٦٨]، وقوله عزّ وجلّ: ﴿بَلْ يَدَاهُ مَبْسُوطَتَانِ يُنْفِقُ كَيْفَ يَشَاءُ﴾ [المائدة: ٦٤]، ونحو ذلك ممّا هو كثير في الكتاب والسنّة.

§21.1 As for the first matter – namely, essential necessitation: that is, the belief that the Exalted Essence brings contingent beings (*mumkināt*) into existence not by choice, but by way of causality (*ʿillah*) and nature – there is no doubt regarding the disbelief of one who holds this view.

For among the necessary entailments of this doctrine is the denial of the past-eternal capability and will, the assertion of the world's pre-eternity, and the rejection of the Qurʾān in His saying – exalted is He: "And your Lord creates what He wills and chooses,"[20] and His saying – mighty and majestic: "Rather, both His hands are outstretched; He spends as He wills,"[21] and the like of that, which is abundant in the Book and the Sunnah.

§٢١-٢ والفرق بين العلّة والطبيعة: أنّ العلّة تقتضي معلولها وتلازمه، ولا يمكن انفكاكه عنها أصلًا، والطبيعة تقتضي مطبوعها عند توفّر الشروط وانعدام الموانع، وقد يتخلّف عنها المطبوع لتخلّف شرط أو وجود مانع.

§21.2 The difference between the cause (*ʿillah*) and nature (*ṭabīʿah*) is that the cause necessitates its effect and is concomitant with it,

20 al-Qaṣaṣ: 28:68.
21 al-Māʾidah: 5:64.

and separation from it is absolutely impossible. Nature, however, necessitates what is natural to it upon the availability of conditions and the nonexistence of impediments, and what is natural to it may fail to occur due to the nonexistence of a condition or the presence of an impediment.

وهذا المذهب ظاهر الفساد؛ فإنّ البرهان القطعيّ قد دلّ على وجوب القدم لمولانا جلّ وعزّ، ووجوب الحدوث لكلّ ما سواه تعالى، ودلّ أيضًا على استحالة حوادث لا أوّل لها، فيتعيّن على سبيل القطع واليقين أنّ المولى تبارك وتعالى إنّما أوجد العالم بطريق الاختيار، لا بطريق اللزوم في الأزليّ؛ وهو طريق التعليل، ولا بطريق اللزوم فيما لا يزال؛ وهو طريق الطبع؛ إذا قدر تخلّف شرط أو وجود مانع في الأزل لوجود العالم؛ لأنّه لو تخلّف شرطها في الأزل لم يمكن أن توجد أبدًا؛ لنقل الكلام إلى ذلك الشرط فيلزم فيه التسلسل، ولو وجد لها مانع من وجودها في الأزل لكان ذلك المانع قديمًا، فيستحيل عدمه، والعوالم قد توقّفت على عدمه، فلا يمكن وجودها أبدًا.

This doctrine is manifestly corrupt. Decisive proof has established the necessity of pre-eternity for our Master (glorious and mighty is He), and the necessity of origination for everything other than Him (exalted is He), and has likewise established the impossibility of an infinite regress of originated events without a beginning.

It is therefore decisively and certainly determined that the Master (blessed and exalted is He) brought the world into being by way of volition – not by way of necessitation in past-eternity (which is the path of causal explanation), nor by way of necessitation in perpetuity (which is the path of nature).

If it were supposed that a condition was lacking or an impediment present in past-eternity for the world's existence, then if that condition were absent in past-eternity, it would never be possible for the world to exist at all – for the discussion would transfer to that condition, leading to infinite regress (*tasalsul*). And if there were an impediment in past-eternity, then that impediment would be eternal, making its nonexistence impossible, while the existence of the worlds depends on its nonexistence – and so their existence would never be possible.

§٢١-٣ وأمّا الأمر الثاني؛ وهو التحسين العقليّ: فقد نشأ عنه كفر صريح مجمع عليه؛ وهو كفر البراهمة؛ فإنّهم أنكروا النبوّة، وكذّبوا الرسل عليهم الصلاة والسلام فيما بلّغوه عن المولى تبارك وتعالى؛ من إيجاب الركوع والسجود، وإباحة ذبح البهائم للأكل، ونحو ذلك، وهذا كلّه عندهم قبيح، يستحيل أن يشرعه الحكيم.

§21.3 As for the second matter – namely, rational moral appraisal (*taḥsīn ʿaqlī*) – it has given rise to explicit disbelief, unanimously agreed upon: namely, the disbelief of the Brahmins. For they denied prophethood and declared the messengers (peace be upon them) to be liars in what they conveyed from the Lord (blessed and exalted is He) – such as the obligation of bowing and prostration, the permissibility of slaughtering animals for consumption, and the like.

All of this, according to them, is repugnant – and it is impossible, in their view, that the Wise One should legislate it.

ولو تأمّلوا أدنى تأمّل لعرفوا فساد رأيهم؛ لأنّه لو قبح ذلك في حكمه تعالى لقبح في فعله جلّ وعلا، ومن المعلوم قطعًا أنّ المولى تبارك وتعالى قد يجعل شخصًا بمرض أو كبر على هيئة الراكع أو على هيئة الساجد، بل قد يسلب عقله حتى يصدر منه ما هو أعظم من هذا؛ من كشف العورة، وأكل العذرة وسائر النجاسات، والتلطّخ بها! فإذا

كان له تعالى أن يفعل ما يشاء.. فله جلّ وعلا أن يحكم في عبيده بما يشاء.

Had they reflected even slightly, they would have recognised the falsity of their view; for if such a thing were reprehensible in His judgement (exalted is He), it would be equally reprehensible in His action (majestic and sublime is He).

And it is certainly known that the Master (blessed and exalted is He) may cause a person, due to illness or old age, to assume the posture of one bowing or prostrating; and He may even deprive him of his intellect, such that he commits acts more grievous than these – such as exposing his private parts, consuming excrement and other impurities, and defiling himself with them.

So if it is within His capability (exalted is He) to do as He wills, then it is likewise within His capability (majestic and sublime is He) to legislate among His servants as He wills.

ولو توقّفت أفعاله سبحانه وأحكامه على الأغراض.. لزم احتياجه تعالى إلى الأفعال ليحصّل بها غرضه، وذلك ينافي جلاله وعظمته ووجوب غناه جلّ وعلا عن كلّ ما سواه تعالى.

And were His (exalted is He) actions and judgements dependent upon purposes, it would entail His need for actions to realise His aims – and that is contrary to His Majesty and His Greatness, and to the necessity of His absolute self-sufficiency (glorious and exalted is He) above all that is other than Him.

ونشأ عن هذا الأصل الفاسد بدعة المعتزلة: في إيجابهم مراعاة الصلاح والأصلح للعباد في حقّه تعالى، وكون الأحكام الشرعيّة تابعة لتحسين العقل وتقبيحه، ونحو ذلك من بدعهم.

From this corrupt principle arose the innovation of the Muʿtazilah: their claim that it is obligatory for Allah to act in accordance with what is good or better (*al-ṣalāḥ wa-al-aṣlaḥ*) for His servants, and that legal rulings are based on the intellect's appraisal of good and evil – and other such innovations of theirs.

§٢١-٤ وأمّا الأمر الثالث؛ وهو التقليد الرديء: فقد نشأ عنه كفر صريح مجمع عليه؛ وهو تقليد الجاهليّة آباءهم في الشرك وعبادة الأصنام، وتقليد عامّة اليهود وعامّة النصارى لأحبارهم في إنكار نبوّة نبيّنا ومولانا محمّد صلّى الله عليه وسلّم، ونحو ذلك من كلّ تقليد في كفر صريح.

§21.4 As for the third matter – which is vile imitation – it has given rise to explicit disbelief, unanimously agreed upon: the imitation by the people of ignorance of their forefathers in polytheism and the worship of idols; the imitation by the masses of the Jews and Christians of their priests in denying the Prophethood of our Prophet and Master, Muḥammad (peace be upon him); and all other forms of imitation that entail explicit disbelief.

ونشأ عنه بدعة مختلف في كفر صاحبها: كتقليد عامّة المعتزلة والمرجئة والمجسّمة لقدمائهم فيما دانوا به من هذه البدع، وقد سبق ما في ذلك من الخلاف.

It also gave rise to an innovation about which there is disagreement concerning the disbelief of its adherent – such as the imitation by the common people among the Muʿtazilah, the Murji'ah, and the corporealists (*mujassimah*) of their predecessors in what they adopted of these innovations. The disagreement concerning this has already preceded.

§٢١-٥ واحترز بـ (التقليد الرديء) من التقليد الحسن؛ كتقليد عامّة المؤمنين لعلمائهم في الفروع.

§21.5 His use of the term "vile imitation" is intended to exclude sound imitation – such as the imitation of the common believers to their scholars in matters of subsidiary rulings.

§٢١-٦ واختلف في تقليد عامّة المؤمنين لعلماء أهل السنّة في أصول الدين: هل يكفي ذلك أم لا؟

§21.6 There is a difference of opinion regarding the imitation of the common believers of the scholars of the People of Truth in the principles of religion: is it sufficient or not?

وكثير من المحقّقين قالوا: إنّ ذلك كاف إذا وقع منهم التصميم على الحقّ، لا سيّما فيمَن يعسر عليه فهم الأدلّة.

Many of the verifiers have said that it is sufficient, provided they have firm resolve upon the truth – especially in the case of those for whom understanding the evidences is difficult.

§٢١-٧ وأمّا الأمر الرابع؛ وهو الربط العاديّ: فلا شكّ أنّه قد نشأ عنه كفر صريح مجمع عليه؛ ككفر الطبائعيّين القائلين بقدم الأفلاك وتأثيرها بطباعها في العوالم الأرضيّة، وكفر الجاهليّة المنكرين للبعث وأحوال الآخرة بسبب الاغترار بالربط العاديّ.

§21.7 As for the fourth matter – which is customary association (*rabṭ ʿādī*) – it has unquestionably given rise to explicit disbelief, unanimously agreed upon. Such as the disbelief of the naturalists who assert the pre-eternity of the celestial spheres and their influence by their natures upon the terrestrial realms, and the disbelief of the pre-Islamic pagans who denied resurrection and the realities of the Hereafter on account of their delusion with customary association.

ونشأ عنه بدعة مختلف في كفر صاحبها: كبدعة من اعتقد حدوث الأسباب العاديّة وتأثيرها بجعل اللّٰه تعالى فيها قوّة لذلك، ولو شاء لم تؤثّر، وقد سبق ما في ذلك من الخلاف.

And from it arose an innovation concerning which there is disagreement regarding the disbelief of its proponent. Such as the innovation of one who believes that customary causes are originated and effect things by Allah placing within them a power to do so – though, if He willed otherwise, they would not effect anything. The aforementioned disagreement on this has already been mentioned.

§٢١-٨ وأمّا الأمر الخامس؛ وهو الجهل المركّب الذي هو اعتقاد أمر على خلاف ما هو عليه: فلا شكّ أنّه سبب للتمادي على الكفر إن كان ذلك الكفر هو الذي وقع الجهل باعتقاده؛ كجهل الفلاسفة باعتقاد قدم الأفلاك، واعتقادهم تأثير الإله بطريق التعليل، ونحو ذلك من كفرياتهم.

§21.8 As for the fifth matter – which is compound ignorance (*jahl murakkab*), that is, believing something to be as it is not – there is no doubt that it is a cause for continued disbelief, when the disbelief itself is the object of that ignorance. Such as the ignorance of the philosophers in their belief in the pre-eternity of the celestial spheres, or their belief that the Deity acts by way of causal necessitation, and other such doctrines of theirs that entail disbelief.

وهو أيضًا سبب في التمادي على البدعة إن كانت تلك البدعة هي التي وقع الجهل باعتقادها؛ كجهل القدريّة باعتقادهم استقلال الحيوانات بإيجادها أفعالها الاختياريّة، واعتقادهم وجوب مراعاة

الصلاح والأصلح في حقّ المولى تبارك وتعالى، ونحو ذلك من سائر البدع الاعتقاديّة.

It is also a cause for persistence in innovation when that innovation itself is the object of one's ignorance – such as the ignorance of the Qadariyyah in their belief that living creatures independently produce their voluntary acts, and their belief that it is obligatory for the Master (blessed and exalted is He) to act in accordance with what is good and most beneficial – and other such doctrinal innovations.

§٢١-٩ وإنّما كان الجهل المركّب سببًا وأصلًا للتمادي على الكفر والبدعة؛ لأجل عدم شعور صاحبه بجهله، واعتقاده الصواب والحقّ في جهله، ومن كان على هذه الصفة فإنّه لا يطلب الخروج عن جهله؛ لأنّه هو الصراط المستقيم عنده، وإذا اتّفق أن يجيء من يشكّكه في معتقده، أو يردّه إلى ما هو الحقّ في نفس الأمر.. يمتنع من الاستماع له، ومن قبول قوله، بخلاف الجهل البسيط؛ وهو عدم إدراك أمر من الأمور، فإنّ صاحبه يطلب العلم بما جهله إن شعر بعدم إدراكه، وإن غفل عن ذلك وجاء من ينبّهه لطلب العلم بذلك، أو جاء من يعلمه ما جهله.. فإنّه يجيب إلى ذلك ويقبله؛ لِما جبلت عليه النفوس من النفرة عن الجهل البسيط، ومحبّة تحصيل العلم بما ليس معلومًا لها.

§21.9 *Compound ignorance* (*jahl murakkab*) is a cause and foundation of persistence in disbelief and innovation, because the one afflicted by it is unaware of his ignorance and believes his ignorance to be correctness and truth. A person in this condition does not seek to exit his ignorance, for he regards it as the straight path. And if someone happens to come along who casts doubt on his belief or attempts to return him to what is, in reality, the truth, he refuses to listen or accept what is said.

This is in contrast to *simple ignorance* (*jahl basīṭ*), which is merely the failure to grasp a matter. The one afflicted with it will seek knowledge of what he is ignorant of, if he becomes aware of his lack of understanding. And if he is heedless of that, and someone comes to alert him to the need to seek knowledge, or to teach him what he does not know, he responds and accepts it – because souls are naturally averse to simple ignorance and inclined to acquire knowledge of what is unknown to them.

§٢١-١٠ وسبب الجهل المركّب: وثوق النفس في العقليّات بما ليس برهانيًّا من الأدلّة، وتحسين الظنّ بما يستبد به من أنظارها واستنباطها، لا سيّما عندما تظهر لها الإصابة للحقّ في بعض أنظارها، فتزهو وتعجب حينئذٍ، وتقيس سائر أنظارها على ذلك النظر الذي من المولى الكريم تبارك وتعالى فيه بالتوفيق لدرك الحقّ، فضلًا منه جلّ وعلا.

§21.10 The cause of compound ignorance is the soul's confidence in rational matters on the basis of evidences that are not demonstrative, and its favourable presumption regarding the independent speculations and inferences it formulates – especially when it happens to perceive that it has arrived at the truth in some of its views. At that point, it becomes proud and self-admiring, and proceeds to analogise all its other views to that one view in which the Generous Lord (blessed and exalted is He) had granted it success in apprehending the truth, as a grace from Him (majestic and sublime).

فعوقب هذا الناظر بالحرمان وعدم التسديد في سائر الأنظار؛ لتكبّره، وإهماله شكر نعمة درك الصواب التي انفرد بإسدائها المولى جلّ

وعلا، وليس للعقل ولا للفكرة ولا للدليل الصحيح مادّةً وتركيبًا فيه تأثير ألبتّة؛ لا بطريق التولّد، ولا بطريق التعليل، وإهماله لزوم التواضع والفقر إلى المولى الكريم جلّ وعلا في كلّ نظر يقف بباله، قال اللّه عزّ وجلّ: ﴿سَأَصْرِفُ عَنْ آيَاتِيَ الَّذِينَ يَتَكَبَّرُونَ فِي الْأَرْضِ بِغَيْرِ الْحَقِّ﴾ [الأعراف: ١٤٦].

Thus, this observer was punished with deprivation and a lack of success in all his other reflections, due to his arrogance and his failure to show gratitude for the blessing of attaining correctness – a blessing uniquely granted by the Master (majestic and exalted is He). Neither the intellect, nor speculation, nor sound evidence – whether in its matter or its form – has any effect in this whatsoever: neither by way of causal generation nor by way of causal necessitation.

He also neglected the obligation of humility and neediness before the Generous Master (majestic and exalted is He) in every reflection that arises in his mind.

Allah (mighty and majestic) said: “I shall turn away from My signs those who are arrogant upon the earth without right.”[22]

ويكون أيضًا هذا الجهل المركّب في الشرعيّات كما يكون في العقليّات، ويكون من المقلّدين كما يكون من الناظرين.

This compound ignorance also occurs in revealed doctrines just as it occurs in rational doctrines, and it may be found among the imitators just as it is found among the speculative reasoners.

§٢١-١١ وأمّا الأمر السادس؛ وهو التمسّك في عقائد الإيمان بمجرّد ظواهر الكتاب والسنّة من غير تفصيل بين ما يستحيل ظاهره منها وما لا يستحيل: فلا خفاء في كونه أصلًا للكفر أو البدعة.

---

22 al-Aʿrāf: 7:146.

§21.11 As for the sixth matter – which is adhering, in matters of faith, to the mere outward sense of the Book and the Sunnah without distinguishing between what is impossible in its outward sense and what is not – there is no doubt that this is a foundational source of disbelief or innovation.

أمّا الكفر: فكأخذ الثنويّة القائلين بألوهيّة النور والظلمة من قوله تعالى: ﴿اللَّهُ نُورُ السَّمَاوَاتِ وَالْأَرْضِ﴾ [النور: ٣٥]: أنّ النور أحد الإلهين واسمه: اللّه، ولم ينظروا إلى استحالة كون النور إلهًا؛ لأنّه متغيّر حادث، يوجد وينعدم، والإله يستحيل عليه التغيّر، ويجب له القدم والبقاء.

As for disbelief: it is like the interpretation of the dualists, who asserted the divinity of light and darkness, and took from His saying – exalted is He – "Allah is the Light of the heavens and the earth"[23] that light is one of the two gods, and that its name is Allah.

They gave no thought to the impossibility of light being a deity, for it is changeable and originated – coming into and out of existence – whereas it is impossible for the deity to be subject to change, and pre-eternity and perpetuity are necessary for Him.

§٢١-١٢ وإذا كان كذلك وجب حمل الآية على خلاف ظاهرها:

§21.12 And if that is the case, then it becomes necessary to interpret the verse contrary to its apparent meaning:

(١) إمّا مع التفويض إلى المولى تبارك وتعالى في تعيين المراد منها؛ وهو مذهب السلف في جنس هذه الظواهر.

(1) Either by consigning the determination of its intended meaning to the Exalted Lord (blessed and exalted is He) – and this is the

23 al-Nūr: 24:35.

doctrine of the early generations (*al-salaf*) regarding this general category of apparent texts.

(٢) وإمّا مع تعيين معنى يصحّ إرادته بهذا اللفظ في لغة العرب؛ لأنّ القرآن نزل بألسنتهم، وهو مذهب إمام الحرمين وكثير من الأئمّة.

(2) Or by specifying a meaning that it is valid to intend by this wording in the Arabic language, for the Qur'ān was revealed in their tongue – and this is the position of Imām al-Ḥaramayn and many of the Imāms.

ولهم في ذلك تأويلات مذكورة في كتب التفسير، من جملتها أنّه يحتمل أن يكون اللفظ خرج مخرج الاستعارة، أو التشبيه البليغ؛ بأنّ جعل العدم كظلمة استتر فيه وجود الكائنات من السموات والأرض وما بينهما، ولما توقّف خروجها من العدم إلى الوجود في ذواتها وصفاتها على إيجاد المولى العظيم تبارك وتعالى لها؛ كما توقّف ظهور الأشياء المستترة بالظلمة على انتشار النور عليها.. أُطلق بهذا الاعتبار على المولى جلّ وعلا أنّه نور السموات والأرض؛ أي: هو جلّ وعلا المظهر للسماوات والأرض ولجميع الكائنات؛ بخلقه لها أوّلًا، وإمدادها ثانيًا؛ بإبقاء ذواتها بما والى عليها من نفقات الأعراض المتكاثرة كثرةً لا يحصي عددها إلّا هو جلّ وعلا.

They have, in this regard, interpretations recorded in the books of *tafsīr*. Among them is the view that the expression may have been uttered in the mode of metaphor or emphatic simile – such that nonexistence is likened to a darkness in which the existence of beings was concealed: the heavens, the earth, and all that lies between them.

Since the emergence of these beings from nonexistence into existence, in both their essences (*dhawāt*) and their attributes, depended upon the origination of the Exalted Lord (blessed and exalted is He) – just as the appearance of things hidden in darkness depends upon the diffusion of light over them – it was, by this consideration, ascribed to the Lord (glorious and exalted is He) that He is the Light of the heavens and the earth; meaning: He (glorious and exalted is He) is the one who manifests the heavens, the earth, and all created beings: first, by creating them; and second, by sustaining them – by preserving their very essences through the ongoing succession of accidents, in such multiplicity that none can enumerate them but He (glorious and exalted is He).

فلولا المولى تبارك وتعالى بما نشر على وجود الممكنات من أنوار قدرته وإرادته وعلمه.. لوجب بقاؤها في ظلمة العدم أبد الآباد، ولهذا إذا طوى سبحانه عن هذه العوالم ما نشر على وجودها من نور تعلّق صفاته بإبقائها وإمدادها.. خربت وفنيت، ودخلت في ظلمة عدمها الذي كانت عليه، حتى يقابل أيضًا وجودها بأنوار قدرته وإرادته وعلمه عند البعث والنشأة الثانية، فتصبح حينئذٍ ترفل في أثواب وجودها ذاهبة وجائية، كلّ صائر إلى ما حكم به المولى العظيم جلّ وعلا وأراده في أزله.

Were it not for the Lord (blessed and exalted is He), who diffused upon the existence of contingent beings the lights of His capability, will, and knowledge, they would necessarily have remained in the darkness of nonexistence for all eternity.

Thus, when He – glorified is He – withdraws from these worlds what He had diffused upon their existence of the light of His attributes' linkage to their preservation and sustenance, they collapse and perish, returning to the darkness of nonexistence in which they once were.

Then, once again, their existence is met with the lights of His capability, will, and knowledge at the time of resurrection and the second origination; and they shall then don the garments of their existence, coming and going – each proceeding toward that which the mighty Lord (majestic and exalted is He) decreed and willed in His past-eternity.

فصحّ إذًا أن يقال على طريق مجازات لغة العرب واستعاراتها، وتفنّنها في بدائع تشبيهاتها: ﴿اللَّهُ نُورُ السَّمَاوَاتِ وَالْأَرْضِ﴾.

It is thus sound to say, following the figurative usages of the Arabic language, its metaphors, and its artistic variety in exquisite similes: "Allah is the light of the heavens and the earth."

ويحتمل أن يكون المراد بقوله تعالى: ﴿اللَّهُ نُورُ السَّمَاوَاتِ وَالْأَرْضِ﴾ أنّه به تعالى ظهرت أنوارها الحسّيّة؛ من شمس وقمر ونجوم وسرج، وأنوارها المعنويّة؛ كعلوم الملائكة وعلوم الأنبياء والرسل والأقطاب والأولياء والصالحين والعلماء وأحوالهم السنيّة التابعة لتلك العلوم والمعارف.

It is also possible that the intended meaning of His (exalted is He) saying "Allah is the light of the heavens and the earth" is that, through Him (exalted is He), their sensory lights appeared – such as the sun, moon, stars, and lamps – and likewise their intelligible lights. Such as the knowledge of the angels, the prophets, the messengers, the spiritual poles (*aqṭāb*), the allies (*awliyā'*), the righteous, and the scholars, as well as their noble states that proceed from such knowledge and cognisance.

فالمعنى: أنّ تلك القلوب والجوارح إنّما استنارت بتلك العلوم والأحوال والأعمال بإنارة المولى العظيم لها بذلك، لا بحولها ولا بقوّتها، فهو تعالى إذا نور السموات والأرض.

The meaning, then, is that those hearts and limbs were illumined by those knowledges, states, and acts through the illumination of the Almighty Lord for them by means of that – not by their own power, nor by their own capability. For He (exalted is He) is the one who illumines the heavens and the earth.

ومثل هذا المجاز أو التشبيه مألوف اليوم في عرف الناس؛ يقولون فيمَن تتوقّف عليه أمور البلد وتصفات أهلها بطريق السداد والعافية: فلان هو نور هذه المدينة؛ أي: به استنارت وظهرت محاسنها، والله تعالى أعلم بمراده.

Such a metaphor or simile is familiar today in common usage. People say of someone upon whom the affairs of a town and the well-being of its people depend – through sound judgement and upright conduct – "So-and-so is the light of this city," meaning that through him it is illumined and its virtues become manifest. And Allah (exalted is He) knows best His intent.

وأمّا البدعة الناشئة عن تقليد مجرّد ظواهر الكتاب والسنّة: فكثير جدًّا؛ كأخذ المجسّمة الجسميّة من ظواهر قوله تعالى: ﴿لِمَا خَلَقْتُ بِيَدَيَّ﴾ [ص: ٧٥] ونحوه، والاختصاص بجهة فوق بطريق التحيّز وعمارة الفراغ كاختصاص الأجسام.. من قوله تعالى: ﴿الرَّحْمَنُ عَلَى الْعَرْشِ اسْتَوَى﴾ [طه: ٥]، وقوله تعالى: ﴿يَخَافُونَ رَبَّهُمْ مِنْ فَوْقِهِمْ﴾ [النحل: ٥٠] ونحو ذلك، وكأخذهم أيضًا الجسميّة والجهة والانتقال بالحركة والسكون من قوله صلّى الله عليه وسلّم: «ينزل ربّنا إلى السماء الدنيا إذا كان الثلث الأخير من الليل».

As for the innovation arising from the mere imitation of the outward expressions of the Book and the Sunnah, it is exceedingly widespread.

Among these are the corporealists' (*mujassimah*) derivation of corporeality from the outward sense of His (exalted is He) saying, "What I created with My two hands"[24] and similar verses; and their attribution of a direction of "above" by way of spatial delimitation and the occupation of void – just as bodies are characterised by delimitation – based on His (exalted is He) saying, "The All-Merciful *istawā ʿalā* the Throne,"[25] and His saying, "They fear their Lord above them,"[26] and the like.

Also included is their derivation of corporeality, spatial direction, and locomotion – through motion and rest – from his (peace and blessings be upon him) saying, "Our Lord descends to the lowest heaven when the last third of the night remains."[27]

§٢١-١٣ ومشكلات الكتاب والسنّة كثيرة جدًّا، وقد صنّف العلماء في جمعها والكلام عليها تصانيف، والضابط الجمليّ في جميعها: أنّ كلّ مشكل منها مستحيل الظاهر فإنّه ينظر فيه:

§21.13 The ambiguous passages (*mushkilāt*) of the Book and the Sunnah are exceedingly numerous, and scholars have composed treatises collecting them and commenting on them. The general rule in all such cases is this: every ambiguous passage whose apparent meaning is impossible is to be examined in the following manner.

فإن كان لا يقبل من التأويل إلّا معنى واحدًا.. وجب أن يحمل عليه؛ كقوله تعالى: ﴿وَهُوَ مَعَكُمْ أَيْنَ مَا كُنْتُمْ﴾ [الحديد: ٤]، فإنّ المعيّة بالتحيّز والحلول في المكان مستحيلة على المولى تبارك وتعالى؛ لأنّها من صفات الأجسام، فتعيّن صرف الكلام عن ظاهره، ولا يقبل هنا

24 Ṣād: 38:75.
25 Ṭāhā: 20:5.
26 al-Naḥl: 16:50.
27 Cf. al-Bukhārī, no. 7494; Muslim, no. 758.

إلّا تأويلًا واحدًا دلّ عليه السياق؛ وهو المعيّة بالإحاطة علما وسمعًا وبصرًا.

If it admits of only one possible interpretation, then it must be adopted – such as His (exalted is He) saying, "And He is with you wherever you are."[28]

For accompaniment (*ma'iyyah*) by way of spatial delimitation or indwelling in place is impossible for the Lord (blessed and exalted is He), since such characteristics belong to bodies. It thus becomes necessary to divert the verse from its apparent meaning, and in this case, it admits of only one interpretation, indicated by the context: namely, accompaniment through His encompassing knowledge, hearing, and sight.

وإن كان يقبل من التأويل أكثر من معنى واحد؛ كقوله تعالى: ﴿تَجْرِي بِأَعْيُنِنَا﴾ [القمر: ١٤]، وقوله جلّ وعلا: ﴿لِمَا خَلَقْتُ بِيَدَيَّ﴾ [ص: ٧٥]، وقوله تعالى: ﴿الرَّحْمَنُ عَلَى الْعَرْشِ اسْتَوَى﴾ [طه: ٥] ونحوه.. فقد اختلفت العلماء في ذلك على ثلاثة مذاهب:

And if it admits more than one meaning by way of interpretation – such as His (exalted is He) saying, "Sailing under Our eyes,"[29] His (majestic and sublime) saying, "That which I created with My two hands,"[30] and His (exalted is He) saying, "The All-Merciful *istawā 'alā* the Throne,"[31] and similar verses – then the scholars have differed regarding them into three positions.

المذهب الأوّل: وجوب تفويض معنى ذلك إلى الله تعالى بعد القطع بالتنزيه عن الظاهر المستحيل: وهو مذهب السلف، ولهذا لمّا سأل

28 al-Ḥadīd: 57:4.
29 al-Qamar: 54:14.
30 Ṣād: 38:75.
31 Ṭāhā: 20:5.

السـائل مالـك بن أنس رضي اللّٰه تعالـى عنه عن قوله تعالى: ﴿على العرش استوى﴾ قال في جوابه: (الاسـتواء معلوم، والكيف مجهول، والسؤال عن هذا بدعة)، وأمر بإخراج السائل.

يعنـي رضـي اللّٰه عنه: أنّ الاسـتواء معلوم من لغـة العرب محامله المجازيـة التـي تصحّ في حـقّ مولانا جلّ وعلا، والمراد في الآية منها أو مـن غيرهـا بمـا لم نعلمه.. مجهول لنا، والسـؤال عن تعيين ما لم يرد نصّ فيه من الشـرع بتعيينه.. بدعة، وصاحب البدعة رجل سـوء، مجانبته وإخراجه عن مجالس العلم؛ لئلا يدخل على المسلمين فتنة بسبب إظهار بدعته.

The first position: It is obligatory to consign the meaning of such expressions to Allah (exalted is He) after decisively affirming His transcendence above the impossible apparent sense. This is the doctrine of the early generations (*al-salaf*). For this reason, when someone asked Mālik ibn Anas (may Allah be pleased with him) about the saying of the Exalted: "The All-Merciful *istawā* over the Throne," he replied: "The *istiwā'* is known, its modality is unknown, and asking about it is an innovation," and he ordered the questioner to be removed.

He (may Allah be pleased with him) meant that *istiwā'* is known from the Arabic language, along with its figurative usages that are valid in reference to our Master (majestic and exalted is He). As for the intended meaning in the verse – whether it lies within those usages or beyond them but remains unknown to us – it is, in any case, hidden from us. To inquire into the specification of something for which no textual designation has come from the divine legislation is an innovation, and the one who engages in such questioning is a man of deviance. He is to be avoided and removed from the gatherings of knowledge, lest he introduce tribulation among the Muslims by publicly displaying his innovation.

المذهـب الثانـي: جـواز تعيين التأويل للمشـكل، ويترجّـح على غيره ممّا يصحّ بدلالة سياق أو بكثرة استعمال العرب للفظ المشكل فيه؛ فتحمل العين على العلم أو البصر أو الحفظ، وتحمل اليد على القدرة أو النعمـة، ويحمـل الاسـتواء على القهر، وهذا مذهـب إمام الحرمين وجماعة كثيرة من العلماء.

The second position: the permissibility of specifying the interpretation (*ta'wīl*) of an ambiguous expression, and of preferring one valid interpretation over others – either by contextual indication or by the frequency with which the Arabs use the ambiguous term in a given sense. Thus, *ayn* may be interpreted as knowledge, sight, or preservation; *yad* as capability, or beneficence; *istiwā'* as subjugation or mastery.

This is the position of Imām al-Ḥaramayn and a large group of scholars.

المذهـب الثالـث: حمـل تلك المشـكلات على إثبـات صفات لله تعالى تليق بجلاله وجماله لا يعرف كنهها، وهذا مذهب شـيخ أهل السنّة الشيخ أبي الحسن الأشعريّ رحمه اللّٰه تعالى ورضي عنه.

The third position: Interpreting those ambiguous passages as affirming attributes for Allah (exalted is He) that befit His majesty and beauty, whose true nature (*kunh*) is unknown.

This is the position of the Shaykh of the People of the Sunnah, Shaykh Abū al-Ḥasan al-Ash'arī (may Allah – exalted is He – have mercy on him and be pleased with him).

قلت: والظاهر أنّ مَن احتاط، وعبّر بما يذكره من تأويل لذلك المشكل بلفـظ الاحتمـال؛ فيقول: يحتمل أن يكون المراد من الآية والحديث

كذا.. فقد سلم من التجاسر وسوء الأدب بالجزم بتعيين ما لم يقم الدليل القطعيّ على تعيينه، والله تعالى أعلم.

I say: It appears that whoever exercises caution and expresses his interpretation of that ambiguous passage using the language of possibility – saying, "It is possible that the intended meaning of the verse or ḥadīth is such-and-such" – has thereby avoided audacity and impropriety by asserting with certainty that for which no definitive proof exists for its specification. And Allah (exalted is He) knows best.

§٢١-١٤ وأمّا الأمر السابع؛ وهو الجهل بالأحكام العقليّة وباللسان العربيّ وفنّ البيان: فلا شكّ أنّ الجهل بذلك قد يجرّ إلى الكفر؛ كفهْم بعضهم مذهب النصارى بتركيب الإله وكون عيسى عليه الصلاة والسلام جزءًا منه.. من قوله تعالى: ﴿وَرُوحٌ مِنْهُ﴾ [النساء: ١٧١]، فجعل (من) للتبعيض، ولا شكّ أن معه جهلين:

§21.14 As for the seventh matter – which is ignorance of rational judgements, the Arabic language, and the art of rhetoric – there is no doubt that such ignorance may lead to disbelief. For example: When some have understood the Christian doctrine to imply composition within the Godhead, and that ʿĪsā (peace be upon him) is a part of it, based on His (exalted is He) saying, "and a spirit from Him,"[32] interpreting *min* ("from") as partitive. There is no doubt that this involves two layers of ignorance.

أحدهما: الجهل بالقواعد العقليّة؛ إذ لو عرف أنّ هذا المعنى يستلزم حدوث الإله؛ للزوم مشابهته للحوادث في التغيّر والافتقار إلى التخصيص بمقدار مخصوص من المقادير المركّبة، ويستلزم انعدام

32 al-Nisāʾ: 4:171.

حقيقة الألوهيّة بالكلّيّة؛ لأنّه إذا كان عيسى عليه الصلاة والسلام إنّما حصل فيه جزء من الإله فقد انعد إذًا الإله؛ لوجوب انعدام الحقيقة المركّبة بانعدام جزئها، وعيسى عليه السلام إنّما حصل فيه جزء الإله، وجزء الإله ليس بإله، فقد انعد إذًا الإله بالكلّيّة.

The first is ignorance of rational principles. For had it been known that such a notion entails the origination of the deity – by necessitating His resemblance to originated things in change, and in dependence upon specification by a particular quantity among composite quantities – it would also be clear that this entails the total negation of the reality of divinity.

For if ʿĪsā (peace be upon him) possessed only a part of the deity, then the deity would thereby have ceased to exist; for the essence of a composite necessarily ceases to exist when one of its parts ceases. And ʿĪsā (peace be upon him) possessed only a part of the deity, and a part of the deity is not a deity – therefore, the deity has entirely ceased to exist.

الثاني: جهلهم باللغة العربيّة؛ حيث حصروا معنى (من) في التبعيض، ويلزمهم أن يفهموا أيضًا التبعيض منها في قوله تعالى: ﴿وَسَخَّرَ لَكُم مَّا فِي السَّمَوَاتِ وَمَا فِي الأَرْضِ جَمِيعًا مِّنْهُ﴾ [الجاثية: ١٣] كما فهموه في قوله تعالى: ﴿وَرُوحٌ مِنْهُ﴾، ولو كانوا عارفين باللغة العربيّة لفهموا أنّ (من) في قوله تعالى: ﴿وَرُوحٌ مِنْهُ﴾ ليست للتبعيض، وإنّما هي لابتداء الغاية؛ أي: وروح جاء منه تعالى خلقًا واختراعًا، كما أنّ معناها ذلك في قوله تعالى: ﴿وَسَخَّرَ لَكُم مَّا فِي السَّمَوَاتِ وَمَا فِي الأَرْضِ جَمِيعًا مِّنْهُ﴾ [الجاثية:١٣].

The second is their ignorance of the Arabic language – specifically, in restricting the meaning of *min* to partitivity (*tabʿīḍ*). This would require them also to understand partitivity in His (exalted is He) saying, "And He subjected to you all that is in the heavens and all that is in the earth, all from Him (*minhu*),"[33] just as they understood it in His saying, "and a spirit from Him."

Had they possessed knowledge of the Arabic language, they would have known that *min* in His (exalted is He) saying, "and a spirit from Him (*minhu*)" is not partitive, but rather denotes the commencement of origination – that is, a spirit that came from Him (exalted is He) by way of creation and origination – just as it has that meaning in His saying (exalted is He): "And He subjected to you all that is in the heavens and all that is in the earth, all from Him."

ومن الجهل باللغة العربيّة: أخذ الجسميّة وأعضائها في حقّه تبارك وتعالى من قوله جلّ وعلا: ﴿يَا حَسْرَتَى عَلَى مَا فَرَّطْتُ فِي جَنْبِ اللَّهِ﴾ [الزمر: ٥٦]، وقوله تعالى: ﴿لِمَا خَلَقْتُ بِيَدَيَّ﴾ [ص: ٧٥] ونحوهما، ومَن عرف اللغة العربيّة، ومارس استعمالات العرب.. فهم أنّ الجنب والجانب يستعملان كثيرًا بمعنى جهة الحقوق؛ إذ كثيرًا ما يقول الإنسان: فرطت في جنب فلان؛ أي: جانبه، ومراده: التفريط في جهة حقّه، وليس مراده قطعًا البدن ولا أجزاءه، وعليه يخرج قوله تعالى: ﴿عَلَى مَا فَرَّطْتُ فِي جَنْبِ اللَّهِ﴾ أي: في جهة حقوقه وأوامره ونواهيه.

وكذا يعرف مَن خالط اللغة العربيّة أنّ اليد كما تستعمل في الجارحة المخصوصة.. تستعمل بمعنى القدرة والنعمة.

Among the manifestations of ignorance of the Arabic language is the attribution of corporeality and bodily parts to Him (blessed and exalted is He) based on His (glorious and exalted) saying,

33 al-Jāthiyah: 45:13.

"Alas, my grief over what I neglected in the side of Allah,"[34] and His (exalted is He) saying, "For what I created with My two hands,"[35] and other such verses.

Whoever is knowledgeable of the Arabic language and accustomed to the idiomatic usage of the Arabs understands that *janb* and *jānib* are frequently used to mean "the aspect of rights." It is common for someone to say, "I fell short in the *janb* of so-and-so," meaning: in his *jānib* – that is, in fulfilling what was due to him – without intending by it the body or any of its parts.

Accordingly, the meaning of His (exalted is He) saying, "over what I neglected in the side of Allah" is: in the matter of His rights, His commands, and His prohibitions.

Likewise, one who is familiar with the Arabic language knows that *yad* ("hand"), just as it is used for a physical limb, is also used to mean capability (*qudrah*) and blessing (*ni'mah*).

ومن الجهل بقواعد الإعراب: جعل بعض المعتزلة جملة (خلقناه) من قوله تعالى: ﴿إِنَّا كُلَّ شَيْءٍ خَلَقْنَاهُ بِقَدَرٍ﴾ [القمر: ٤٩] في موضع الصفة لـ (شيء) حتى أخذ من مفهوم الصفة أنّ هناك شيئًا غير مخلوق لله تعالى؛ وهي أفعال الحيوانات الاختياريّة على مذهبه الفاسد، ولو عرف قواعد الإعراب لفهم أنّ جملة (خلقناه) لا محلّ لها من الإعراب؛ لأنّها مفسّرة للعامل في (كلّ) من باب الاشتغال، فيؤخذ حينئذٍ من تعميم الخلق لكلّ شيء بطلان مذهب القدريّة.

Among the manifestations of ignorance regarding the rules of grammatical inflection is that some Mu'tazilah took the clause *khalaqnāhu* ("We created it") in His (exalted is He) saying, "Indeed, all things We created with measure,"[36] to be in the syntactic

34 al-Zumar: 39:56.
35 Ṣād: 38:75.
36 al-Qamar: 54:49.

position of an attributive clause (*ṣifah*) for "thing" (*shay'*). From the implication of that syntactic construction, they inferred that there exists something not created by Allah (exalted is He) – namely, the voluntary acts of living creatures, according to their corrupt doctrine.

Had they known the rules of grammatical inflection, they would have understood that the clause *khalaqnāhu* has no syntactic position at all, for it functions to clarify the operative element in *kulla* ("all") by way of the grammatical principle of *ishtighāl*. In that case, the generality of creation encompassing all things would establish the invalidity of the Qadarite doctrine.

ومن الجهل بفنّ علم المعاني والبيان: أخذ المعتزلة تعليل أفعال المولى تبارك وتعالى بالأغراض من قوله جلّ وعلا: ﴿وَمَا خَلَقْتُ الْجِنَّ وَالْإِنْسَ إِلَّا لِيَعْبُدُونِ﴾ [الذاريات: ٥٦]، فجعلوا اللام للتعليل حقيقةً، ولو خالطوا فن البيان لعرفوا أنّ الآية من باب الاستعارة التبعيّة، وأنّه شبّه التكليف بالعبادة في ترتّبه على الخلق بالعلّة الغائيّة التي تترتّب على الفعل ويقصد الفعل لأجلها، فجعلت العبادة -أي: التكليف بها- لأجل هذا الشبه علّة غائيّة بطريق الاستعارة، فتبع ذلك استعارة اللام الموضوعة للتعليل، ودخلت في العبادة للدلالة على العلّة المجازية.

Among the manifestations of ignorance concerning the discipline of rhetorical semantics (*ma'ānī*) and rhetoric (*bayān*) is the Mu'tazilites' construing the acts of the Exalted Lord (blessed and exalted is He) as being motivated by purposes, based on His (glorious and exalted) saying, "And I did not create the jinn and mankind except that they worship Me."[37] They took the *lām* to indicate real causality (*ta'līl*) in the literal sense.

37 al-Dhāriyāt: 51:56.

Had they been acquainted with the discipline of rhetoric, they would have known that the verse belongs to the category of derivative metaphor (*isti'ārah taba'iyyah*), wherein the obligation of worship is likened – by virtue of its ordering upon creation – to the final cause: that which follows an act and for the sake of which the act is performed. Worship – meaning the obligation to perform it – was thus made, due to this resemblance, a final cause by way of metaphor. Accordingly, the *lām*, which is originally assigned to denote causality, was metaphorically borrowed and applied to worship to signify a figurative cause.

وكذا من الجهل بفنّ المعاني والبيان: اعتقاد صدور حوادث من غير المولى تبارك وتعالى؛ كاعتقاد زيادة الإيمان من سماع آيات القرآن؛ أخذًا من قوله تعالى: ﴿وَإِذَا تُلِيَتْ عَلَيْهِمْ آيَاتُهُ زَادَتْهُمْ إِيمَانًا﴾ [الأنفال: ٢]، وستر العورة من اللباس؛ أخذًا من قوله تعالى: ﴿يَا بَنِي آدَمَ قَدْ أَنْزَلْنَا عَلَيْكُمْ لِبَاسًا يُوَارِي سَوْءَاتِكُمْ﴾ [الأعراف: ٢٦]، وإثارة الرياح للسحاب ونشرها؛ أخذًا من قوله تعالى: ﴿اللَّهُ الَّذِي يُرْسِلُ الرِّيَاحَ فَتُثِيرُ سَحَابًا﴾ [الروم: ٤٨]، ونحو ذلك ممّا هو في القرآن والسنّة كثير.

Likewise, among the manifestations of ignorance in the disciplines of rhetorical semantics (*ma'ānī*) and rhetoric (*bayān*) is the belief that events originate from other than the Exalted Lord – such as the belief that faith increases through the mere hearing of the verses of the Qur'ān, based on His (exalted is He) saying, "And when His verses are recited to them, it increases them in faith";[38] the belief that the covering of nakedness comes from clothing, based on His (exalted is He) saying, "O children of Ādam, We have sent down to you clothing to cover your nakedness";[39] the

38 al-Anfāl: 8:2.

39 al-A'rāf: 7:26.

belief that the winds stir up and spread the clouds, based on His (exalted is He) saying, "Allah is the One who sends the winds, and they stir up clouds"[40]; and the like of that, which is abundant in the Qur'ān and the Sunnah.

ومَـن خالـط فـنّ البيان عـرف أنّ الإسـناد في جميع ذلـك من باب الإسناد المجازيّ العقليّ؛ وهو إسناد الفعل أو ما في معناه إلى ملابَسٍ له غيرِ ما هو له في الظاهر عند المتكلّم.

Whoever has engaged with the discipline of rhetoric knows that the predication in all such cases falls under the category of figurative predication of the rational type (*isnād majāzī 'aqlī*): it is the attribution of an act – or something akin to an act in meaning – to an associated entity other than the one to which it apparently belongs, according to the speaker.

وإذا عرفـت أنّ الجهـل بهـذه العلوم يوقع صاحبه فـي كفر أو بدعة.. تعيّـن علـى مَن له قابليّة لفهمها أن يجتهـد في تحصيلها، ومَن ليس له قابليّة لفهمها وجب عليه أن يتعلّم ما هو فرض عين عليه من علم التوحيد، ومهما سـمع في الكتاب أو السـنّة ما يقتضي ظاهره خلاف مـا عـرف في علـم التوحيد.. يقطع بأنّ ذلك الظاهر المسـتحيل غير مـراد لله تعالـى ولا لرسـوله صلّـى الله عليه وسـلّم، وأنّ لذلك الكلام معنـى صحيحًـا، وتأويلًا ممكنًا مليحًا، ويؤمن على سـبيل القطع بأنّ كلام الله تعالى وكلام رسوله صلّى الله عليه وسلّم حقّ، لا تناقض فيه ولا اخـتلاف، ولا باطـل فيـه ولا جهل ولا وهم ولا حيد عن الصواب ولا غلط ولا انحراف، ولا يضرّه بعد ذلك الجهل بالمراد؛ لأنّ القلب

40 al-Rūm: 30:48.

محشو باعتقاد تنزيه المولى تبارك وتعالى ورسله عليهم الصلاة والسلام عن كلّ نقص وخلل وفساد، وبالله تعالى التوفيق، لا ربّ غيره.

§21.15 If you have understood that ignorance of these sciences leads its possessor into disbelief or innovation, then it becomes incumbent upon whoever has the capability (*qudrah*) to understand them to exert effort in acquiring them.

As for one who does not have the capacity to understand them, it is obligatory upon him to learn what is individually obligatory (*farḍ ʿayn*) for him from the science of *tawḥīd* and whenever he hears in the Book or the Sunnah something whose apparent meaning contradicts what is known in the science of *tawḥīd*, he must be certain that such an impossible apparent meaning is not intended by Allah (exalted is He) or by His Messenger (peace and blessings be upon him). Rather, that statement has a sound meaning and a possible, commendable interpretation.

He must believe with certainty that the speech of Allah (exalted is He) and the speech of His Messenger (peace and blessings be upon him) is true: containing no contradiction, no inconsistency, no falsehood, no ignorance, no delusion, no deviation from correctness, no error, and no distortion.

And his ignorance of the intended meaning does not harm him after that, because his heart is filled with conviction in the transcendence (*tanzīh*) of the Master (blessed and exalted is He) and of His messengers – upon them be peace – above every deficiency, flaw, and corruption.

And with Allah (exalted is He) is success; there is no Lord besides Him.

THE FIFTH PROLEGOMENON

ON EXISTENTS

المقدّمة الخامسة في الموجودات

§٢٢ والموجوداتُ بالنسبةِ إلى المحلِّ والمخصِّصِ أربعةُ أقسامٍ:

١. قسمٌ غنيٌّ عنِ المحلِّ والمخصِّصِ: وهو ذاتُ مولانا جلا وعلا.

٢. وقسمٌ مُفتَقِرٌ إلى المحلِّ والمخصِّصِ: وهو الأعراضُ.

٣. وقسمٌ مُفتَقِرٌ إلى المُخصّصِ دونَ المحلِّ: وهو الأجرامُ.

٤. وقسمٌ موجودٌ في المحلّ ولا يَفْتَقِرُ إلى مخصِّصٍ: وهو صفاتُ مولانا جلَّ وعزَّ.

§22 Existent things (*mawjūdāt*), with respect to a substrate (*maḥall*) and a specifier (*mukhaṣṣiṣ*), are of four categories:

1. A category that is independent of both substrate and specifier – namely, the essence of our Lord (majestic and exalted is He).
2. A category that is dependent upon both substrate and specifier – namely, accidents.
3. A category that is dependent upon a specifier but not a substrate – namely, bodies.
4. A category that exists in a substrate but is independent of a specifier – namely, the attributes of our Lord (majestic and mighty is He).

§٢٢-٠ مراده بالمحلّ: الذات التي تقوم بها الصفات، لا المكان الذي تجاوره الأجسام.

§22.0 His intent by *substrate* (*maḥall*) is the essence (*dhāt*) in which attributes subsist, not the place adjacent to which bodies are situated.

ومعنى افتقار الشـيء إلى المحلّ أو وجوده في المحلّ: قيامه به على سبيل الاتّصاف.

The meaning of a thing's *dependence upon a substrate* or its *existence in a substrate*, is its subsistence in it by way of qualification.

ومعنى المخصّص: الفاعل المختار الذي يخصّص الممكن الحادث بجائز أراده دون جائز لم يرده.

The meaning of the *specifier* (*mukhaṣṣiṣ*) is the volitional agent who specifies an originated contingent with one permissible option that He wills, rather than another permissible option that He does not will.

ومعنى افتقار الشيء إلى المحلّ أو وجوده فيه: اتّصاف ذلك المحلّ به.

The meaning of a thing's *dependence upon a substrate* or its *existence within it*, is that the substrate is qualified by it.

ومعنى استغنائه عن المحلّ: أن يكون في نفسه ذاتًا موصوفًا بالصفات، لا صفة.

The meaning of its *independence from a substrate* is that it is, in itself, an essence qualified by attributes, not itself an attribute.

ومعنـى افتقار الشـيء إلـى المخصّص: أن يكون حادثـًا محتاجًا إلى فاعل يخصّصه بالوجود بدلًا عن العدم الذي كان عليه.

The meaning of a thing's *dependence upon a specifier* is that it is originated and in need of an agent who specifies it with existence rather than the nonexistence it was upon.

§٢٢-١ فإذا عرفت هذا: اتّضح لك ما ذكرناه في الأصل؛ أنّ ذات مولانا تبارك وتعالى غنيّ عن المحلّ والمخصّص.

§22.1 If you have understood this, then it becomes clear to you what we stated at the outset: that the essence of our Master (blessed and exalted is He) is independent of both substrate and specifier.

أمّا غناؤه جلّ وعلا عن المحلّ: فلأنّه ذات موصوف بالصفات العليّة، وليس بصفة؛ إذ لو كان صفةً لاستحال أن يتّصف بالصفات الوجوديّة؛ وهي صفات المعاني، وبلوازمها؛ وهي الصفات المعنويّة، كيف والبرهان القطعيّ دلّ على وجوب اتّصاف مولانا جلّ وعلا بصفات المعاني؛ وهي القدرة والإرادة والعلم والحياة والسمع والبصر والكلام، وبلوازمها؛ وهي كونه تعالى قادرًا ومريدًا وعالمًا وحيًّا وسميعًا وبصيرًا ومتكلّمًا؟!

As for His (glorious and exalted is He) independence from a substrate: it is because He is an essence qualified by exalted attributes, and not Himself an attribute. For if He were an attribute, it would be impossible for Him to be qualified by existential attributes – namely, the entitative attributes (*ṣifāt al-maʿānī*) – and by their necessary concomitants – namely, the derivative attributes (*ṣifāt maʿnawiyyah*).

How so, when definitive proof has established the necessity that our Master (glorious and exalted is He) is qualified by the entitative attributes – namely, capability, will, knowledge, life, hearing, sight, and speech – and by the derivative attributes: namely, His being capable, willing, knowing, living, hearing, seeing, and speaking?

ودليل استحالة اتّصاف الصفة بالصفات الوجوديّة ولوازمها: أنّ الصفة لو قبلت أن تقوم بها الصفات الوجوديّة كما تقوم بالذات.. ألا تعرى عنها كالذوات؛ إذ القبول نفسيّ لا يتخلّف، وذلك يستلزم دخول ما

لا نهاية له في الوجود؛ لأنّ الصفة القائمة بالصفة على هذا التقدير.. يلزم أن تكون هي أيضًا قابلةً للصفة كالأولى فيلزم ألا تعرى عن الصفة، ثمّ ننقل الكلام إلى الصفة القائمة بها فيلزم فيها أيضًا ما لزم فيما قبلها، وهكذا إلى ما لا نهاية له.

The proof for the impossibility of an attribute being qualified by existential attributes and their concomitants is that if an attribute were to admit of existential attributes inhering in it, just as such attributes subsist in the essence, would it not inevitably be unable to be devoid of them, just as essences are? For receptivity is intrinsic and does not fail. And this would entail the entrance of what has no end into existence.

For the attribute inhering in another attribute – on this assumption – must itself also be receptive to yet another attribute, just like the first, and so must not be devoid of qualification. Then the discourse would transfer to the attribute inhering in that one, and the same consequence would follow as with the one before it, and so on, *ad infinitum*.

وأمّا غناؤه جلّ وعلا عن المخصّص؛ وهو الفاعل الموجد: فلأنّه تبارك وتعالى واجب الوجود، لا يتصوّر في العقل عدمه في الأزل؛ لوجوب قدمه، ولا فيما لا يزال؛ لوجوب بقائه؛ إذ لو قبل جلّ وعلا العدم أزلًا وأبدًا.. لزم أن يكون جائز الوجود، وكلّ جائز الوجود فهو مفتقر إلى فاعل موجد يخصّصه بالوجود بدلًا عن العدم، وإذا لزم على هذا التقدير افتقار موجد العوالم إلى فاعل.. لزم افتقار فاعله أيضًا إلى فاعل؛ لتماثلهما في الألوهيّة، ثمّ كذلك أبدًا؛ فإن انحصر عدد الفاعلين لزم الدور، وإن لم ينحصر العدد لزم التسلسل، وكلاهما مستحيل.

As for His (majestic and exalted is He) independence from a specifier – that is, the agent who brings into being – it is because He (blessed and exalted is He) is necessarily existent in and of Himself (*wājib al-wujūd bi-dhātih*). Nonexistence is inconceivable for Him in past-eternity, due to the necessity of His pre-eternality, and likewise in everlasting futurity, due to the necessity of His perpetuity.

For if nonexistence were conceivable for Him (majestic and exalted is He) either in past-eternity or in the everlasting future, it would follow that He is a contingent being (*mumkin al-wujūd*). And every contingent being is in need of an agent who brings it into existence and specifies it with existence rather than nonexistence.

Now, if – under this assumption – the originator of the worlds required an agent, it would follow that that agent would also require an agent, given their equivalence in divinity. And so on, endlessly.

If the number of such agents were finite, circularity (*dawr*) would follow; and if infinite, infinite regress (*tasalsul*) would follow. Both are impossible.

وأيضًا: لو كان الإله جائزًا مفتقرًا إلى الفاعل.. لزم حدوثه وعجزه كسائر الحوادث، وذلك يبطل ألوهيّته.

Moreover: if the deity were possible (*jā'iz*) and in need of an agent, it would follow that He is originated and incapable – like all other originated things. And that invalidates His divinity.

ويلزم أيضًا على هذا التقدير: التمانع بينه وبين فاعله؛ إذ كلّ واحد منهما يجب له من عموم القدرة والإرادة ما وجب لصاحبه.

It also follows, on this assumption, that there would be mutual hindrance between it and its agent; for each of the two would necessarily possess, in terms of universal capability and will, what is required of the other.

ويلـزم أيضًـا على هذا التقدير: التحكّم والترجيـح بلا مرجّح؛ إذ ليس تقدير أحد الإلهين مفعولًا لصاحبه بأولى من تقديره فاعلًا له.

It also follows, on this assumption, arbitrariness and preference without a preponderating factor; for positing one of the two deities as the effect of the other is no more warranted than positing it as the agent over the other.

وبهذا الذي اتّضح لك من وجوب غنى مولانا جلّ وعلا عن المخصّص: يتّضح لك استـحالة كونه تعالى من جنس الأجرام المتحيّزة؛ لوجوب الحـدوث لجميعهـا، واحتياجهـا إلـى مخصّـص يخصّصهـا بالوجود بـدلًا عـن العدم، وبالمقدار المخصوص بها بدلًا عن غيره، وبالمكان المخصـوص، والزمـان المخصـوص، والصفـة المخصوصـة، والجهة المخصوصة.. بدلًا عن مقابلاتها.

By what has become clear to you regarding the necessary independence of our Master (majestic and exalted is He) from any specifier, it likewise becomes clear that it is impossible for Him (exalted is He) to belong to the genus of spatially delimited bodies.

For all such bodies are necessarily originated and in need of a specifier to specify them with existence rather than nonexistence, the particular magnitude they possess rather than another, a specific place, a specific time, a specific attribute, and a specific direction – rather than their opposites.

وبهـذا تعـرف أيضًـا: تنزّهه تعالى عن خواصّ الأجـرام؛ من المقادير، والأزمنـة، والأمكنـة، والأعراض المتغيّره، والجهات، فلا مثل له تبارك وتعالـى فـي الوجود الخارجـيّ، ولا في التقدير العقلـيّ، ولا الوهميّ، ولا الخياليّ.

And by this you also know His exalted transcendence above the properties of bodies – such as magnitudes, times, places, changing accidents, and directions.

There is no likeness to Him – blessed and exalted is He – in external ontological actuality (*wujūd ʿaynī*), nor in rational estimation (*taqdīr ʿaqlī*), nor in imaginative estimation (*taqdīr wahmī*), nor in fantastical representation (*taqdīr khayālī*).

§٢٢-٢ وأمّا ما ذكرناه من افتقار القسم الثاني؛ وهو الأعراض -أي: الصفات القائمة بالأجرام؛ من ألوان وطعوم وروائح وحركات وسكنات وغيرها- إلى المحلّ والمخصّص: فظاهر؛ لأنّها لمّا كانت صفاتٍ استحال أن تقوم بأنفسها، بل لا يمكن أن تكون موجودةً إلّا في محلّ؛ أي: ذات تقوم بها، ولمّا كانت حادثةً وجب افتقارها إلى مخصّص موجد لها.

§22.2 As for what we have mentioned regarding the dependence of the second category – namely, accidents (*aʿrāḍ*), that is, attributes subsisting in bodies, such as colours, tastes, odours, motions, rests, and the like – upon a substrate and a specifier, this is evident.

For since they are attributes, it is impossible for them to subsist on their own; rather, they can only exist in a substrate – that is, an essence in which they inhere. And since they are originated, it is necessary that they depend upon a specifier who brings them into existence.

§٢٢-٣ وأمّا ما ذكرناه من افتقار القسم الثالث -وهو الأجرام- إلى المخصّص دون المحلّ: فلأنّها لمّا كانت حادثةً؛ بدليل لزومها للأعراض الحادثة؛ من حركة وسكون وغيرهما.. لزم افتقارها إلى مخصّص موجد لها ابتداءً، وممدّ مبق لها بموالاة خلق أعراضها

دوامًـا، فافتقارهـا إلى المولى جلّ وعلا لا يمكـن أن تعرى عنه ابتداءً ولا دوامًا.

§22.3 As for what we have mentioned regarding the dependence of the third category – namely, bodies – upon a specifier (*mukhaṣṣiṣ*) rather than a substrate (*maḥall*): it is because they are originated, as evidenced by their inseparability from originated accidents – such as motion, rest, and the like.

It therefore follows that they require a specifier who brings them into existence in the first instance, and who sustains and preserves them by continuously creating their accidents. Their dependence upon the Master (glorious and exalted is He) cannot be absent – neither initially nor continually.

§٢٢-٤ وأمّـا وجـوب غنائها عن المحلّ: فلأنّها ليسـت صفاتٍ، بل هـي ذوات موصوفـة بالصفـات، فلو قام جـرم منها بجرم آخـر لزم أن يتّحـد حيّزهما، وذلك يسـتلزم أن يكون الجرمـان جرمًا واحدًا، وذلك لا يعقل.

§22.4 As for the necessity of their independence from a substrate: it is because they are not attributes, but rather essences (*dhawāt*) qualified by attributes. So if one body were to inhere in another, it would follow that their spatial loci coincide – thereby entailing that the two bodies are in fact one body. And that is inconceivable.

وأيضًـا: لو افتقر الجرم إلـى المحلّ كافتقار العرض إليه.. لزم الترجيح بلا مرجّـح؛ إذ ليـس جعـل أحـد الجرميـن مـحلًّا للآخـر بأولـى من العكس.

Moreover: were a body (*jirm*) to require a substrate (*maḥall*) in the same way an accident (*ʿaraḍ*) requires one, this would entail preference without a preponderating factor – for designating one of the two bodies as the substrate of the other would be no more warranted than the reverse.

وأيضًا: يلزم في محلّه من الافتقار إلى محلّ ما لزم فيه، فإن كان الحالّ محلًّا أيضًا لمحلّه.. لزم الدور، وإن كان غيره لزم التسلسل، ودخول ما لا نهاية له في الوجود.

And moreover: it follows that the substrate itself would require a further substrate in which it inheres. If the inhering entity (*ḥāll*) were the substrate of its own substrate, circularity (*dawr*) would ensue; and if it were something else, infinite regress (*tasalsul*) would follow – and the admission of what has no end into existence.

§٢٤-٥ وأمّا ما ذكرناه في القسم الرابع -وهو صفات مولانا جلّ وعلا- من وجوب قيامها بذاته العليّة، ووجوب غنائها عن المخصّص: فلأن كونها صفاتٍ يوجب استحالة قيامها بأنفسها؛ لِما يلزم عليه من قلب الحقائق، إذ حقيقة الصفة تستلزم موصوفًا يتّصف بها، فلو قامت بنفسها لم تكن صفةً، لكن مفارقة الصفة لحقيقتها التي هي كونها صفةً لموصوف.. محال، فقيامها إذا بنفسها الذي استلزم مفارقتها لحقيقة نفسها.. محال.

§22.5 As for what we mentioned in the fourth category – namely, the attributes of our Master (majestic and exalted is He) – concerning the necessity of their inhering in His exalted essence, and the necessity of their independence from any specifier: this is because their very being as attributes entails the impossibility of their subsisting on their own.

For that would result in an inversion of realities, since the true reality (*ḥaqīqah*) of an attribute entails the presence of a subject that is qualified by it. If it were to subsist on its own, it would not be an attribute. But for an attribute to be severed from its own true reality – that is, from being an attribute of a subject – is impossible. Therefore, its subsistence by itself, which would entail its separation from its own quiddity, is likewise impossible.

فإن قلت: قصارى ما أنتج دليلكم أنّ الصفة لا تعقل حقيقتها بدون موصوف بها، ولا يلزم من استلزامها موصوفًا بها أن تقوم بذلك الموصوف؛ لاحتمال أن تكون صفةً لموصوف ولا تقوم به.

Should you say: The utmost that your proof establishes is that an attribute cannot be intellectually conceived in its reality without a subject that possesses it. But it does not follow from its requiring a subject that it inheres in that subject – for it is possible that it be an attribute of a subject without actually inhering in it.

فالجواب: أنّه لا معنى لكونها صفةً لموصوف إلّا قيامها به؛ إذ لو لم تقم به لم يمكن أن تكون صفةً له دون غيره؛ لِما يلزم عليه من الترجيح بلا مرجّح، فلو لم تقم إذا بموصوفها لم تكن صفةً له ولا لغيره؛ لعدم موجب الاختصاص، فقد لزم إذًا من قيامها بنفسها وجود الصفة بلا موصوف، وذلك إبطال لحقيقتها، وذلك عين ما ألزمناه في البرهان السابق.

The answer is that there is no meaning to its being an attribute of a subject except its inhering in it. For if it did not inhere in it, it could not be an attribute of it rather than of something else – due to the entailment of preference without a preponderating factor.

Therefore, if it did not inhere in its subject, it would not be an attribute of it nor of anything else, due to the absence of a cause for specification. It would then follow, if it subsisted by itself, that there would exist an attribute without a subject – thereby nullifying its reality.

And that is precisely what we affirmed in the preceding demonstration.

§٢٤-٦ وإنّما عدلنا عن ذكر الافتقار إلى الذات في صفة المولى تبارك وتعالى؛ لأنّ الافتقار والفقر يقتضيان لغةً وعرفًا الحاجة إلى أمر مفقود يطلب حصوله؛ فيقال: الجائع يفتقر إلى الأكل، فإذا أكل وشبع لم يوصف بالافتقار إلى الأكل، وكما يقال: العريان مفتقر إلى كسوة، فإذا اكتسى لم يطلق عليه الافتقار إلى الكسوة، وقس على هذا.

§22.6 We have refrained from describing the Lord (blessed and exalted is He) as being "in need of the Essence" because both the term dependence (*iftiqār*) and poverty (*faqr*) – linguistically and conventionally – imply need for something absent whose attainment is sought.

Thus it is said: a hungry person is in need of food; but once he eats and is satiated, he is no longer described as being in need of food. Likewise, it is said: a naked person is in need of clothing; but once he is clothed, he is no longer described as being in need of clothing. And analogise accordingly.

ولا شكّ أنّ صفات مولانا تبارك وتعالى يستحيل عليها الافتقار؛ لأنّه إن كان لتحصيل وجودها فوجودها حاصل واجب غنيّ عن الفاعل أزلًا وأبدًا، وإن كان لتحصيل وجود موصوفها فهو ذات مولانا جلّ وعزّ، وهو أيضًا حاصل واجب غنيّ لا يتصوّر عدمه أزلًا ولا أبدًا، غنيّ عن كلّ ما سواه، ومفتقر إليه كلّ ما عداه، فمعنى الفقر إذًا لا يتصوّر في الذات ولا في صفاتها، فيمنع إطلاق لفظه على الصفات الأزليّة.

There is no doubt that the attributes of our Master (blessed and exalted is He) are necessarily precluded from neediness (*faqr*). For if such neediness were for the attainment of their existence, their existence is already actual, necessary, and independent of any agent – past-eternally and perpetually. And if it were for the attainment of the existence of their subject, that is the essence of our Master (majestic and mighty is He), then that too is actual, necessary, and self-sufficient – whose nonexistence is inconceivable, in past-eternity and everlastingness, independent of all other than Him, while all else is in need of Him.

Thus, the very meaning of neediness is inconceivable in relation to either the Essence or its attributes. Accordingly, the application of this term to the past-eternal attributes is to be rejected.

وقد غفل الفخر فأساء الأدب، وأطلق عليها الفقر إلى الذات العليّة؛ نظرًا منه إلى استحالة قيامها بأنفسها، ووجوب قيامها بموصوفها، ولم يتنبّه إلى ما يوهمه الفقر والافتقار من فقد أمر يحتاج إلى حصوله، والله سبحانه المسؤول أن يسمح لنا وله ولسائر المؤمنين والمؤمنات، وأن يعامل جميعنا دنيًا وأخرى بما هو أهل له من كثرة العفو والغفران لعظيم الزلات، ولا يعاملنا بما نحن له أهل من النقم وأنواع العقوبات، والطرد دنيًا وأخرى عن جميع الخيرات؛ بجاه نبيّه ومصطفاه سيّدنا ومولانا محمّد صلّى الله عليه وسلّم وعلى آله وصحبه، فهو وسيلتنا العظمى وذخيرتنا الكبرى وملجؤنا الأعزّ والأرفع في الحياة وبعد الوفاة.

Fakhr al-Dīn was heedless and acted discourteously when he attributed to them poverty in relation to the Exalted Essence (*al-dhāt al-ʿaliyyah*), on the basis of his view that it is impossible for them to subsist by themselves and that they must necessarily inhere in their subject. He failed to attend to what the terms poverty (*faqr*) and need (*iftiqār*) imply – namely, the absence of something whose attainment is sought.[41]

41 (Tr:) The editor points out that others – including al-Ījī and al-Taftāzānī – agree with Fakhr al-Dīn al-Rāzī (p225, fn 2). In *Sharḥ al-Kubrā* (p326), the author quotes a passage from Sharaf al-Dīn ibn al-Tilmisānī's *Sharḥ Maʿālim*

We ask Allah (exalted is He) to be generous with pardon toward us, toward him, and toward all believing men and women, and to treat all of us – both in this life and in the next – in accordance with what befits Him: abundant pardon and forgiveness for grave transgressions, and not in accordance with what we deserve – of vengeance, forms of punishment, and expulsion in this world and the next from all goodness – by the rank of His Prophet and Chosen One, our Master and Patron Muḥammad (may Allah bless him and grant him peace), and upon his family and companions. For he is our greatest means, our supreme treasure, and our most noble and exalted refuge in life and after death.

---

uṣūl al-dīn. The editor points out that Fakhr al-Dīn al-Rāzī's did not actually endorse this in his larger *Al-Arbaʿūn fī Uṣūl al-Dīn*.

THE SIXTH PROLEGOMENON

ON MUTUALLY CONTRADICTORY POSSIBLES

المقدّمة السادسة في الممكنات المتقابلات

§٢٣ والممكناتُ المُتَقَابِلاتُ ستةٌ: الوجودُ والعدمُ، والمقاديرُ، والصفاتُ، والأزمنةُ، والأمكنةُ، والجهاتُ.

§23 The mutually opposing (*mutaqābilāt*) possibilities (*mumkināt*) are six:

1. **existence and nonexistence,**
2. **magnitudes,**
3. **attributes,**
4. **times,**
5. **places, and**
6. **directions.**

§٢٣-٠ مراده بـ (الممكنات): الجائزات، (المتقابلات)؛ أي: المتنافرات التي يقبل الجرم كلّ واحد منها قبولًا مساويًا لقبول منافره، ثمّ مع ذلك اختصّ من كلّ متقابلين متساويين في القبول بأحدهما، وترجّح له على صاحبه، وغلبة أحد المتساويين لمساويه ورجحانه عليه بلا مغلّب ولا مرجّح.. مستحيل؛ لأنّه جمع بين متنافيين؛ وهما رجحان أمر لنفسه على مقابله، ومساواته له بنفسه أيضًا.

§23.0 His intent by *mumkināt* is "possibles" (*jā'izāt*), and by *mutaqābilāt* he means mutually opposed contraries – such that a body equally admits each of them, just as it admits its opposite.

Yet despite this equal receptivity, one of the two contraries is specified and preferred over its counterpart.

Now, for one of two equal contraries to predominate over the other, and be preferred without a predominating factor or preferrer, is impossible. For this would entail the conjunction of two incompatible states: that a thing be preferred over its opposite by itself, and that it be equal to it by itself as well.

§٢٣-١ فتعيّن على سبيل القطع واليقين الضروريّ بعد هذا التأمّل افتقار كلّ جرم إلى مخصّص؛ أي: فاعل يخصّصه بالوجود بدلًا عن العدم مساويه في القبول والإمكان على قول، أو هو أرجح من الوجود -لأصالته في كلّ حادث- على قول، ويخصّصه أيضًا بالمقدار المخصوص؛ في الطول والقصر والتوسّط بينهما بدلًا عن سائر المقادير التي يقبل الجرم جميعها على السواء، ويخصّصه أيضًا بصفة معيّنة؛ من حركة أو ضدّها، أو بياض أو ضدّه، أو علم أو ضدّه، إلى غير ذلك من سائر الصفات المتقابلات، ويخصّصه أيضًا بالوجود في زمن معيّن بدلًا عمّا يقابله؛ من زمن متقدّم أو متأخّر، ويخصّصه أيضًا بمكان مخصوص بدلًا عن سائر ما يقابله من الأمكنة، ويخصّصه أيضًا بجهة مخصوصة؛ من جنوب أو شمال، أو مشرق أو مغرب، بدلًا عمّا يقابله من سائر الجهات.

§23.1 It is thus established – by way of definitive and immediate (*ḍarūrī*) certainty after this reflection – that every body requires a specifier (*mukhaṣṣiṣ*), that is, an agent who specifies it with existence rather than nonexistence. According to one view, both are equal in receptivity and possibility; according to another, existence is preponderant due to its primacy in every originated thing.

He likewise specifies it with a particular magnitude: whether long, short, or intermediate – rather than any of the other magnitudes which the body equally admits.

He also specifies it with a particular attribute: motion or stillness, whiteness or its opposite, knowledge or its opposite, and so on among all opposing attributes.

He specifies it with existence in a particular time – rather than an earlier or later one.

He specifies it with a particular place – rather than one of the other possible locations.

And He specifies it with a particular direction: whether south or north, east or west – rather than its counterparts among the remaining directions.

وبهذا يتّضح لك: أنّ كلّ جرم من أجرام العوالم؛ من السموات والأرضين، والعرش والكرسيّ، والإنس والجن والملائكة، وسائر أنواعها وأشخاصها.. حادث مفتقر إلى المولى تبارك وتعالى افتقارًا ضروريًّا لازمًا.

Thus it becomes clear to you that every body among the bodies of the worlds – whether of the heavens and the earths, the Throne and the Footstool, humans, jinn, angels, and all their kinds and individual instances – is originated, and necessarily and inescapably dependent upon the Master (blessed and exalted is He).

يشهد بوجوب حدوثه ووجوب افتقاره إلى المولى تبارك وتعالى: اختصاصه بالوجود بدلًا عن العدم الذي يقبله، وقد اتّصف به كثير من أمثاله المتخيّلة.

§23.2 What testifies to the necessity of its origination and its necessary dependence upon the Master (blessed and exalted is He) is its being specified with existence rather than nonexistence, which it admits of – while many of its imagined counterparts have been characterised by nonexistence.

ويشهد أيضًا بذلك: مقداره المخصوص، ووصفه المخصوص، وزمانه المخصوص، ومكانه المخصوص، وجهته المخصوصة.

This is also attested by its specific magnitude, its specific attribute, its specific time, its specific place, and its specific direction.

فكلّ جرم من أجرام العالم ينادي ناظره بلسان الحال الذي هو أفصح وأصدق من لسان المقال: كلّ ما وقع عليه بصرك منّي، أو جال فيه فكرك من أحوالي.. ليس مقابله أولى بالعدم منه لولا تخصيص مريد قادر قاهر، لا يقف لمعارضة سطوة قهره ممكن، ولا يتعاصى على إرادته للتغيير قويّ من الجائزات، ولا راسخ منها متمكن، فتبارك المولى العظيم الرحمن الرحيم ربّ العالمين.

Every body among the bodies of the world proclaims to its observer, with the tongue of its state (*ḥāl*) – which is more eloquent and more truthful than the tongue of speech: Everything upon which your sight falls of me, or over which your thought ranges among my states – none of it is more entitled to existence than its opposite would be to nonexistence, were it not for the specification of a willing, capable, overpowering agent: one before whose might no possible being can oppose His dominion, and against whose will no contingent – however strong – can resist change, nor is any among them firmly rooted or secure.

Exalted is the great Master, the All-Merciful, the Ever-Merciful, Lord of the worlds.

THE SEVENTH PROLEGOMENON ON THE PAST-ETERNAL ENTITATIVE ATTRIBUTES

المقدّمة السابعة في صفات المعاني الأزليّة

§٢٤ والقدرةُ الأزليَّةُ: عبارةٌ عن صفةٍ يَتَأَتَّى بها إيجادُ كلِّ ممكنٍ وإعدامُهُ على وَفْقِ الإرادةِ.

§٢٥ والإرادةُ: صفةٌ يَتَأَتَّى بها تخصيصُ الممكنِ ببعضِ ما يجوزُ عليهِ.

§24 Past-eternal capability (*qudrah*) is an attribute through which every contingent being is brought into existence and brought out of existence – in accordance with the will.

§25 Will (*irādah*) is an attribute through which a contingent being is specified with some of its possibilities.

§٢٤-٠ شرع هنا في بيان صفات المعاني؛ وهي الصفات الوجوديّة التي يتّصف بها مولانا تبارك وتعالى؛ فإنّ صفاته تبارك وتعالى تنقسم إلى أقسام:

§24.0 He begins here to explain the entitative attributes (*ṣifāt al-maʿānī*) – the existential attributes by which our Master (blessed and exalted is He) is qualified. For His attributes (blessed and exalted is He) are divided into categories:

§٢٤-١ الأوّل: ما يعبّر به عن نفس الذات العليّة؛ وهي الوجود.

§24.1 First: that which expresses the very essence (*dhāt*) of the Most High – and that is existence (*wujūd*).

§٢٤-٢ الثاني: ما يرجع معناه إلى سلب نقص مستحيل على مولانا تبارك وتعالى؛ وهي خمس صفات:

§24.2 Second: that whose meaning entails the negation of a deficiency impossible for our Master (blessed and exalted is He); and these are five attributes:

(١) القدم: وهو عبارة عن سلب العدم في الأزل.

(٢) والبقاء: وهو عبارة عن سلب العدم فيما لا يزال.

ويجمعهما معا: وجوب الوجود؛ لأنّه عبارة عن عدم قبول العدم أزلًا وأبدًا.

(1) Pre-Eternity (*qidam*): It is the negation of nonexistence in past-eternity.

(2) Everlastingness (*baqā'*): it is the negation of nonexistence in perpetuity.

What unites them both is the necessity of existence (*wujūb al-wujūd*): it is the non-admissibility of nonexistence, in past-eternity and in perpetuity.

(٣) والمخالفة للحوادث: وهو عبارة عن سلب الجرميّة والعرضيّة وخواصّهما.

(3) Dissimilarity to originated things (*mukhālifah li-l-ḥawādith*): it consists in the negation of corporeality and accidentality and their properties.

(٤) والقيام بالنفس: وهو عبارة عن سلب الافتقار إلى المحلّ والمخصّص.

(4) Self-Subsistence (*qiyām bi-l-nafs*): it is the negation of dependence upon a substrate or a specifier.

(٥) والوحدانيّة: وهو عبارة عن سلب النظير في الذات والصفات والأفعال.

(5) Unicity (*waḥdāniyyah*): it is the negation of any peer (*naẓīr*) in essence, attributes, and acts.

§٢٤-٣ الثالث: صفات المعاني: وهي عبارة عن الصفات الوجوديّة القائمة بالذات العليّة؛ وهي سبع صفات: القدرة، والإرادة، والعلم، والحياة، والسمع، والبصر، والكلام.

§24.3 Third: the entitative attributes (*ṣifāt al-maʿānī*). These are existential attributes subsisting in the exalted Essence, and they are seven in number:

1. capability (*qudrah*),
2. will (*irādah*),
3. knowledge (*ʿilm*),
4. life (*ḥayāh*),
5. hearing (*samʿ*),
6. sight (*baṣar*), and
7. speech (*kalām*).

واختلف في زيادة صفات؛ وهي: إدراك المشمومات، وإدراك المذوقات، وإدراك الملموسات، وإدراك اللذائذ والآلام:

There is disagreement regarding the addition of further attributes, namely: the perception of smells, the perception of tastes, the perception of tactile objects, and the perception of pleasures and pains.

فقيل بثبوت زيادتها على الصفات السبع، وتكون متعلّقة بكلّ موجود من غير اتّصال بالأجسام، ولا تكييف باللذات والآلام، وقيل: ترجع في حقّه تعالى إلى العلم، وقيل بالوقف، وهو أحسنها.

It was said that their establishment (*thubūt*) is affirmed as an addition to the seven attributes, and that they link to every existent without connection to bodies, nor qualification by pleasures and pains.

It was also said that, with respect to Him (exalted is He) they return to knowledge.

And it was said that one should withhold judgement, and this is the best of them.

§٢٤-٤ الرابع: الصفات المعنويّة: وهي صفات الذات اللازمة لصفات المعاني؛ وهي: كونه تعالى قادرًا، ومريدًا، وعالمًا، وحيًّا، وسميعًا، وبصيرًا، ومتكلّمًا.

§24.4 Fourth: the derivative attributes (*ṣifāt maʿnawiyyah*). These are attributes of the essence that necessarily follow from the entitative attributes (*ṣifāt al-maʿānī*). They are His being

1. capable (*qādir*),
2. willing (*murīd*),
3. knowing (*ʿālim*),
4. living (*ḥayy*),
5. hearing (*samīʿ*),
6. seeing (*baṣīr*), and
7. speaking (*mutakallim*).

§٢٤-٥ وزاد بعضهم قسما خامسًا: وهو صفات الأفعال: وهي عبارة عن التعلّق التنجيزيّ للقدرة والإرادة بالممكنات؛ كخلقه تعالى ورزقه وإماتته وتحريكه وتسكينه، وإن شئت قلت: هي عبارة عن صدور الممكنات عن القدرة والإرادة؛ وهي تنقسم إلى قسمين:

صفة فعليّة وجوديّة: كالأمثلة المذكورة.

وصفة فعليّة سلبيّة: كعفوه تعالى عمّن شاء من أهل المعاصي؛ فإنّه عبارة عن ترك العقوبة لمَن يستحقّها، ولا شكّ أنّ هذا الترك متأخّر عن المعصية الحادثة، وهو فعل بناءً على أنّ الترك فعل، أو سلب فعل العقوبة لمستحقّها بناءً على أنّه ليس بفعل.

§24.5 Some have added a fifth category: the attributes of action (*ṣifāt al-afʿāl*). These are defined as the executive link (*taʿalluq tanjīzī*) of capability and will to contingent beings – such as His creating, providing, causing death, moving, and stilling.

If you prefer, you may say: they are the issuance of contingent beings from capability and will.

These attributes are divided into two types:

1. An existential active attribute – such as the aforementioned examples.
2. A negative active attribute – such as His (exalted is He) pardon of whomever He wills from among the people of disobedience. For this is the abandonment of punishment for one who deserves it. There is no doubt that this abandonment occurs after the newly committed disobedience. It is considered an act – on the view that abandonment is a kind of act – or the negation of the act of punishment for one who deserves it – on the view that it is not, in itself, an act.

§٢٤-٦ وزاد بعضهم قسمًا سادسًا: وهو الصفات الجامعة لسائر أقسام الصفات؛ كالألوهيّة والكبرياء والعظمة.

§24.6 Some have added a sixth category: the attributes that encompass all other categories of attributes – such as divinity (*ulūhiyyah*), majesty (*kibriyāʾ*), and greatness (*ʿaẓamah*).

وإنّما تعرضنا في هذه المقدّمات لبيان قسم واحد؛ وهي صفات المعاني؛ اعتناءً بثبوتها، وإشارةً إلى وجوب وجودها؛ ردًّا على المعتزلة الذين قالوا بنفيها ولم يثبتوا منها إلّا الكلام، وجعلوه صفةً فعليّةً بناءً منهم على حصر الكلام في الحروف والأصوات، فمعنى كونه تعالى متكلّمًا عندهم: أنّه فاعل للكلام، خالق له في محلّ، وسيأتي إن شاء اللّه تعالى الردّ عليهم عند تعرّضنا لشرح الكلام القديم.

We have addressed in these prolegomena only one category – namely, the entitative attributes (*ṣifāt al-maʿānī*) – out of concern for affirming their establishment (*thubūt*) and to indicate the necessity of their existence, in refutation of the Muʿtazilites, who denied them and affirmed only speech, which they classified as an active attribute. This was based on their restriction of speech to letters and sounds.

Thus, according to them, the meaning of His being a speaker is that He is the agent of speech, its creator in a substrate.

A refutation of their position will follow, if Allah wills, when we turn to the explanation of pre-eternal speech.

وأثبت أيضًا معتزلة البصرة: الإرادة، إلّا أنّهم جعلوها صفةً حادثةً قائمةً بنفسها، لا في محلّ.

The Muʿtazilites of Basra also affirmed will, except that they held it to be an originated attribute subsisting by itself, not in a substrate.

§٧-٢٤ والحاصل: أنّ المعتزلة كلّهم أنكروا صفات المعاني التي أثبتها جماعة أهل السنّة، ووافقوهم على اتّصافه تعالى بأحكامها المعنويّة؛ وهي كونه تعالى قادرًا، ومريدًا، وعالمًا، وحيًّا، وسميعًا، وبصيرًا، ومتكلّمًا، وقالوا: يجب أن تكون هذه الأحكام واجبةً لذاته تعالى، ولا نعلّلها بصفات المعاني كما في الشاهد؛ لِما يلزم على تعليلها في حقّه تعالى: من جوازها، وافتقارها إلى علّلها، وذلك يستلزم حدوثها، واتّصافه تعالى بالحوادث مستحيل، وأيضًا: يلزم على إثباتها كثرة القدماء، والإجماع على أنّ القديم واحد، بل ويلزم على إثباتها: تعدّد الإله؛ لأنّها تكون حينئذٍ مشاركةً للإله في القدم، والقدم أخصّ صفات الإله، والمشاركة في الأخصّ توجب المشاركة في الأعمّ، فيلزم أن تشاركه تعالى في سائر صفات الألوهيّة.

§24.7 The upshot is that all the Muʿtazilites denied the entitative attributes (*ṣifāt al-maʿānī*) affirmed by the community of the People of the Sunnah, while agreeing with them that He (exalted is He) is described by their derivative predicates – namely, that He is capable, willing, knowing, living, hearing, seeing, and speaking.

They argued that these predicates must be necessary by virtue of His Essence, and that they should not be explained by recourse to entitative attributes, as is done in observable reality. For, to explain them in His case by attributes would imply their possibility and dependence upon causes, which in turn implies their origination – and for Him (exalted is He) to be described by originated attributes is impossible.

Moreover, affirming such attributes would entail a multiplicity of pre-eternal entities, whereas there is consensus that the pre-eternal is one. Indeed, affirming them would entail a multiplicity of gods, for they would then share with Allah in pre-eternity, and pre-eternity is the most specific of divine attributes. But sharing in what is most specific entails sharing in the more general – so it would follow that they share with Him in all the attributes of divinity.

وهذا الذي تخيّلوه فاسد:

(١) أمّا ما اغترّوا به من إطلاق تعليل الأحكام المعنويّة بالمعاني: فلا يلزم منه جوازها ولا حدوثها؛ لأنّ معنى تعليلها بها: أنّها ملازمة لها، لا يمكن ثبوتها بدونها، وكلّ منهما قديم واجب، وليس معناه أنّ صفات المعاني أثرت في ثبوت الصفات المعنويّة وأفادتها الثبوت والحصول، وإذا كان التعليل بمعنى التلازم فلا يدلّ على جواز ولا على حدوث؛ إذ كما يتلازم جائزان في الشاهد يتلازم واجبان في الغائب، ولا يقدح ذلك في وجوبها، وذلك كما تقول: كونه تعالى قادرًا ملازم لكونه تعالى مريدًا، وهما متلازمان لكونه تعالى عالمًا.

This notion they have imagined is invalid.

(1) As for what they have been deluded by – namely, the unqualified attribution of the causation (*taʿlīl*) of the derivative predicates (*aḥkām maʿnawiyyah*) to the entitative attributes (*ṣifāt al-maʿānī*) – this does not entail their possibility or origination.

For the meaning of attributing their causation to them is simply that they are concomitant with them, such that their establishment (*thubūt*) is not conceivable without them; and each of them is eternal and necessary. It does not mean that the entitative attributes bring about or effect the actuality of the derivative predicates.

And when causation is understood in the sense of necessary concomitance, it does not imply possibility or origination. Just as two possible things may be concomitant in the observable realm, so too may two necessary things be concomitant in the unseen. This does not undermine their necessity.

This is like saying: His being capable is concomitant with His being willing, and both are concomitant with His being knowing.

وإنّما أطلقوا على صفات المعاني العلل دون المعنويّة: لأنّ صفات المعاني صفات وجوديّة تتميّز وتعقل على حيالها، والصفات المعنويّة صفات ثبوتيّة لا تعقل على حيالها، وإنّما تعقل بصفات المعاني، فلمّا كانت تابعةً لها في التعقّل.. أطلقوا على ما كان أصلاً في التعقّل: علّةً، وعلى ما كان تابعًا له في التعقّل: معلولاً.

They applied the term "causes" to the entitative attributes (*ṣifāt al-maʿānī*) rather than to the derivative attributes (*ṣifāt maʿnawiyyah*) because the entitative attributes are existential attributes that are distinct and intelligible in themselves, whereas the derivative attributes are attributes of establishment (*thubūt*) that are not intelligible in themselves but are only intelligible through the entitative attributes.

Since the latter are dependent upon the former in intelligibility, they applied the term "cause" to that which is primary in intelligibility, and the term "effect" to that which is dependent upon it in intelligibility.

(٢) وأمّا ما ألزموه من مخالفة الإجماع بتكثير القدماء: ففاسد؛ لأنّ الشيء لا يتكثّر بكثرة صفاته، فالذات القديمة واحدة بإجماع وإن تعدّدت صفاتها، فمتعلّق الإجماع وحدة الذات الموصوفة بصفات الألوهيّة، لا وحدة الموصوف بالقدم من غير تقييد بكونه ذاتًا.

(2) As for their imputation of contravening consensus by positing a multiplicity of pre-eternals, it is invalid; for a thing is not multiplied by the multiplicity of its attributes. The eternal Essence is one by consensus, even if its attributes are multiple. The object of consensus is the unity of the essence described by the attributes of divinity, not the unity of that which is described as pre-eternal without qualification as to its being an essence.

(٣) وأمّا ما ألزموه من تعدّد الألوهيّة بسبب اشتراكها في أخصّ صفات الإله؛ وهو القدم: ففاسد؛ لأنّ القدم ليس صفةً نفسيّةً؛ بدليل تعقّل وجود الذات قبل تعقّل قدمها، والأخصّ لا يكون إلّا صفةً نفسيّةً لا يمكن تعقّل الذات بدونها؛ كالحيوانيّة للإنسان، بل هو أخصّ الصفات النفسيّة؛ كالناطقيّة للإنسان.

(3) As for what they have asserted – namely, the multiplicity of divinity due to the sharing of the most specific attribute of the divine, which is pre-eternity – is invalid. This is because pre-eternity is not an essential attribute (*ṣifah nafsiyyah*); as evidenced by the fact that the existence of the essence is conceived prior to the conception of its pre-eternity. The most specific attribute can only be an essential attribute, without which the essence cannot be conceived – such as animality for the human being. Rather, it

is the most specific of the essential attributes – such as rationality (*nāṭiqiyyah*) for the human being.

ولمّا تقرّرت الملازمة عقلًا بين الصفات المعنويّة وبين صفات المعاني في الشاهد بطريق التعليل، أو الشرطيّة، أو الحقيقة، أو الدلالة العقليّة.. وجب طرد تلك الملازمة شاهدًا وغائبًا؛ إذ اللزوم العقليّ لا يمكن تخلّفه بوجه من الوجوه.

Once the concomitance between the derivative attributes and the entitative attributes in the observable realm was established intellectually – whether by way of causation, conditionality, essential reality, or rational indication – it became necessary to apply that concomitance uniformly to both the observable and the unobservable. For rational concomitance cannot, in any way whatsoever, be subject to failure.

§٢٤-٨ فإذا عرفت هذا: فقوله في المقدّمة: (القدرة الأزليّة) يعني: القديمة؛ وهي قدرة مولانا جلّ وعزّ، لا القدرة الحادثة؛ وهي قدرة الحيوانات.

§24.8 If you have understood this, then his statement in the introduction, "past-eternal capability," means: the pre-eternal; and it is the capability of our Master (majestic and exalted is He) not the originated capability, which is the capability of living creatures.

قوله: (يتأتّى بها إيجاد كلّ ممكن وإعدامه) يعني: يتيسّر بها إخراج كلّ ممكن من العدم إلى الوجود، وإخراجه من الوجود إلى العدم.

His statement, "through which every contingent being is brought into existence and brought out of existence" means: it becomes feasible by it to bring every contingent being out of nonexistence into existence, and to bring it out of existence into nonexistence.

وقد مرّ القول في جعل العدم الطارئ أثرًا للقدرة الأزليّة مباشرةً على مذهب القاضي، وهو الأصحّ في النظر؛ لأنّ المصحّح لتأثير القدرة الأزليّة إن قلنا: هو الإمكان مع الحدوث، أو الإمكان بشرط الحدوث، أو الحدوث فقط، أو الإمكان فقط.. فذلك كلّه محقّق ثابت للعدم الطارئ، ولا يلزم في أثر القدرة أن يكون وجوديًّا كما صار إليه إمام الحرمين، بل إنّما يلزم فيه أن يكون متجدّدًا حادثًا، كان ذلك المتجدّد وجوديًّا أو عدميًّا، وهذا هو الحقّ الذي لا شكّ فيه، والله تعالى أعلم.

The discussion has already passed regarding the attribution of the incidental nonexistence as a direct effect of the past-eternal capability according to the doctrine of al-Qāḍī, which is the more correct view in speculative (*naẓarī*) reasoning.

For that which validates the effect of the past-eternal capability – whether we say it is: possibility (*imkān*) along with origination (*ḥudūth*), possibility conditional upon origination, origination alone, or mere possibility – all of that is indeed realised and established in the case of incidental nonexistence.

It is not necessary for the effect of capability to be existential, as Imām al-Ḥaramayn held; rather, what is necessary is that it be something renewed and originated, whether that renewal be existential or privative. This is the truth in which there is no doubt. And Allah (exalted is He) knows best.

وقد ذهب بعض الأئمّة المحقّقين إلى أنّ العدم الممكن السابق عن وجود الحوادث فيما لا يزال.. مقدور للبارئ تبارك وتعالى؛ كالعدم والوجود الطارئين؛ بمعنى: أنّه في قبضة قدرته تعالى يتأتّى منه جلّ وعلا إبقاؤه، وإزالته بجعل الوجود الحادث في مكانه.

Some verifying imāms have held that the contingent nonexistence antecedent to the existence of originated things in perpetuity is within the capability of the Creator (blessed and exalted is He) just like the incidental nonexistence and existence; meaning: it lies within the grasp of His capability (majestic and sublime is He) to maintain it or to remove it by placing originated existence in its stead.

وإطلاق المقدوريّة بأقلّ من هذا مستعمل في اللغة والعرف؛ يقال: الملك يقدر على الناس ولا يقدرون عليه؛ بمعنى: أنّه يملك على سبيل المجاز تغيير بعض أحوالهم؛ كإعزاز أو إذلال ونحوهما، فكيف لا يطلق على ذلك العدم الممكن أنّه مقدور لله تعالى؟! فإنّه جلّ وعلا يملك إبقاءه وتغييره بما شاء وكيف شاء على الحقيقة، لا على المجاز، فملء الفم بأنّه ليس مقدورًا للمولى تبارك وتعالى؛ نظرًا إلى أنّ حقيقته ليست بوجوديّة ولا طارئة.. سوء أدب؛ بإطلاق ما يوهم عجزًا في قدرته جلّ وعلا.

The application of 'being subject to capability' (*maqdūriyyah*) to less than this is employed in language and convention; it is said: "The king has power over the people, and they have no power over him," meaning that he possesses – by way of metaphor – the ability to alter some of their states – such as honouring or humiliating and the like.

So how could it not be said of that contingent non-being that it is an object of capability for Allah, exalted is He? For He, majestic and sublime, truly possesses the power to maintain it or alter it as He wills and how He wills – not metaphorically, but in reality.

Therefore, to emphatically declare that it is not an object of capability for the Exalted Lord, on the basis that its reality is neither existent nor accidental, is a grave impropriety – issuing a statement that implies deficiency in His capability (exalted is He).

وهـذا الـذي اختاره هذا الإمام هو الآتي على أن مصحّح تعلّق القدرة الأزليّـة بالممكـن.. الإمـكان فقط، فكلّ ممكن علـى هذا؛ وجوديًّا كان أو عدميًّـا، سـابقًا كان أو لاحقًـا.. فهـو مقـدور لمولانـا تبـارك وتعالـى، ومقدوريّـة كلّ حقيقـة من هذه الحقائـق بما يليق بها، وهذا القول أقرب للغة والعرف، وأسلم من سوء الأدب وإيهام النقص، واللّه سبحانه أعلم.

This view, which this Imām has chosen, is the following: that the sole factor validating the relation of the past-eternal capability to the contingent (*mumkin*) is merely possibility (*imkān*). Thus, every contingent – whether existent or non-existent, prior or subsequent – is an object of capability for our Master (blessed and exalted is He), and the being subject to capability (*maqdūriyyah*) of each of these realities occurs in a manner appropriate to it.

This view accords more closely with language and customary usage, and is safer from impropriety and any suggestion of deficiency. And Allah (exalted is He) knows best.

وقولـه فـي تعريف القدرة الأزليّة: (يتأتّى بها إيجاد كلّ ممكن) يعني: سواء كان جرمًا أو عرضًا، مكتسبًا للحيوان أو غيرَ مكتسب، ففيه تنبيه على فسـاد مذهب القدريّة الذين أخرجوا أفعال الحيوانات الاختياريّة عـن تعلّـق قدرة اللّـه تعالى، وعلى فسـاد مذهـب الطبائعيّيـن الذين أسندوا بعض الممكنات لقوى الطبائع العلويّة والسفليّة.

His statement in the definition of the past-eternal capability: "through which every contingent being is brought into existence" – he means: whether it be a substance or an accident, acquired by a living creature or not acquired.

In this is an indication of the invalidity of the doctrine of the Qadarites, who excluded the voluntary acts of living creatures from the scope of the capability of Allah (exalted is He), and of the invalidity of the doctrine of the naturalists, who ascribed some contingents to the forces of the upper and lower natures.

وقولـه: (علـى وفـق الإرادة) إشـارة إلـى أنّ فعلـه للكائنـات إنّمـا هو بطريق الاختيار، لا بطريق اللزوم، كفعل العلّة والطبيعة عند الفلاسفة والطبائعيّين.

His statement, "in accordance with the will," is an indication that His act of bringing things into being occurs by way of volition, not by way of necessity, as is the case with the act of the cause and nature according to the philosophers and naturalists.

§٢٥-١ وقولـه: (والإرادة: صفـة يتأتّى بهـا تخصيص الممكن ببعض مـا يجـوز عليه) يعنـي: أنّ الممكنـات لمّا كانت نسـبتها إلى قدرته تعالى على حدّ السـواء؛ فلو اختصّت بوجود بعضها دون بعض.. لزم العجـز، فإذًا لا بـدّ لتخصيص بعض الممكنات بالوقوع دون مقابله.. من صفة أخرى، وليست إلّا صفة الإرادة؛ إذ لا يلزم نقصٌ في قولنا: أراد اللّـه تعالـى وجود هذا الممكن، ولم يرد هذا الممكن الآخر، بل أراد عدمـه، بـل ذلـك دليل على غاية الكمـال؛ فإن تصفه جلّ وعلا فـي الممكنات بمحـض الإرادة والاختيار، ولا باعث له على ممكن منها ولا إكراه ولا إجبار، كما قال جلّ وعلا: ﴿وَرَبُّكَ يَخْلُقُ مَا يَشَاءُ وَيَخْتَارُ﴾ [القصص: ٦٨].

§25.1 His statement, "Will (*irādah*) is an attribute through which a contingent being is specified with some of its possibilities." – he means: that since all contingent beings (*mumkināt*) stand in equal relation to His capability (exalted is He) then if some of them were singled out for existence over others, deficiency would follow. Therefore, it is necessary that the specification of some contingent beings with actualisation over their counterparts be due to another attribute – and that is none other than the attribute of will.

For there is no imperfection entailed in saying, "Allah (exalted is He) willed the existence of this contingent being, and did not will this other contingent being; rather, He willed its nonexistence." Rather, that is evidence of utmost perfection – for He, exalted and sublime, engages with contingent beings purely by will and choice, and there is no motive for Him toward any of them, nor compulsion, nor coercion. As He (exalted is He) said: "And your Lord creates what He wills and chooses."[42]

ولو قلت: قدر اللّٰه تعالى على هذا الممكن الموجود، ولم يقدر على مقابله.. لكان فاسدًا؛ لِما فيه من لزوم نقيصة العجز.

Were you to say: "Allah (exalted is He) had capability over this existent contingent (*mumkin*), but not over its counterpart," it would be invalid; due to the entailment therein of the deficiency of incapacity.

وأمّا سائر الصفات -كالعلم، والكلام، والسمع، والبصر- فلا يصحّ التخصيص بها؛ لأنّ التخصيص تأثير، وهذه الصفات ليست مؤثّرةً في متعلّقاتها.

As for the rest of the attributes – such as knowledge, speech, hearing, and sight – they cannot validly serve as the basis for specification, because specification is an act of effectuation, and these attributes do not exert effect upon their objects.

وأشار بالعموم في قوله: (الممكن) إلى فساد مذهب المعتزلة الذين خصّصوا تعلّق الإرادة بالخير دون الشرّ، وبالصلاح والأصلح دون مقابليهما.

42 al-Qaṣaṣ: 28:68.

He alluded generally in his statement, "a contingent being (*mumkin*)," to the invalidity of the doctrine of the Muʿtazilah, who restricted the linking of will to good and not to evil, and to the good (*ṣāliḥ*) and the better (*aṣlaḥ*) and not to their opposites.

§٢٦ والعلمُ: صفةٌ يَنْكَشِفُ بها المعلومُ على ما هو بِهِ.

§26 Knowledge (*ʿilm*) is an attribute through which what is known is revealed as it truly is.

§٢٦-٠ يعني بالمعلوم: كلّ ما يصحّ أن يعلم؛ وهو: كلّ واجب، وكلّ مستحيل، وكلّ جائز.

§26.0 What is meant by "what is known" (*maʿlūm*) is everything that can rightly be known – that is: every necessary (*wājib*), every impossible (*mustaḥīl*), and every possible (*jāʾiz*).

ومعنى (ينكشف): أنّه يتّضح ذلك المعلوم لمَن قامت به تلك الصفة ويتميّز عن غيره اتّضاحًا لا خفاء معه.

The meaning of "it is disclosed" is that the object of knowledge becomes clear to the one in whom that attribute subsists, and it becomes distinguished from other things with a clarity that admits no obscurity.

وهذا مخرج للظنّ والشكّ والوهم؛ فإنّ الاحتمال القائم فيها انكشاف ذلك المظنون والمشكوك والموهوم، ويوجب له خفاء.

This excludes conjecture, doubt, and illusion; for the contingency inherent in them impedes the disclosure of the conjectured, doubted, or imagined object, and necessitates obscurity with respect to it.

ويخرج أيضًا: الاعتقاد الجازم، مطابقًا كان أو غير مطابق؛ لأنّه يحتمل النقيض بتشكيك مشكّك، فلا يستمرّ معه الانكشاف.

Also excluded is firm belief (*i'tiqād jāzim*), whether it accords with reality or not; for it admits of contradiction through a sceptic's challenge, and thus disclosure does not persist with it.

والتعبير بالمضارع في الانكشاف يقتضي دوام الانكشاف واستمراره؛ بحيث لا يحتمل النقيض بوجه، وذلك لاستناد هذه الصفة إلى ضرورة أو برهان.

The use of the present tense in "disclosure" (*inkishāf*) entails the perpetuity and continuity of the disclosure, such that its contrary is in no way conceivable. This is because this attribute is grounded in immediate knowledge (*'ilm ḍarūrī*) or demonstration (*burhān*).

وقوله: (على ما هو به) زيادة في البيان، وتصريح علل سبيل التوكيد بإخراج الجهل المركّب؛ وهو اعتقاد أمر على خلاف ما هو به.

His statement, "as it truly is," is an elaborative clarification and a form of emphatic specification, serving to exclude *compound ignorance* (*jahl murakkab*) – which is the belief in something contrary to what it in fact is.

والمقصود من هذا التعريف: التقريب على سبيل الاختصار؛ لعسر تعريف العلم بما يسلم من كلّ مناقشة.

The purpose of this definition is approximation by way of brevity, due to the difficulty of defining knowledge in a manner free from all disputation.

ويدخل في العلم على مقتضى هذا التعريف: إدراك السمع والبصر وسائر الإدراكات، فهي إذا أنواع من العلم، وهذا مذهب الشيخ الأشعريّ رضي اللّه تعالى عنه.

According to this definition, included under knowledge is the apprehension of hearing, sight, and all other forms of apprehension;

these, then, are types of knowledge. This is the position of Shaykh al-Ashʿarī (may Allah – exalted is He – be pleased with him).

§٢٧ والحياةُ: صفةٌ يصحُّ ممَّنْ قامَتْ بهِ الإدراكُ.

§27 Life (*ḥayāh*) is an attribute by which the one in whom it subsists is capable of perception.

§٢٧-٠ يعني: أنّ الحياة ليست من الصفات المتعلّقة؛ وهي ما يقتضي لذاته زائدًا على القيام بمحله؛ كالقدرة؛ فإنّها تقتضي زائدًا على القيام بمحلّها؛ وهو المقدور الذي يتأتّى بها إيجاده وإعدامه، والإرادة تقتضي لذاتها مرادًا يتخصّص بها، والعلم يقتضي معلومًا ينكشف به، والكلام يقتضي معنى يدلّ عليه، والسمع يقتضي مسموعًا يسمع، والبصر يقتضي مبصرًا، والحياة لا تقتضي زائدًا على القيام بمحلّها، وإنّما هي صفة مصحّحة للإدراك؛ بمعنى: أنّها شرط عقليّ له، يلزم من عدمها عدم الإدراك، ولا يلزم من وجودها وجود الإدراك ولا عدمه، وبالله تعالى التوفيق.

§27.0 Meaning: That Life is not among the relational attributes; these are those which, by their very essence, entail something additional to their inherence in their substrate. Capability, for instance, entails something beyond its inherence in its substrate – namely, the object of capability, which can be brought into or out of existence by it. Will entails, by its very essence, an intended object specified by it. Knowledge entails an object known, through which it becomes manifest. Speech entails a meaning indicated by it. Hearing entails an audible object that is heard. Sight entails a visible object.

Life, however, does not entail anything beyond its inherence in its substrate. Rather, it is an attribute that validates perception – in the sense that it is an intellectual (*ʿaqlī*) condition for it. That is, the nonexistence of life necessitates the nonexistence of perception, but the existence of life does not necessitate either the existence or the nonexistence of perception.

And success is from Allah (exalted is He).

§٢٨ والسمعُ الأزليُّ: صفةٌ يَنْكَشِفُ بها كلُّ موجودٍ على ما هو بِهِ انكشافًا يُبَايِنُ سواهُ ضرورةً، والبصرُ مثلُهُ، والإدراكُ على القولِ بِهِ مثلُهما.

§28 Past-eternal hearing (*samʿ*) is an attribute through which every existent is revealed as it truly is – with a disclosure necessarily distinct from that of any other attribute.

Sight (*baṣar*) is like it.

Perception (*idrāk*), according to the view that affirms it, is like the two.

§٢٨-٠ هذه الصفات مشتركة في تعلّقها بالموجود، قديمًا كان أو حادثًا، إلّا أنّها في الشاهد مختصّة ببعض الموجودات؛ لتخصيصه تعالى لها بذلك، ولو خرق سبحانه وتعالى العادة في ذلك لصحّ أن تتعلّق بسائر الموجودات، ولهذا جازت رؤية المخلوق لمولانا تبارك وتعالى على مذهب أهل الحقّ، وجاز سماعهم لكلامه القديم القائم بذاته العليّة جلّ وعلا، مع أنّ الرؤية في الشاهد إنّما جرت العادة بتعلّقها بالأجرام وألوانها وأكوانها، والسمع في الشاهد إنّما جرت العادة بتعلّقه بالحروف والأصوات.

§28.0 These attributes are common in their link to existent things, whether eternal or originated. However, in the observable realm, they are specific to certain existents due to His (exalted is He) specification of them as such. Were He (glory be to Him, exalted is He) to suspend the customary order in this regard, it would be valid for them to pertain to all existents.

For this reason, the vision of our Master (blessed and exalted is He) by created beings is possible according to the doctrine of the people of truth. Likewise, it is possible for them to hear His eternal speech subsisting in His exalted essence (majestic and sublime is He) even though vision in the observable realm customarily links only to bodies, their colours, and their modes of being (*akwān*), and hearing in the observable realm customarily links only to letters and sounds.

ولمّـا اسـتحال دخول التخصيص فـي صفات المولى تبـارك وتعالى؛ لاسـتلزامه الافتقار إلى المخصّص المستلزم للحدوث.. وجب تعميم تعلّـق صفاتـه تعالـى بكلّ ما تصلـح له؛ لأنّها واجبـة، فلا يمكـن أن تتّصـف بمـا يقتضي حدوثهـا، والقاعدة: أنّ كلّ مـا يقبله تعالى من الصفات الذاتيّة وكمالاتها.. فهو واجب له؛ لاسـتحالة اتّصافه تعالى بالجائزات.

Since the admission of specification (*takhṣīṣ*) into the attributes of the Exalted Lord is impossible – because it entails dependence upon a specifier, which in turn entails origination – it is necessary to generalise the scope of His attributes' link to everything to which they are suited; because they are necessary, they cannot be characterised by anything that would entail their origination.

The principle is that everything that is admissible for Allah (exalted is He) from among the essential attributes and their perfections is necessary for Him – for it is impossible for Him (exalted is He) to be characterised by possibles.

وقـد اتّفـق أهـل الحـقّ قاطبةً علـى جواز تعلّـق البصر بـكلّ موجود، واختلفوا في جواز تعلّق ما عدا الرؤية من الإدراكات بكلّ موجود:

All adherents of the truth are unanimously agreed on the possibility of sight linking to every existent, while they have differed concerning the possibility of other forms of perception – apart from sight – linking to every existent.

§٢٨-١ فذهب القدماء منهم؛ كعبد اللّه بن سعيد الكلابيّ والقلانسيّ: إلى أنّ هذا العموم مختصّ بالرؤية، وبقية الإدراكات لا يجوز أن تعمّ الموجودات.

§28.1 The ancients among them – such as ʿAbd Allāh ibn Saʿīd al-Kullābī and al-Qalānisī – held that this universality is specific to vision, and that other forms of perception are not permitted to be universal with respect to existents.

ونقل عن إمام أهل السنّة وشيخهم الشيخ أبي الحسن الأشعريّ مخالفيهما في ذلك، وصار إلى جواز عموم كلّ إدراك لكلّ موجود.

It was transmitted from the Imām of the Sunnis and their shaykh, Shaykh Abū al-Ḥasan al-Ashʿarī (may Allah be pleased with him), that he opposed them in that matter and held the possibility of the universality of every perception with respect to every existent.

ونقل عن عبد اللّه بن سعيد: أنّه لمّا خصّ تعلّق السمع بالأصوات.. ذهب إلى أنّ الكلام الأزليّ لا يصحّ أن يسمع؛ يعني واللّه تعالى أعلم: بل يدرك بصفة العلم، وفي قوله ذلك مخالفة لقواطع السمع.

It was transmitted from ʿAbd Allāh ibn Saʿīd that, since hearing is specifically linked to sounds, he held that the past-eternal speech cannot rightly be heard – meaning, and Allah knows best, rather it is known by the attribute of knowledge. In this statement of his is an opposition to the definitive evidences of hearing.

والشيخ أبو الحسن رضي اللّه تعالى عنه لمّا قال: إدراك السمع يعمّ كلّ موجود.. جوّز تعلّقه بكلام اللّه تعالى، وقال بوقوع ذلك الجائز على ما ورد به السمع في حقّ موسى عليه الصلاة والسلام.

And Shaykh Abū al-Ḥasan (may Allah be pleased with him), when he said, "Auditory perception encompasses every existent," permitted its linkage to the speech of Allah (exalted is He), and affirmed the occurrence of that possible matter as reported in the transmitted texts in the case of Mūsā (upon him be blessings and peace).

§٢٨-٢ وعمدة الشيخ في ذلك: ما ثبت في فصل الرؤية من أنّ الوجود هو المصحّح للرؤية؛ بمعنى: أنّه متعلّقها، فلا فرق بين موجود وموجود؛ فإذا رئي موجود أو أدرك بغير الرؤية.. جاز تعلّقهما بكلّ موجود.

§28.2 The Shaykh's principal argument in this regard is what has been established in the section on vision: that existence is what renders vision admissible, in the sense that it is its object. Thus, there is no distinction between one existent and another; so if an existent is seen or perceived by means other than vision, it is possible for each to link to any existent.

وقد اختلف الأصحاب في الأكوان التي هي متعلّق الرؤية في وقتنا اتّفاقًا: هل هي متعلّق لإدراك اللمس أم لا؟ فذهب بعضهم إلى أنّ إدراك اللمس يتعلّق بها، واحتجّ على ذلك: بأنّ من لمس شيئًا واضطرب تحت يده.. أدرك حركته، وإذا تفرّقت أجزاؤه في يده أدرك تفرّقتها، ومن الأصحاب من أنكر ذلك، وزعم أنّه يعلم ذلك عند اللمس، ولم يتعلّق إدراك اللمس به، قال المقترح: (والتحقيق: الأوّل).

The colleagues differed concerning the actualities (*akwān*) that are, by agreement, the object of vision in our time: are they also the object of tactile perception, or not?

Some held that tactile perception links to them, and argued this by stating that when one touches something and it moves beneath one's hand, one perceives its motion; and when its parts separate in one's hand, one perceives their separation.

Others among the colleagues denied this, claiming that such things are known at the time of touch, but that tactile perception does not link to them.

Al-Muqtaraḥ said: "The correct view is the first."

وأورد على أهل السنّة في قولهم: (إنّ الرؤية تتعلّق بكلّ موجود) لزوم التسلسل؛ وذلك أنّ الرؤية المتعلّقة هي من جملة الموجودات، فيجب أن تصحّ رؤيتها، فإذا لم نر رؤيتنا فإنّما لم نرها لمانع؛ كما في حقّ غيرها من الموجودات التي لا نراها، ثمّ ننقل الكلام إلى ذلك المانع فنقول: هو موجود، فيجوز أن يرى، فيحتاج أيضًا إلى تقدير مانع يمنع من رؤيته، وكذلك الكلام في مانع المانع إلى ما لا نهاية له.

An objection is raised against the Sunnis in their claim that "vision links to every existent," namely, the entailment of infinite regress (*tasalsul*). This is because the vision that links is itself among the totality of existents, and thus it must be valid for it to be seen. If we do not see our vision, then it is due to an impediment – just as is the case with other existents that we do not see. We then turn to that impediment and say: it is an existent, so it is valid for it to be seen; it too, then, requires the positing of an impediment that prevents its being seen. Likewise, the discourse continues regarding the impediment of the impediment, to no end.

وأجاب القاضي عن ذلك: بأنّ المانع الأوّل يمنع من رؤية ما هو مانع منه، ومانع أيضًا من رؤية نفسه، فلا يحتاج إلى تقدير مانع آخر حتى يلزم التسلسل.

The Qāḍī responded to that by saying: the first impediment prevents seeing that which it obstructs, and also prevents itself being seen; thus, there is no need to posit another impediment, and infinite regress (*tasalsul*) does not follow.

واعترض عليه: بأنّ المانع إذا كان يمنع من رؤية نفسه فيكون امتناع رؤيته صفةً نفسيّةً له تمنع من تقدير مانع بالنسبة إلى رؤيته، وذلك ممّا يقدح في طرد دلالة الوجود على صحّة تعلّق الرؤية بكلّ موجود.

An objection was raised against it: that if the impediment prevents seeing itself, then the impossibility of its being seen is an essential attribute that precludes positing an impediment for its being seen. This undermines the universality of the indication of existence for the validity of vision linking to every existent.

فأجاب القاضي رضي اللّٰه تعالى عنه: بأنّ المانع من صفة نفسه أن يمنع من قام به رؤيته؛ لا غير من قام به، فيجوز أن يراه غير مَن قام به؛ إذ الحكم لا يثبت للمعنى إلّا في محلّ قام به ذلك المعنى، فصحّت الكلّيّة المذكورة؛ وهي أن كلّ موجود تصحّ رؤيته.

The Qāḍī (may Allah be pleased with him) answered: the impediment is an essential attribute that prevents the one in whom it inheres from seeing it – not one in whom it does not inhere. Therefore, it is possible for someone other than the one in whom it inheres to see it. For a ruling applies to a meaning only in the substrate in which that meaning inheres. Thus, the aforementioned universal holds true: namely, that every existent is valid to be seen.

فإن قلت: إذا وجب تعلّق هذه الإدراكات في حقّه تعالى بكلّ موجود، والعلم أيضًا قد تعلّق بها، فيلزم إمّا تحصيل الحاصل، أو اجتماع المثلين إن كان ما تعلّقت به غير ما تعلّق به العلم، وإمّا خفاء بعض المعلومات عن العلم إن كان ما تعلّقت به تلك الإدراكات لم يتعلّق به العلم، وكِلا الأمرين مستحيل.

Should you say: If it is necessary, in His regard (exalted is He), that these perceptions link to every existent, and knowledge also links to them, then it follows either the acquisition of what has already been acquired, or the conjunction of two similars – if that to which the perceptions link is other than that to which knowledge links – or that some known things are hidden from knowledge, if that to which those perceptions link is not that to which knowledge links. Both alternatives are impossible.

قلت: نختار من القسمين الأوّل؛ وهو أنّ ما تعلّقت به تلك الإدراكات هو عين ما تعلّق به العلم، ولا يلزم من ذلك تحصيل الحاصل ولا اجتماع المثلين؛ وذلك أنّ هذه الإدراكات لمّا كانت غير متّحدة الحقيقة، سواء قلنا: إنّها أنواع العلم أو لا، فتعلّقاتها كذلك غير متّحدة، فاجتماع تعلّقاتها في متعلّق واحد ليس من تحصيل الحاصل، ولا من اجتماع الأمثال، بل كلّ متعلّق منها له حقيقة من الانكشاف تخصّه ليست عين حقيقة سواه، وكلّ حقيقة منها عامّة لما تصحّ له.

I say: We choose the first of the two divisions – that what these perceptions link to is the very same as what knowledge links to. This does not entail the acquisition of what has already been acquired, nor the conjunction of similars.

This is because these perceptions, since they are not unified in reality – whether we say they are types of knowledge or not – their modes of linkage are likewise not unified. So the conjunction of their linkages upon a single object is neither an acquisition of the acquired nor a conjunction of similars.

Rather, each linkage possesses a distinct reality of disclosure particular to it, which is not identical to the reality of another. And each of these realities is general with respect to that to which it rightly applies.

وهـذا كمـا تقـدّم: أنّ متعلّق القدرة والإرادة واحـد؛ وهو الممكنات، ولا يلزم من اجتماعهما في متعلّق واحد تحصيل الحاصل؛ لاختلاف حقيقتَـي تعلّقهمـا، وكلّ منهمـا عامّ بتعلّقه الخـاصّ بحقيقته لجميع الممكنات، ولهذا أشرنا بقولنا: (يباين سواه ضرورةً).

As previously stated: the object of capability and will is one and the same – that is, contingents (*mumkināt*). The fact that both link to a single object does not entail the acquisition of what has already been acquired, due to the difference in the realities of their respective linkages. Each of them is universal in its specific linkage – according to its own reality – to all contingents.

Thus we indicated by our statement, "a disclosure that necessarily differs from all else."

ومـا ثبـت أنّ المشـاهدة أقـوى مـن العلم إنّمـا يصحّ ذلـك في حقّ الحادث؛ لنقص علمه وعدم إحاطته، فقد ينكشف له عند المشاهدة أمـور لـم يتعلّـق بها علمـه أصلًا، أو تعلّق لكن على سـبيل الاجمال لا على سـبيل التفصيل، فيسـتفيد بسبب السمع والبصر علمًا بما لم يكن معلومًا عنده.

وهذا مسـتحيل في حقّه تعالى؛ فإنّ السـمع والبصر لا ينكشـف بهما في حقّه تبارك وتعالى شـيء لم يكن منكشـفًا لعلمه جلّ وعلا؛ لوجـوب إحاطـة علمـه تبـارك وتعالـى بجميـع المعلومـات؛ جملتها وتفصيلها، وإنّما السـمع والبصر يزيدان على العلم في حقّه جلّ وعلا بحقيقتهما وتعلّقهما الخاصّ بهما، ولا يزيدان في حقيقة علمه تعالى شيئًا أصلًا.

As for the claim that witnessing (*mushāhadah*) is stronger than knowledge, that is valid only in the case of the originated being, due to the deficiency of his knowledge and its lack of comprehensiveness. For it may be that, upon witnessing, things become manifest to him that his knowledge had not encompassed at all, or had encompassed only in a general manner, not in detail. Thus, through hearing and sight, he acquires knowledge of that which was previously unknown to him.

This is impossible with respect to Him (exalted is He), for hearing and sight do not disclose to Him (blessed and exalted is He) anything that was not already disclosed to His knowledge, due to the necessary comprehensiveness of His knowledge (blessed and exalted is He) of all objects of knowledge, both in totality and in detail.

Rather, hearing and sight add to His knowledge only by their own realities and their specific modes of linkage, and they add nothing whatsoever to the reality of His knowledge (exalted is He).

قوله: (والإدراك على القول به مثلهما) يعني: مثلهما في وجوب تعلّقه بكلّ موجود، وأنّه لا يختصّ بما اختصّ به في الشاهد، وقد تقدّم فيه ثلاثة أقوال لأهل السنّة، وباللّه تعالى التوفيق.

His statement, "Perception (*idrāk*), according to the view that affirms it, is like the two" – that is, it is like the two in the necessity of its linking to every existent, and that it is not restricted to what it is restricted to in the seen world. Three positions on this matter have already been mentioned from the Sunnis. And success is from Allah (exalted is He).

§٢٩ والـكلامُ الأزليُّ: وهو المعنى القائمُ بالذاتِ، المُعَبَّرُ عنهُ بالعباراتِ المختلفـاتِ، المُبَايِـنُ لجنـسِ الحروفِ والأصـواتِ، المُنَزَّهُ عـنِ البعضِ والكلِّ، والتقديمِ والتأخيرِ، والتجدُّدِ والسكوتِ، واللحنِ والإعرابِ، وسائرِ أنواعِ التغيُّراتِ، المتعلِّقُ بما يتعلَّق بهِ العلمُ مِنَ المتعلَّقاتِ.

§29 Past-eternal speech (*kalām*) is a meaning subsisting in the essence, expressed through various different expressions. It is distinct from the genus of letters and sounds, and is transcendent above part and whole, priority and posteriority, origination and silence, incorrectness and grammatical inflection, and all other types of change. It links to the same objects to which knowledge links.

§٢٩-٠ لا شـكّ أنّ الكتاب والسـنّة والإجماع مصرّحة بإثبات الكلام لمولانـا تبـارك وتعالى؛ من أمر ونهي، ووعد ووعيد، وتبشـير وتحذير، إخبار.

§29.0 There is no doubt that the Book, the Sunnah, and consensus explicitly affirm the speech of our Master (blessed and exalted is He): command and prohibition, promise and threat, glad tidings and warning, and report.

ودليـل العقـل أيضًا يـدلّ بالطريق القطعيّ: أنّ كلّ عالم بأمر يصحّ أن يتكلّـم بـه، ومولانا جـلّ وعلا عالم بجميع المعلومـات، فصحّ أن له كلامًـا يتعلّـق بهـا، وكلّ ما صـحّ أن يتّصف به جـلّ وعلا وجب له؛ لاستحالة اتّصافه بصفة جائزة، فالكلام إذًا واجب له.

The intellect's proof also indicates, in a definitive manner, that every knower of a matter is validly able to speak about it. And our Master (majestic and exalted is He) is a knower of all objects of knowledge; thus, it is valid that He has speech pertaining to them. And everything that it is valid for Him (majestic and exalted is He) to be described with is obligatory for Him, due to the impossibility of His being described with a possible attribute. Therefore, speech is obligatory for Him.

ثمّ اختلفت الناس بعد هذا على فرق:

Thereafter, humanity diverged into factions.

فذهب الحشويّة: إلى أنّ هذا الكلام الذي يتّصف به مولانا جلّ وعزّ حروف وأصوات قائمة بذاته على حسب ما ثبت في الكلام اللسانيّ في الشاهد، وزعموا أنّه مع كونه حرفًا وصوتًا قديم، بل زعموا أنّ المداد حادث، فإذا كتب به القرآن صار بعينه قديمًا!

The Ḥashwiyyah held that this speech by which our Master (majestic and exalted is He) is described consists of letters and sounds subsisting in His Essence, in accordance with what is established regarding spoken language in the seen world. They claimed that, despite being a letter and a sound, it is eternal. Indeed, they asserted that while the ink is originated, when the Qur'ān is written with it, it becomes itself eternal.

وهذا المذهب واضح الفساد؛ إذ من المعلوم أنّ الحروف والأصوات لا تعقل إلّا حادثة؛ لتجدّدها بعد عدم، وعدمها بعد تجدّد، فالعدم يكتنفها سابقًا ولاحقًا، والقديم لا يقبل العدم لا سابقًا ولا لاحقًا.

This doctrine is manifestly unsound; for it is known that letters and sounds are intelligible only as originated, due to their renewal after nonexistence and their cessation after renewal. Nonexistence encompasses them both before and after, whereas that which is eternal does not accept nonexistence – neither prior nor subsequent.

وذهبت المعتزلة: إلى أنّ كلامه تعالى حروف وأصوات كما قالت الحشويّة، إلّا أنّهم خالفوهم بأنّ قالوا: إنّ كلامه تعالى فعل من أفعاله؛ كرزقه وعطائه، فلا يصحّ أن يقوم بذاته تعالى؛ لاستحالة قيام الحوادث به، فإذا أراد اللّه تعالى أن يتكلّم بأمر أو نهي أو غيرهما من سائر أنواع الكلام.. خلق ذلك في جرم من الأجرام، وأسمع ذلك من شاء من ملائكته وأنبيائه ورسله.

The Muʿtazilah held that His speech (exalted is He) is composed of letters and sounds, as the Ḥashwiyyah claimed. However, they diverged from them by asserting that His speech (exalted is He) is an act from among His acts, like His provision and His giving. Therefore, it is not valid for it to subsist in His Essence, due to the impossibility of accidents subsisting in Him.

When Allah (exalted is He) wills to speak a command, a prohibition, or any other type of speech, He creates that in a body from among the bodies and makes whomever He wills from among His angels, prophets, and messengers hear it.

وهـذا المذهـب أيضًا واضح الفسـاد؛ لأنّه يسـتلزم امتنـاع ما علمت صحّتـه مـن الـكلام في حقّ العالـم، وأيضًا: إذا لـم يكن في الذات العليّـة أمـر ولا نهي، ولا وعد ولا وعيد، وإنّما هي موجودة في الأجرام الحـادثة.. فالمكلّفون إذًا عابدون لتلك الأجرام؛ إذ هي الآمرة الناهية.

This doctrine is also clearly unsound, for it entails the impossibility of what is known to be valid regarding speech with respect to created beings. Moreover, if there is in the exalted Essence neither command nor prohibition, nor promise nor threat, and these are instead found in originated bodies – then the obligated agents are, in effect, serving those bodies, for they are the ones issuing the commands and prohibitions.

فإن قالـوا: إنّ مـا خلـق فيهـا دالّ علـى ما عنـد اللّٰه تعالـى من الأمر والنهي، والوعد والوعيد، فهي كالمبلّغة عنه تبارك وتعالى.

If they say: What has been created therein indicates what is with Allah (exalted is He) of command and prohibition, promise and threat – then it is like one conveying from Him (blessed and exalted is He).

فالجـواب: أنّ الـذات العليّـة عندهـم عارية عـن الـكلام أصلًا؛ فلا أمـر فيهـا ولانهـي ولا خبـر، ولا وعد ولا وعيد، ومن شـرط تبليغ هذه الحقائق أن يتّصف بها المبلّغ عنه أوّلًا، ثمّ تبلّغ عنه.

The response is that the Exalted Essence (*al-dhāt al-ʿaliyyah*), according to them, is entirely devoid of speech; thus, it contains neither command nor prohibition, nor report, nor promise nor threat. And among the conditions for conveying these realities is that the one from whom they are conveyed must first be described by them – then they may be conveyed from him.

ومذهبهم: أنّ هذه الحقائق إنّما وجدت ابتداءً في تلك الأجرام، ولم يكن لها وجود أصلًا في ذاته تبارك وتعالى، فليس إذًا عنده حكم ولا خبـر يبلّغـان عنـه، وإذا كان كذلك فالناس إذًا عابـدون لتلك الأجرام التي سمع منها الأمر والنهي، والوعد والوعيد.

Their doctrine is that these realities came into existence initially in those bodies, and had no existence whatsoever in His Essence (exalted is He). Therefore, He possesses neither judgement nor report that could be conveyed from Him. If that is the case, then people are, in effect, serving those bodies from which command and prohibition, promise and threat were heard.

ولا يخلصهـم مـا زعمـوه: أنّ لله تعالى إرادة للخير، فهي التي تمتثل، وهـي التـي بلغّتها الأجرام عنـه بصيغة الأمر والنهـي، والوعد والوعيد، ونحـو ذلك من الألفـاظ الدالّة على الأحكام؛ لأنّ هذا الذي تخيّلوه باطل؛ لِما ثبت من البرهان القاطع أنّ إرادته تعالى عامّة للخير والشرّ، والطاعـة والمعصية، والكفـر والإيمان، فيلزم إذًا أن لا معصية أصلًا؛ لأنّ الخلق كلّهم متصرّفون على وفق إرادته تعالى.

What they have claimed does not save them: that Allah (exalted is He) possesses a will that pertains to good, and that it is this will that is to be obeyed, and that the bodies conveyed it from Him in the form of command and prohibition, promise and threat, and other such expressions indicative of rulings.

For this notion they have imagined is false, due to the conclusive proof that His will (exalted is He) is universal – encompassing good and evil, obedience and disobedience, disbelief and faith. It would then follow that there is no disobedience at all, since all creatures act in accordance with His will (exalted is He).

والحامل لهؤلاء المبتدعة على هذه الأقوال الفاسدة: إنكارهم كلامًا غير حرف ولا صوت، وقد نقض عليهم علماء أهل السنّة بما نجد في أنفسنا من الكلام الدالّ على المعاني؛ للقطع بأنّه مغاير لِما في النفس من العلوم والإرادات، والظنون والشكوك والأوهام.

What impelled these innovators to adopt these corrupt doctrines was their denial of speech that is neither letter nor sound.

The scholars of the People of the Sunnah refuted them by what we find within ourselves of speech indicative of meanings, with certainty that it is distinct from what is within the soul of knowledge, volitions, suppositions, doubts, and delusions.

وإذا ثبت في الشاهد كلام ليس بحرف ولا صوت.. بطل ما عوّلوا عليه من حصر الكلام في الحروف والأصوات، واتّضح أنّ الحقّ ما أجمع عليه أهل السنّة من ثبوت كلام للمولى تبارك وتعالى؛ ليس من جنس الحروف والأصوات، منزّهًا عن التقدّم والتأخر، والجزء والكلّ، واللحن والإعراب والسكوت، ونحوها من خواصّ كلامنا الحادث، لسانيًّا كان أو نفسيًّا؛ لاستلزام ذلك كلّه النقص والبكم والحدوث، وإنّما كلامه جلّ وعلا صفة واجبة القدم والبقاء، متعلّقة بجميع ما

تعلّق به علمه، وكنهه محجوب عن العقل؛ إذ لا مثل له لا عقليًّا ولا وهميًّـا ولا خياليًّـا، ولا موجـودًا ولا مقدّرًا، وذلك كذاته العليّة وسـائر صفاته.

And if it is established in the seen world that there is speech which is neither letter nor sound, then what they relied upon in restricting speech to letters and sounds is invalidated. It becomes clear that the truth is what the People of the Sunnah have unanimously affirmed: that there is speech affirmed for the Exalted Lord (blessed and exalted is He) which is not of the genus of letters and sounds, transcendent above precedence and subsequence, part and whole, grammatical error and inflection, silence, and the like from among the particular properties of our originated speech – whether linguistic or mental – for all of that entails deficiency, muteness, and origination.

Rather, His speech (majestic and exalted is He) is an attribute necessarily pre-eternal and everlasting, linked to all that His knowledge is linked to. Its true reality (*ḥaqīqah*) is veiled from the intellect, for there is nothing like it – neither intellectually, nor imaginatively, nor in estimation by the faculty of illusion, nor in actual existence, nor as a hypothetical construct. And it is, in that regard, as His Essence and the rest of His attributes.

§٢٩-١ فإن قلـت: قول أهـل الحقّ: إنّ الكلام الأزليّ متعلّق بجميع متعلّقات العلم الأزليّ قد يقدح فيه أنّ أمر اللّه تعالى بعض المكلّفين بمـا علم سـبحانه أنّه لا يقع منهم.. يسـتلزم أنّ أمـره تعالى قد تعلّق بوقـوع ذلـك المأمـور ولـم يتعلّق بعدمـه، وعلمه قد تعلّـق بعدم ذلك المأمـور، فقـد تعلّـق علمـه سـبحانه بما لـم يتعلّق به أمـره الذي هو كلامه، فالعلم إذا أعمّ تعلّقًا من الكلام.

§29.1 Should you say: The assertion of the people of truth that the past-eternal speech is linked to all the objects of past-eternal knowledge may be undermined by the fact that Allah commands some morally responsible agents with what He knows will not occur from them. This entails that His command is linked to the occurrence of the commanded act, and not to its non-occurrence, while His knowledge is linked to the non-occurrence of that same act. Thus, His knowledge is linked to what His command – namely, His speech – is not linked to. Therefore, knowledge is more general in linkage than speech.

قلت: الكلام المذكور الأزليّ له تعلّقات كثيرة لا نهاية لها، وليس تعلّقه منحصرًا في التعلّق الأمريّ، فإن كان لم يتعلّق كلامه تبارك وتعالى بترك المأمور في المثال بطريق الأمر.. فقد تعلّق به بطريق النهي وبطريق الوعيد وبطريق الخبر بعدم الوقوع، وهذه كلّها تعلّقات الكلام الأزليّ، فإذًا لا يمكن أن ينفرد العلم الأزليّ بمتعلّق لا يكون متعلّقًا للكلام الأزليّ بوجه من وجوه التعلّقات.

I would say: The aforementioned past-eternal speech has numerous, endless linkages, and its linkage is not confined to the imperative mode. For if His speech (blessed and exalted is He) did not link to the abandonment of the commanded act in the example by way of command, then it did link to it by way of prohibition, by way of threat, and by way of report of its non-occurrence. All of these are modes of linkage of the past-eternal speech. Therefore, it is not possible for past-eternal knowledge to have an object to which the past-eternal speech does not link by some mode of linkage.

فصحّ ما قاله أئمّة أهل السنّة رضي اللّه تعالى عنهم: أنّ الكلام الأزليّ يتعلّق بجميع ما تعلّق به العلم الأزليّ، وبطل اعتراض من اعترض

عليهـم بالمثال السـابق الذي انتفى بـه بعض تعلّقات الكلام الأزليّ، ومن المعلوم: أنّه لا يلزم من نفي تعلّق الأخصّ نفي تعلّق الأعمّ.

What the Imāms of the People of the Sunnah (may Allah be pleased with them) have said is thus verified: that the past-eternal speech links to all that past-eternal knowledge links to, and the objection raised against them by means of the aforementioned example – by which some linkages of the past-eternal speech were negated – is invalidated. It is known that the negation of the two specific linkages does not entail the negation of a general one.

§٢٩-٢ وإذا عرفـت مذهـب أهـل الحقّ في كلام اللّٰه تعالى.. عرفت أنّ إطلاق السـلف رضـي اللّٰـه تعالى عنهم علـى كلام اللّٰه تعالى أنه محفوظ في الصدور، مقروء بالألسـنة، مكتوب في المصاحف.. هو بطريق الحقيقة، لا بطريق المجاز، وليس يعنون بذلك حلول كلام اللّٰه تعالـى القديـم في هذه الأجـرام تعالى اللّٰه عن ذلك، وإنّما يريدون أنّ كلامـه عـزّ وجلّ مذكور مدلول عليه: بتلاوة اللسـان، وكلام الجنان، وكتابـة البنـان، فهو موجود فيها فهمًا وعلمًا لا حلولًا؛ لأنّ الشـيء له وجـودات أربـع: وجود فـى الأعيان، ووجود فى الأذهـان، ووجود في اللسان، ووجود بالبنان؛ أي: بالكتابة بالأصابع.

§29.2 When you understand the doctrine of the people of truth regarding the speech of Allah (exalted is He), you will understand that the statement of the pious predecessors (may Allah be pleased with them) that the speech of Allah is preserved in hearts, recited by tongues, and written in codices is to be taken in the literal sense, not metaphorically.

They did not mean by this that the eternal speech of Allah indwells these bodies (exalted is Allah above such a claim!) but rather that His speech (mighty and majestic) is mentioned and indicated by the recitation of the tongue, the speech of the heart, and the writing of the fingers. Thus, it exists in these by way of understanding and knowledge, not by way of indwelling.

For a thing has four modes of existence:

1. existence in external ontological actuality (*wujūd ʿaynī*),
2. mental existence (*wujūd dhihnī*),
3. existence in speech, and
4. existence in writing – that is, by inscription with the fingers.

فالوجـود الأوّل هو الوجود الذاتيّ الحقيقيّ، وسـائر الوجودات إنّما هي باعتبار الدلالة والفهم، وبهذا تعرف أنّ التلاوة غير المتلو، والقراءة غير المقروء، والكتابة غير المكتوب؛ لأنّ الأوّل من كلّ قسم من هذه الأقسام حادث، والثاني منها قديم لا نهاية له، وبالله تعالى التوفيق.

The first existence is the true essential existence, and all other modes of existence are only by way of indication and understanding. By this, you come to know that the recitation is not the recited, the reading is not the read content, and the writing is not the written content – because the first in each of these categories is originated, while the second is eternal without end. And with Allah (exalted is He) is success.

§٣٠ والكلامُ ينقسمُ إلى خَبَرٍ وإنشاءٍ.

فالخبرُ: ما يَحْتَمِلُ الصدقَ والكَذِبَ لذاتِهِ.

والإنشاءُ: ما لا يحتملُ صدقًا ولا كذبًا لذاتِهِ.

§30 Speech divides into declarative and non-declarative types.

A declarative expression (*khabar*) is that which, by its very essence, admits of truth or falsehood.

A non-declarative expression (*inshāʾ*) is that which, by its very essence, does not admit of truth or falsehood.

§٣٠-٠ يعني: أنّ كلّ كلام -وهو ما أفاد نسبة مقصودة لذاتها- فهو منحصر في قسمين؛ وهما: الخبر، والإنشاء.

§30.0 Meaning: that every speech (*kalām*) – which is that which conveys a relation intended in itself – is confined to two categories: the declarative and the non-declarative.

§٣٠-١ فالخبر: هو الكلام الذي يقبل الصدق والكذب لأجل ذاته؛ أي: لأجل حقيقته، من غير نظر إلى المخبر والمادّة التي تعلّق بها الكلام؛ كأن تكون من الأمور الضروريّة التي لا يقبل إثباتها إلّا الصدق، ولا يقبل نفيها إلّا الكذب.

§30.1 A *declarative* (*khabar*) is speech that, by its very essence, admits of truth or falsehood – that is, by its own essence – without regard to the speaker or to the subject matter to which the speech pertains; such as when it concerns necessary (*ḍarūrī*) matters that admit only affirmation as true and negation as false.

§٣٠-٢ فخرج بالقيد الأوّل -وهو احتمال الصدق والكذب- الإنشاءات؛ كالأمر، والنهي، والاستفهام، والتمني، والعرض، والتحضيض، والنداء.

§30.2 What is excluded by the first qualification – that is, the admission of truth and falsehood – are *non-declarative expressions* (*inshā'āt*), such as command, prohibition, question, wishing, proposal, incitement, and vocative address.

ودخل في الخبر بسبب تقييد احتمال الصدق والكذب بالذات ثلاثة أقسام:

Included under the declarative (*khabar*), due to the restriction of the admission of truth and falsehood to the essence, are three categories.

الأوّل: ما يحتمل الصدق والكذب مطلقًا؛ أي: يقبلهما بالنظر إلى حقيقة ذلك الكلام، وبالنظر إلى زائد عليه؛ وهو المخبر به، والمعنى المخبر به.

The first [category]: That which admits of truth or falsehood absolutely – that is, it accepts both with respect to the reality of that speech and with respect to what is additional to it, namely the one who conveys it and the meaning conveyed.

ومثاله: قول قائل غير معصوم من الكذب: فلان من أهل الجنّة، وفلان من أهل النار، ونحو ذلك؛ فإنّ هذا الكلام يحتمل الصدق والكذب مطلقًا، سواء نظرنا إلى صورة نسبته، أو إلى مادّته ومعناه، أو إلى المتكلّم به.

An example of this is the statement of a person who is not infallible: "So-and-so is among the people of Paradise," and "So-and-so is among the people of the Fire," and the like. This speech absolutely admits of truth and falsehood, whether we consider the form of its attribution, or its matter and meaning, or the speaker.

القسم الثاني: ما يحتمل الصدق والكذب بالنظر إلى صورة نسبته فقط، مع قطع النظر إلى زائد على ذلك، أمّا إذا نظرنا إلى زائد على صورة نسبته فإنّه ينتفي عنه الاحتمال، ويتحتّم له الصدق بلا ارتياب.

The second category: That which admits of truth and falsehood with respect only to the form of its predicative relation, disregarding anything beyond that. However, if we consider something beyond the form of its predicative relation, then the possibility is negated, and it becomes necessarily true without doubt.

ومثال ذلك: إخبار مولانا جلّ وعزّ، وإخبار رسله عليهم الصلاة والسلام؛ كقوله تعالى: ﴿إِنَّ الْمُتَّقِينَ فِى جَنَّاتٍ وَنَهَرٍ﴾ [القمر:

٥٤]، وقولـه جلّ وعلا: ﴿وَالسَّـابِقُونَ السَّـابِقُونَ * أُولَئِـكَ الْمُقَرَّبُونَ﴾ [الواقعة: ١٠-١١]، وقوله سبحانه: ﴿وَنَادَى أَصْحَابُ الْجَنَّةِ أَصْحَابَ النَّـارِ...﴾ [الأعـراف: ٤٤] الآية، ونحو ذلك من سـائر أخباره تبارك وتعالى، ومثل قوله عليه الصلاة والسلام: «لا نبيّ بعدي»، ونحوه من سائر أخباره عليه الصلاة والسلام.

An example of this is the report of our Master (majestic and exalted is He) and the reports of His messengers (upon them be blessings and peace), such as His saying (exalted is He): "Indeed, those who are mindful of Allah are in gardens and rivers"[43]; and His saying (majestic and sublime): "And the foremost, the foremost – those are the ones brought near"[44]; and His saying (glory be to Him): "And the companions of the Garden will call out to the companions of the Fire..."[45]; and the like of that among His other reports (blessed and exalted is He).

And likewise, his saying (upon him be blessings and peace): "There will be no prophet after me,"[46] and the like of that among his other reports (upon him be blessings and peace).

فإنّ هـذه الأخبـار كلّهـا إذا نظرنا إلى مجرّد حقائقهـا اللغويّة، وقطعنا النظـر عمّا زاد على ذلـك.. فإنّا نجدها تقبل بمجرّد صورتها الصدق والكـذب، أمّـا إذا نظرنـا إلى زائد على حقائقها وصـور تراكيبها؛ وهو كـون المخبـر بها هو مولانا جلّ وعلا المنزّه عن نقيصة الكذب عقلاً

43 al-Qamar: 54:54.

44 al-Wāqiʿah: 56:10–11.

45 al-Aʿrāf: 7:44.

46 al-Suyūṭī, *Jāmiʿ al-aḥādīth*, no. 35060 (Ibn Abī Shayba, no. 32074; *Kanz al-ʿummāl*, no. 36489).

al-Suyūṭī, *Jāmiʿ al-aḥādīth*, no. 35061 (al-Ṭayālisī, no. 209; al-Bukhārī, no. 4154; Muslim, no. 2404; Abū Nuʿaym, *Ḥilyat al-awliyāʾ*, 7:196; *Kanz al-ʿummāl*, no. 36489).

ونـقلًا، ورسـوله المعصـوم مـن الكـذب عقلًا ونـقلًا صلّـى اللّٰه عليه وسلّم.. فإنّه يرتفع حينئذٍ عن تلك الأخبار احتمال الصدق والكذب، ويتحتّم لها الصدق لا غير.

For all these reports, if we consider merely their linguistic realities and disregard anything beyond that, we find that, by their mere form, they admit of both truth and falsehood.

However, if we consider what lies beyond their realities and the forms of their composition – namely, that the one informing of them is our Master (majestic and exalted is He), who is transcendent above the imperfection of falsehood by reason and transmission, and His Messenger, who is infallible from falsehood by reason and transmission (may Allah bless him and give him peace) – then the possibility of truth and falsehood is thereby removed from these reports, and truth becomes necessary for them alone.

ومـن أمثلة هذا القسـم: ما يخبر بـه من الأمور الضروريّة ابتداءً؛ نحو قولـك: الاثنـان أكثر من الواحـد؛ فإنّ هذا الخبر من حيث النظر إلى صورتـه الخبريّة، مـع الإعراض عن معناه الضروريّ.. محتمل للصدق والكـذب، وإنّمـا يتحتّم صدقه ويرتفع عنـه الاحتمال إذا نظر في زائد علـى صورتـه الخبريّة؛ وهو معناه المعلـوم بالضرورة. وكذلك: ما يخبر به من الأمور الضروريّة انتهاءً عند قيام البرهان القطعيّ على صحّتها؛ كقول أهل الحقّ: العالم حادث، اللّٰه سـبحانه موجود، اللّٰه سـبحانه قديم، قائم بنفسه، مخالف للحوادث، واحد في ذاته وفي صفاته وفي أفعاله، ونحو ذلك؛ فإنّ هذه الأخبار أيضًا محتملة للصدق والكذب فـي ذاتهـا مـن غير نظر إلى زائد على ذلك، أمّا إذا نظرنا إلى براهينها القطعيّة فإنّ الاحتمال حينئذٍ يرتفع، ويجب لها الصدق لا غير.

Among the examples of this category is what is reported of necessary (*ḍarūrī*) matters initially – such as your statement, "Two is more than one." For this report, insofar as one considers only its propositional form while disregarding its necessary meaning, admits of both truth and falsehood. Its truth becomes necessary and the possibility of falsehood is removed only when one considers something beyond its propositional form – namely, its meaning known by necessity.

Likewise, what is reported of necessary matters ultimately, upon the establishment of a definitive demonstration (*burhān qaṭʿī*) for their veracity – such as the statements of the people of truth: "The world is originated," "Allah (exalted is He) exists," "Allah (exalted is He) is pre-eternal," "He subsists by His Essence," "He differs from originated things," "He is one in His Essence, His attributes, and His acts," and the like. These reports, too, in themselves admit of both truth and falsehood when considered apart from anything beyond them. However, when we consider their definitive proofs, the possibility of falsehood is removed, and truth becomes necessary for them exclusively.

القسم الثالث: ما يحتمل الصدق والكذب بالنظر إلى ذاته وصورته فقط، وإذا نظرنا إلى زائد على ذلك تحتّم كذبه، وارتفع احتمال الصدق.

The third category: That which admits of truth and falsehood when considered solely in terms of its essence and its form, but when something additional is considered, its falsehood becomes necessary and the possibility of truth is removed.

ومثال ذلك: قول المعتزلة: الإرادة الأزليّة لا تتعلّق بالكفر ولا بالمعاصي، وإنّما تتعلّق بالخير فقط، والقدرة الحادثة هي المؤثّرة في أفعال العباد على وفق إرادتهم، وأفعال اللّه تعالى وأحكامه تتبع الأغراض، ونحو ذلك من عقائدهم الفاسدة.

An example of that is the statement of the Muʿtazilah: the past-eternal will does not link to disbelief or to acts of disobedience; rather, it links only to what is good. The originated capability is what effects the acts of the servants in accordance with their own will. The acts and judgements of Allah (exalted is He) follow purposes. And the like of that are among their corrupt doctrines.

فهذه أخبار تحتمل الصدق والكذب إذا قصرنا النظر على مجرّد حقائقها اللغويّة، أمّا إذا نظرنا إلى براهين عموم إرادة اللّه تعالى وعموم قدرته الأزليّة، وتنزّه أفعاله وأحكامه عن الأغراض.. ارتفع حينئذٍ عن تلك الأخبار احتمال الصدق والكذب، وتعيّن لها الكذب لا غير.

These are reports that admit of truth or falsehood if we restrict consideration to their mere linguistic realities. However, if we consider the demonstrations of the universality of Allah's will, the universality of His past-eternal capability, and the transcendence of His acts and judgements above purposes, then the possibility of truth is removed from those reports, and falsehood becomes necessary for them exclusively.

ونحوه: الإخبار بخلاف المعلوم ضرورةً؛ نحو: الأربعة أقل من الثلاثة؛ فإنّ هذا يحتمل بالنظر إلى مجرّد صورته الخبريّة الصدق والكذب، وإذا نظرنا إلى مدلوله ومعناه.. ارتفع عنه الاحتمال، وتحتّم كذبه لا غير.

And likewise: reporting what contradicts what is known by immediate knowledge (*ʿilm ḍarūrī*) – such as: "Four is less than three." This, when considered merely in terms of its propositional form, admits of truth and falsehood. But when we consider its referent and meaning, that possibility is removed, and its falsehood becomes necessary and exclusive.

فقد ظهر لك بهذا: فائدة زيادة لفظة (لذاته) في تعريف الخبر؛ لأنّه لو أسقطت لَما تناول التعريف إلّا القسم الأوّل؛ وهو ما يحتمل الصدق والكذب مطلقًا، ويكون حينئذٍ فاسد العكس؛ لخروج القسمين الآخرين منه.

It thus becomes clear that the benefit of adding the phrase "in itself" (*li-dhātihi*) to the definition of the declarative (*khabar*) is that, were it omitted, the definition would apply only to the first category – namely, that which admits of truth and falsehood absolutely – and the definition would then be invalid in its converse, due to the exclusion of the other two categories from it.

ويخرج أيضًا بسبب هذا التقييد: الإنشاء الذي يحتمل الصدق والكذب لا من حيث ذاته، بل من حيث لوازمه الخبريّة، فلولا هذا التقييد لفسد طرد تعريف الخبر كما يفسد عكسه، وباللّه تعالى التوفيق.

Also excluded by this qualification is the non-declarative expression that admits of truth and falsehood not in respect of its own essence, but in respect of its declarative entailments (*lawāzim khabariyyah*). Were it not for this qualification, the positive definition of the declarative (*khabar*) would be invalidated, just as its converse would be invalidated. And with Allah (exalted is He) lies success.

قوله: (والإنشاء: ما لا يحتمل صدقًا ولا كذبًا لذاته) يعني: أنّ الإنشاء هو الكلام الذي لا يحتمل صدقًا ولا كذبًا بالنظر إلى صورته وتركيبه.

§30.3 His statement, "A non-declarative expression (*inshāʾ*) is that which, by its essence, does not admit of truth or falsehood" – meaning that the non-declarative is speech which, when considered in terms of its form and composition, admits neither truth nor falsehood.

ومثاله: الأوامر؛ نحو: قم، واقعد.

Its examples in commands include "Stand" and "Sit."

والنواهي؛ نحو: لا تقم، ولا تقعد، وكقوله تعالى: ﴿وَلَا تَقْرَبُوا الزِّنَى﴾ [الإسراء: ٣٢]، وقوله عزّ وجلّ ﴿وَلا تَقْرَبُوا الْفَوَاحِشَ﴾ [الأنعام: ١٥١]، ﴿وَلَا تَقْرَبُوا مَالَ الْيَتِيمِ﴾ [الأنعام: ١٥٢]، ﴿وَلا يَقْتُلُونَ النَّفْسَ الَّتِي حَرَّمَ اللَّهُ إِلا بِالْحَقِّ﴾ [الأنعام: ١٥١]، ونحو ذلك ممّا هو كثير.

Its examples in prohibitions include "Do not stand" and "Do not sit," – and such as His saying (majestic and exalted is He): "And do not approach fornication";[47] "And do not approach immoralities";[48] "And do not approach the property of the orphan";[49] "And do not kill the soul which Allah has made inviolable except by right;"[50] and the like of that, which are many.

والاستفهام؛ كقولك: هل قام زيد؟ وقوله تعالى: ﴿مَاذَا قَالَ رَبُّكُمْ قَالُوا الْحَقَّ﴾ [سبأ: ٢٣].

Its examples in questions include your saying, "Did Zayd stand?," and His saying (exalted is He): "What did your Lord say? They said: The truth."[51]

والتمني؛ كقولك: ليت زيدًا قائم، وقوله تعالى إخبارًا عن المنافقين: ﴿يَا لَيْتَنِي كُنْتُ مَعَهُمْ فَأَفُوزَ فَوْزًا عَظِيمًا﴾ [النساء: ٧٣].

47 al-Isrā': 17:32.
48 al-An'ām: 6:151.
49 al-An'ām: 6:152.
50 al-An'ām: 6:151.
51 Saba': 34:23.

Its examples in wishes include your saying, "Would that Zayd were standing," and His saying (exalted is He), reporting about the hypocrites: "Would that I had been with them, so I would have attained a great triumph."[52]

والنداء؛ كقولك: يا زيد، وقوله تعالى إخبارًا عن أهل النار: ﴿يَا مَالِكُ﴾ [الزخرف: ٧٧] ونحوه.

Its examples in vocative addresses include your saying, "O Zayd," and His saying (exalted is He) reporting about the people of the Fire: "O Mālik,"[53] and the like thereof.

فإنّ هذه الأمثلة كلّها لا تحتمل صدقًا ولا كذبًا؛ لأنّها لم تحكم بوقوع شيء في الخارج ولا بعدم وقوعه، ولهذا لا يحسن أن يقال للمتكلّم بها: صدقت، ولا: كذبت.

For all these examples do not admit of truth or falsehood, because they do not assert the occurrence of anything in external ontological actuality (*wujūd ʿaynī*) nor its non-occurrence. Therefore, it is not appropriate to say to the one who utters them, "You have spoken truly," or, "You have lied."

وإنّما زدنا أيضًا في تعريف الإنشاء التقييد بقولنا: (لذاته) ليخرج منه القسمان الآخران من أقسام الخبر الثلاثة التي ذكرناها في تعريف الخبر؛ فإنّ كلّ واحد منهما لا يحتمل الصدق والكذب، بل يتحتّم في الأوّل منهما الصدق لا غير، وفي الثاني الكذب لا غير، فلو اقتصرنا في تعريف الإنشاء على قولنا: (وهو ما لا يحتمل صدقًا ولا كذبًا).. لدخل فيه ذانك القسمان من أقسام الخبر، ويكون التعريف حينئذٍ فاسد الطرد، فلمّا زدنا في تعريف الإنشاء تقييد نفي

52 al-Nisāʾ: 4:73.
53 al-Zukhruf: 43:77.

احتمال الصدق والكذب بالذات.. خرج منه ذانك القسمان؛ لأنّهما يحتملان الصدق والكذب بالنظر إلى ذاتهما، فهما إذًا خبر لا إنشاء.

We also added the qualification "in itself" (*li-dhātihi*) to the definition of the non-declarative expression in order to exclude the other two categories of the threefold division of the declarative that we mentioned in its definition.

For each of those two does not admit of truth or falsehood absolutely, but rather, in the first, truth alone is necessary, and in the second, falsehood alone is necessary.

So, were we to define the non-declarative merely by saying, "It is that which does not admit of truth or falsehood," then those two categories of the declarative would fall under it, and the definition would be invalid in its positive formulation.

But when we added the qualification that the non-admission of truth and falsehood is in itself, those two categories were excluded – because they do admit of truth and falsehood when considered in themselves. They are, therefore, declarative expressions, not non-declarative ones.

ويدخل أيضًا في الإنشاء بسبب هذا التقييد: الأمر لشخص بأكل الطعام مثلًا إذا كان الآمر يحتمل ألا يريد من المأمور أكلًا، أو ليس عنده ما يؤكل أصلًا، وإنّما صدر منه الأمر بالأكل بمجرّد رياء ونحو؛ فإنّ هذا الأمر يحتمل الصدق والكذب باعتبار ما دلّ عليه عرفًا؛ من الإخبار بإرادة أكل المأمور به والحث فيه والتمكّن منه، ولهذا كثيرًا ما يقال لمَن فهم منه مجرّد الرياء في هذا الأمر: كذبت، ويقال لمَن فهم منه خلوص المودّة والمحبّة فيما أمر به: صدقت، ولا يحتمل هذا الأمر صدقًا ولا كذبًا من حيث ذاته وحقيقته الطلبيّة.

Also included under non-declarative expression, due to this restriction, is commanding a person to eat food, for example, when the one issuing the command may not actually intend for the person to eat, or has nothing available to be eaten in the first place, and the command is issued merely out of ostentation or the like.

In such a case, this command admits of truth or falsehood in view of what it implies conventionally (*ʿarfan*) – namely, informing of a will for the commanded act of eating, insistence upon it, and the ability to carry it out.

For this reason, it is often said to someone from whom mere ostentation is understood in such a command, "You have lied," and to someone from whom sincere affection and goodwill is understood in the command, "You have spoken the truth." However, the command itself does not admit of truth or falsehood in itself and in its essential character as a request.

فلولا زيادة التقييد بالذات في تعريف الإنشاء لخرج هذا الأمر ونحوه من الإنشاءات المحتملة للصدق والكذب باعتبار لوازمها الخبريّة، ويكون التعريف حينئذٍ فاسد العكس، فقد أصلحت هذه الزيادة طرد التعريف وعكسه في الإنشاء والخبر، وبالله تعالى التوفيق.

Were it not for the additional qualification "by its very essence" (*bi-l-dhāt*) in the definition of the non-declarative expression, this imperative and its like would fall outside the category of non-declarative expressions that do not admit of truth and falsehood, considering their declarative entailments. The definition would then be invalid in its converse.

This addition, therefore, rectified both the positive definition and the converse of the definition in distinguishing the non-declarative from the declarative. And with Allah (exalted is He) lies success.

§٣١ والصدقُ: عبارةٌ عن مُطابَقَةِ الخبرِ لِمَا في نفسِ الأمرِ، خالفَ الاعتقادَ أم لا.

والكذبُ: عدمُ مطابقةِ الخبرِ لِمَا في نفسِ الأمرِ، وافَقَ الاعتقادَ أم لا.

§31 Truth (*ṣidq*) is the declarative statement's correspondence to what is in reality, whether or not it agrees with one's belief.

Falsehood (*kadhib*) is the declarative statement's non-correspondence to what is in reality, whether or not it agrees with one's belief.

§٣١-٠ يعني: أن حقيقة الصدق: هي مطابقة الخبر -الذي عرفته فيما سبق- لِما في نفس الأمر، سواء كان ذلك موافقًا أيضًا لاعتقاد المخبر؛ كقول السنّيّ مثلًا: اللّه سبحانه خالق أفعال العباد كلّها؛ ضروريّها واختياريّها، ولا أثر لقدرهم فيها أصلًا؛ فإنّ هذا الخبر صدق؛ لأنّه مطابق لِما في نفس الأمر؛ لقيام الدليل القطعيّ عقلًا ونقلًا على ذلك، ثمّ هو مطابق أيضًا لاعتقاد كلّ سنّيّ من أهل الحقّ.

§31.0 Meaning: the reality of *truth* (*ṣidq*) is the correspondence of the declarative statement (*khabar*) – which you have previously come to know – to what is in fact the case, whether:

(1) It also accords with the belief of the one reporting.

For example, the statement of a Sunni: "Allah (exalted is He) is the Creator of all the acts of the servants, both necessary and volitional, and their capability has no effect in them at all" – this report is true because it corresponds to what is in fact the case, as definitive proof, both rational and transmitted, establishes that. Moreover, it also conforms to the belief of every Sunni among the people of truth.

أم كان مخالفًا لاعتقاده؛ كهذا الخبر بعينه إذا صدر من المعتزليّ بحضرة أهل السنّة على سبيل التخفّي منهم ببدعته، فهذا الخبر

الصادر منه هو صدق أيضًا؛ لأنّه مطابق لِما في نفس الأمر، ولا يقدح في صدقه مخالفته لاعتقاد المخبر؛ إذ المطابقة للاعتقاد لا يلتفت إليها في حقيقة الصدق عند أهل السنّة.

(2) Or is contrary to his belief – such as this very report, if it were spoken by a Mu'tazilite in the presence of the Sunnis in concealment of his innovation – then this report uttered by him is also true, because it corresponds to what is in fact the case. Its contradiction of the reporter's belief does not undermine its truth, for correspondence to belief is not considered in the reality of truth (*ṣidq*) according to the Sunnis.

ولهذا: يجب التأويل عندهم في قوله تعالى: ﴿إِذَا جَاءَكَ الْمُنَافِقُونَ قَالُوا نَشْهَدُ إِنَّكَ لَرَسُولُ اللَّهِ وَاللَّهُ يَعْلَمُ إِنَّكَ لَرَسُولُهُ وَاللَّهُ يَشْهَدُ إِنَّ الْمُنَافِقِينَ لَكَاذِبُونَ﴾ [المنافقون: ١]؛ فإنّ قول المنافقين: (إِنَّكَ لَرَسُولُ اللَّهِ) هو حقّ صدق؛ لموافقته لِما في نفس الأمر، ولا يلتفت في حقيقة صدقه إلى كونه مخالفًا لاعتقاد المنافقين؛ إذ الموافقة للاعتقاد لا نعتبر في صدق الخبر، وظاهر الآية: تكذيبهم في هذا الخبر، فوجب إذًا تأويل الآية، وصرف التكذيب فيها إلى غير المشهود به؛ ممّا تضمّنته الشهادة من الخبر بمطابقة ألسنتهم لقلوبهم فيما أخبروا به من رسالة سيّدنا ومولانا محمّد صلّى اللّه عليه وسلّم، ولا شكّ أنّ هذا الخبر الذي تضمّنته الشهادة غير مطابق لِما في نفس الأمر عندهم، فصحّ تكذيبهم فيه.

For this reason, they hold that interpretation is necessary in His saying (exalted is He): "When the hypocrites come to you, they say, 'We bear witness that you are indeed the Messenger of Allah.'

And Allah knows that you are indeed His Messenger, and Allah bears witness that the hypocrites are surely liars."[54]

For the statement of the hypocrites – "Indeed, you are the Messenger of Allah" – is a true and truthful statement, as it accords with what is in reality. The truth of a statement is not contingent upon its agreement with the belief of the speaker, for agreement with belief is not considered in the reality of truth (*ṣidq*).

Yet the apparent sense of the verse is that they are being declared liars in this report. Therefore, it becomes necessary to interpret the verse and to redirect the attribution of falsehood therein to something other than the content of the testimony – namely, to what the testimony entails of reporting that their tongues were in conformity with their hearts in what they reported concerning the messengership of our master and patron Muḥammad (may Allah bless him and give him peace).

There is no doubt that this report, which the testimony entails, does not correspond to what is in reality according to them. Thus, their being declared liars in it is valid.

ويحتمل صرف التكذيب إلى المشهود به، لكن في اعتقادهم وزعمهم الفاسد؛ إذ هم يعتقدون الكذب فيما أخبروا به من الرسالة؛ لأنّها في زعمهم الفاسد غير حاصلة في نفس الأمر، ففيه تعيير عليهم بإخبارهم بما يعتقدون كذبه خداعًا ونفاقًا.

It is also possible to interpret the attribution of falsehood as directed toward the content of the testimony – but in their belief and corrupt presumption; for they believe that what they reported concerning the messengership is false, since in their corrupt presumption it does not obtain in reality. Thus, it constitutes a reproach against them for reporting what they believe to be false, as a form of deceit and hypocrisy.

54 al-Munāfiqūn: 63:1.

ويحتمل صرف التكذيب إلى ما هو المقصود الذي أخبروا به بعد تمهيد هذه المقدّمة؛ وهو إظهار إيمانهم وشهادتهم برسالة نبيّنا ومولانا محمّد صلّى اللّه عليه وسلّم، فقدّموا هذه المقدّمة بين يدي المقصود الذي أخبروا به بعدها؛ ليدفعوا بذلك تهمة الكفر الذي اتّهموا به عن أنفسهم؛ وذلك الخبر أنّهم حلفوا على أنّهم لم يصدر منهم ما بلغ عنهم من المقالة لرسول اللّه صلّى اللّه عليه وسلّم؛ وهي قولهم: ﴿لَا تُنْفِقُوا عَلَى مَنْ عِنْدَ رَسُولِ اللَّهِ...﴾ إلى قولهم: ﴿لَيُخْرِجَنَّ الْأَعَزُّ مِنْهَا الْأَذَلَّ﴾ [المنافقون: ٧-٨]، فكذّبهم اللّه تعالى في إنكارهم صدور هذه المقالة منهم، وحقّق صدورها منهم بقوله عزّ وجلّ: ﴿هُمُ الَّذِينَ يَقُولُونَ لَا تُنْفِقُوا...﴾ [المنافقون: ٨] الآية.

It is also possible that the attribution of falsehood is redirected to what was actually intended by what they reported after presenting that introductory premise – namely, their display of faith and their testimony to the Messengership of our Prophet and Master Muḥammad (may Allah bless him and give him peace). They presented that premise before the intended report that followed it in order to deflect from themselves the accusation of disbelief with which they had been charged.

That report is their oath that they had not uttered the statement that had been conveyed from them to the Messenger of Allah (may Allah bless him and give him peace) – namely, their words: "Do not spend on those who are with the Messenger of Allah..." up to their statement, "Surely, if we return to Medina, the more honoured will surely expel the more abased."[55] But Allah (exalted is He) declared them liars in their denial that this statement had issued from them, and affirmed that it had indeed issued from

55 al-Munāfiqūn: 63:7–8.

them with His words (exalted is He): "They are the ones who say: 'Do not spend....'"[56]

ويحتمل أن يكون تجوّز بالكذب؛ فأطلق على غلطهم باستعمالهم كلمة الشهادة التي وضعت لغةً للمعلوم المحقّق في غير موضوعها؛ وهو ما ليس بمعلوم ولا محقّق في قلوبهم.

It is also possible that the term "lie" was used figuratively, being applied to their error in employing the word "testimony" – which, in linguistic usage, is designated for that which is known and verified – in a context where it does not belong, namely, to that which is neither known nor verified in their hearts.

§٣١-١ وبهذا تعرف فساد اعتماد النظّام المعتزليّ على هذه الآية؛ فيما ذهب إليه: أنّ الصدق: عبارة عن مطابقة الخبر لاعتقاد المخبر، وافق ما في نفس الأمر أم لا، والكذب: عدم مطابقة الخبر لاعتقاد المخبر، خالف ما في نفس الأمر أم لا.

§31.1 By this, the invalidity of the Muʿtazilite Naẓẓām's reliance on this verse becomes evident in his view that truth is defined as the correspondence of the report to the belief (*iʿtiqād*) of the reporter, whether or not it accords with the actual state of affairs; and that falsehood is the non-correspondence of the report to the belief of the reporter, whether or not it contradicts the actual state of affairs.

وذهب الجاحظ من المعتزلة: إلى أنّ الصدق: مطابقة الخبر لِما في نفس الأمر مع الاعتقاد لذلك، والكذب: عدم مطابقة الخبر لِما في نفس الأمر مع الاعتقاد لذلك، فشرط في كلّ من الصدق والكذب شرطين، ومهما انتفيا أو أحدهما.. كان الخبر واسطةً؛ لا يوصف بالصدق ولا بالكذب، فأقسام الخبر عنده ستة:

56 al-Munāfiqūn: 63:8.

واحد صدق: وهو المطابق للاعتقاد وما في نفس الأمر.

وواحد كذب: وهو المخالف لِما في نفس الأمر وللاعتقاد.

وأربعة واسطة: وهو المطابق لِما في نفس الأمر مع اعتقاد خلاف ذلك، والمطابق لِما في نفس الأمر مع الشك في ذلك، والمخالف لِما في نفس الأمر مع اعتقاد مطابقته له، والمخالف لِما في نفس الأمر مع الشك في ذلك.

Al-Jāḥiẓ, of the Muʿtazilah, held that truth (*ṣidq*) is the correspondence of a report to what is in reality (*nafs al-amr*) along with belief in it, and that falsehood (*kadhib*) is the non-correspondence of a report to what is in reality along with belief in it. Thus, he stipulated two conditions for both truth and falsehood.

If both conditions – or even one of them – are absent, the report is intermediate (*wāsiṭah*) and cannot be described as either true or false. According to him, the divisions of the declarative statement (*khabar*) are six:

One is truth: that which corresponds to both belief and what is in reality.

One is falsehood: that which contradicts both belief and what is in reality.

And four are intermediates: that which corresponds to what is in reality while one believes the contrary; that which corresponds to what is in reality while one is in doubt regarding it; that which contradicts what is in reality while one believes it corresponds to it; and that which contradicts what is in reality while one is in doubt regarding it.

وشبهته في ذلك وردّها معلوم في فنّ الأصول والبيان.

His specious argument (*shubhah*) in this regard – and its refutation – are well known in the disciplines of legal theory (*uṣūl*) and rhetoric (*bayān*).

§٣١-٢ قولـه: (والكـذب: عدم مطابقة الخبر لِما في نفس الأمر...) إلى آخره.

§31.2 His statement, "Falsehood (*kadhib*) is the declarative statement's non-correspondence to what is in reality,..." to the end.

مثـال الكـذب الذي يوافق الاعتقاد: قـول المعتزليّ: الحيوان المختار موجـد لأفعالـه الاختياريّـة بالقـدرة التي خلق اللّٰه تعالى لـه؛ فإنّ هذا الخبـر كـذب؛ لمخالفته لِما فـي نفس الأمـر؛ لأنّ العقل والنقل من الكتاب والسنّة وإجماع السلف الصالح قبل ظهور البدع.. شاهدة أنّ الكائنات خلق لمولانا تبارك وتعالى، ولا شريك معه في أثر من الآثار، والقدريّـة مجـوس هـذه الأمّة يعتقـدون خلاف هـذا، وأنّ الحيوانات هي المسـتقلّة بإيجاد أفعالها الاختياريّة؛ بما خلق اللّٰه تعالى لها من القدرة.

An example of a falsehood that accords with belief is the statement of the Muʿtazilī: "The volitional animal brings about its voluntary acts through the capability that Allah (exalted is He) created for it." This report is false, for it contradicts what is in reality. Both the intellect and transmission – namely, the Book, the Sunnah, and the consensus of the righteous predecessors before the emergence of innovations – testify that all existents are a creation of our Master (blessed and exalted is He), and that He has no partner in any effect whatsoever.

The Qadarites, the Magians of this Ummah, hold the contrary belief: that living creatures are independent in bringing about their voluntary acts by means of the capability that Allah (exalted is He) created for them.

ومثـال الكـذب الذي يخالف الاعتقاد: هذا الخبر بعينه إذا صدر من سـنّيّ أخبر به بمحضر المعتزلة سـترا لحاله؛ للخوف منهم، فإنّه وإن كان كذبًـا لمخالفتـه لِما فـي نفس الأمر فهو مخالـف أيضًا لاعتقاد السـنّيّ الـذي أخبـر بـه، لكنّـه ارتكب هـذا الكذب المبـاح لدعوى الضرورة إليه.

An example of falsehood that contradicts belief is this very report, if uttered by a Sunnī in the presence of the Muʿtazilah in order to conceal his stance out of fear of them. Although it is false – due to its contradiction of what is in reality – it also contradicts the belief of the Sunnī who reported it. However, he committed this falsehood, which is permitted, on the claim of necessity.

ومن ذلك: من يكره على النطق بكلمة الكفر وقلبه مطمئن بالإيمان.

One such case is one who is coerced into uttering the word of disbelief while his heart is at rest in faith.

§٣١-٣ واعلـم: أنّ تفسـير أهـل الحـقّ للصـدق والكـذب حصل به الوثوق بأخبار الرسول عليه الصلاة والسلام في أحكامه ووعده ووعيده وأحـوال الآخـرة جملةً وتفصـيلًا؛ لأنّا نعلم بالبرهـان القطعيّ صدقه؛ أي: مطابقـة أخبـاره لِمـا في نفس الأمـر، لا لاعتقاده فقط مع جواز مخالفتها لِما في نفس الأمر، وبالله تعالى التوفيق.

§31.3 Know that the definition of the people of truth regarding truth and falsehood is what establishes confidence in the reports of the Messenger (upon him be blessings and peace) concerning his rulings, promises, threats, and the conditions of the Hereafter, both in general and in detail. For we know by decisive proof his truthfulness – that is, the correspondence of his reports to what is in reality, not merely his belief in them while their contrariety to reality remains possible. And with Allah (exalted is He) lies success.

EIGHTH PROLEGOMENON

ON TRUSTWORTHINESS

المقدّمة الثامنة في الأمانة

§٣٢ والأمانــةُ: حفظُ جميعِ الجوارحِ الظاهــرةِ والباطنةِ مِنَ التلبُّسِ بمَنْهِيٍّ عنهُ نهْيَ تحريمٍ أو كراهةٍ.

والخيانةُ: عدمُ حفظِهما مِنْ ذلكَ.

§٣٣ وباللَّهِ تعالى التوفيقُ.

§32 Trustworthiness (*amānah*) is protecting all external and internal faculties from engaging in anything prohibited or reprehensible.

Treachery (*khiyānah*) is failing to protect them from such things.

§33 And success is only through Allah (exalted is He).

§٣٢-٠ لما أن عرف فيما سبق الصدق؛ ليعرف منه الصدق الواجب فــي حــقّ الرســل عليهم الصلاة والــسلام؛ بدلالة المعجــزة النازلة من مولانــا جــلّ وعلا منزلــة قوله: صدق عبــدي في كلّ مــا يبلّغ عنّي.. عــرف هنــا الأمانة؛ ليعرف منهــا أيضًا الأمانة الواجبة في حقّ الرســل عليهم الصلاة والسلام، فذكر أنّها عبارة: عن حفظ المكلّف جوارحه الظاهرة والباطنة من التلبّس بمحرّم أو مكروه.

§32.0 When truthfulness was previously defined so that the obligatory truthfulness in the case of the messengers (upon them be blessings and peace) might be known from it – through the indication of the miracle, which, from our Master (majestic and exalted is He), stands in the place of His saying, "My servant has spoken truthfully in all that he conveys from Me" – trustworthiness was likewise defined here, so that the obligatory trustworthiness in the case of the messengers (upon them be blessings and peace) might be known from it as well.

Thus, it was stated that it is the preservation by the responsible agent of his outward and inward faculties from engaging in what is forbidden or disliked.

وسُمّي صاحبها أمينًا؛ للأمن في جهته من المخالفة لِما حُدّ له وأوصي به.

He was called *trustworthy* (*amīn*) because he is secure, on his part, from contravening what was assigned to him and commanded of him.

ولا شكّ أنّ مولانا جلّ وعزّ قد حدّ لعبيده المكلّفين حدودًا، وأمرهم وأوصاهم ألا يتعدّوا حدوده؛ فحدّ لنا سبحانه الواجب والمندوب والمباح، ونهانا أن نتعدّاها إلى فعل المحرّم أو المكروه من الأفعال، وأوصانا جلّ وعلا بتقواه، وبالفرار من غضبه وعقابه إلى حرم طاعته وما جعله جلّ وعلا بفضله أمارة على رضاه ونعيمه وثوابه.

There is no doubt that our Master (majestic and exalted is He) has set bounds for His responsible servants and has commanded and enjoined them not to transgress His bounds. Thus, He (glorified is He) has delineated for us the obligatory, the recommended, and the permissible, and has forbidden us to transgress these by engaging in prohibited or disliked actions. He (majestic and exalted is He) has enjoined us to fear Him and to flee from His wrath and punishment to the sanctuary of His obedience and to that which He (glorified and exalted is He), by His grace, has made a sign of His good pleasure, His bliss, and His reward.

فمَـن وفقـه اللّٰه للمحافظة علـى وصيّته، وحفظه جلّ وعلا بفضله من مخالفته.. كان أمينًا، ومَن قهره تبارك وتعالى بعدله، وطرده إلى ولوج أبـواب غضبـه ونقمه، وسـدّ عنه أبواب عصمته وفضلـه وكرمه.. كان خائنًا.

Whoever is granted success by Allah to uphold His commandment, and is preserved (majestic and exalted is He) by His grace from violating it, is trustworthy. And whoever is subjected by Him (blessed and exalted is He) through His justice, cast away to enter the gates of His wrath and vengeance, and barred from the gates of His protection, grace, and generosity, is untrustworthy.

§٣٢-١ ولا شكّ أنّ الأنبياء والرسل عليهم الصلاة والسلام قد تفضّل المولـى الكريم سـبحانه على جميعهـم؛ بأن أدخلهم في منيع حفظه ورعايتـه، وحـال بينهم وبين كلّ مخالفة ودناءة بعزيز عصمته وشـريف حبّـه وعظيـم ولايته، فأصبحـوا في حضرة المشـاهدة لجماله وجلاله يتنعّمـون، وفـي أنـوار المعـارف وأنـواع القـرب وملابس أعلـى مراتب الخصوص والولاية يتبخّترون.

§32.1 There is no doubt that the prophets and messengers (upon them be blessings and peace) were all shown favour by the Generous Lord (glorified is He), who encompassed them in the fortress of His protection and care. He placed between them and every act of disobedience and baseness His mighty infallibility, His noble love, and His immense guardianship.

Thus, they came to abide in the presence of witnessing His Beauty and Majesty, delighting in it, and moving through the lights of cognisance (*maʿārif*), the varieties of nearness, and the garments of the highest degrees of distinction and Divine friendship (*wilāyah*).

ثمّ مَنَّ اللّٰه سبحانه على سائر عبيده؛ بأنّ بعث إليهم خواصّه ورسله مكسوين بملابس عصمته، محفوفين بأنواع معجزاته وآياته وكرامته، راكبين مراكب ولايته وهدايته، ليهتدي العبيد إلى نيل رضا المولى تبارك وتعالى دنيًا وأخرى بأقوالهم وأفعالهم ولخظهم وحركاتهم وسكناتهم؛ لطلوع شموس العصمة والرعاية على جميع تصفاتهم.

Then Allah (exalted is He) bestowed His grace upon all His servants by sending to them His elect and His messengers, clothed in the garments of His infallibility, encompassed by the various kinds of His miracles, signs, and marks of honour, borne by the means of His guardianship and guidance – so that the servants might be guided, through their words, deeds, gazes, movements, and stillness, to the attainment of the pleasure of the Master (blessed and exalted is He) in this world and the next, by the rising of the suns of infallibility and divine care over all their states.

فمَن صدقهم واقتدى بأنوارهم، وأعطى القيادة ظاهرًا وباطنًا لشريف سياستهم، وصمّ وعمي عن الالتفات إلى خرائف غيرهم.. فقد فاز ونجا.

Whoever affirms them, follows the light of their guidance, and outwardly and inwardly submits to the noble direction of their governance, while turning a deaf ear and a blind eye to the fables of others – has triumphed and been saved.

ومَن بلي والعياذ باللّٰه بشديد الحمق والعمل؛ حتى لم يشاهد أنوارهم، ولم يفهم عظيم قربهم من المولى العظيم جلّ وعلا واختصاصهم، فقلّد شيطانه اللعين وهواه، وغرّه بما يزايله قريبًا من شهوات دنياه، وأعرض عن اتّباع رسل اللّٰه الهادين إلى طرق رضا اللّٰه تعالى صلوات اللّٰه وسلامه عليهم.. فقد هلك هلاكًا عظيمًا، لا يقدر على الخلاص منه أبدًا، ولا يرتجى إلّا أن يموت على عقد وثيق من تصديقهم،

والتصريح بأنّهم على الحقّ في كلّ ما أتوا به عن المولى تبارك وتعالى، وفي جميع سيرهم وطريقهم، فهذا لا بدّ بفضل اللّه تعالى ووعده الصادق أن يتداركه بالعفو والفوز وإن لقي ما لقي قبل ذلك.

Whoever (may Allah protect us!) has been afflicted with severe foolishness and heedlessness, such that he does not witness their lights nor comprehend their immense nearness to the Great Lord (majestic and exalted is He) and their unique distinction, and so imitates his accursed devil and his caprice, and becomes absorbed in what soon departs from the desires of his worldly life, and turns away from following the messengers of Allah, those who guide to the paths of Allah's good pleasure (may Allah's blessings and peace be upon them) has indeed perished a great perdition, from which he can never be delivered.

There is no hope for him except that he die upon a firm conviction in affirming them, and in explicitly declaring that they are upon the truth in everything they brought from the Master (blessed and exalted is He), and in all their conduct and path. Such a person, by the grace of Allah (exalted is He) and His true promise, will inevitably be overtaken by pardon and triumph, even if he experiences what he experiences before that.

ولا شكّ أنّ إطلاق المولى جلّ وعلا الأمر بالاقتداء بهم ومن غير تأمّل ولا بحث.. دليل قطعيّ على أنّهم معصومون من كلّ مخالفة وعيب في الأقوال والأفعال، والظاهر والباطن.

There is no doubt that the Master's unconditional command (majestic and exalted is He) to emulate them – without reflection or inquiry – is definitive proof that they are infallible against every contravention and flaw, in both words and deeds, outward and inward.

وقد ثبت إجماع أهل الحقّ على أمانة الأنبياء والرسـل عليهم الصلاة والـسلام، وأنّهـم منزّهـون عـن جميـع العيـوب والآثـام، وأنّ أفضلهم وسـيّدهم -بل هو أفضل جميع الخلائق- سـيّدنا ونبيّنا ومولانا محمّد صلّـى اللّـه عليه وسـلّم وعلى آلـه وصحبـه، صلاةً وسلامًا ننجو بهما فـضلًا مـن المولى تبارك وتعالى وكرما مـن كلّ هول وفتنة، في حياتنا وبعـد مماتنـا وفي قبورنا، ويـوم بعث اللّه تعالى لفصـل القضاء جميع الأنام.

It has been established by the consensus of the people of truth that the prophets and messengers (upon them be blessings and peace) possess trustworthiness and are free from all defects and sins. The most virtuous among them, their master – indeed, the most virtuous of all creation – is our master, our prophet, and our patron Muḥammad (may Allah bless him and give him peace, and his family and companions). May such blessings and peace be a means by which we are saved, by the grace and generosity of the Exalted Lord, from every terror and trial: in our lives, after our deaths, in our graves, and on the Day when Allah (exalted is He) resurrects all beings for the final judgement.

CONCLUSION

خاتمة

§٣٢-٢ وهـذا آخـر ما قيّدناه علـى «المقدّمات»، نسأله سـبحانه أن ينفـع بها وبشـرحها الواضـع والمتسـبّب، والقارئ والكاتـب، والناظر والمعلم والمتعلّم، في الحياة وبعد الممات.

§32.2 This is the last of what we have recorded on *al-Muqaddimat* (*The Prolegomena*). We ask Him (glorified is He) to make it beneficial – along with its commentary – for the compiler and the cause, the reader and the writer, the examiner, the teacher, and the learner, in life and after death.

اللّهمّ؛ اجعلني وإيّاهم وسائر الأحبّة والمؤمنين والمؤمنات ممّن أخلص لوجهـك الكريـم العمـل، وقصر في أمور شـهواته ودنيـاه الأمل، وتزوّد للآخرة بلزوم التقوى، وخالف إلى الممات الشيطان والنفس والهوى.

O Allah, make me, them, and all the beloved – believing men and believing women – among those who devote their deeds sincerely to Your noble countenance, who shorten their hopes regarding worldly desires and affairs, who provision for the Hereafter by adhering to piety (*taqwā*), and who oppose Satan, the lower soul (*nafs*), and caprice (*hawā*) until death.

اللّهـمّ؛ اجعلنـا يا مولانا بفضلك من ذوي الألباب، وأرشـدنا يا أرحم الراحميـن فـي أقوالنـا وأفعالنا وظاهرنـا وباطننا إلى سـلوك طريق الحقّ

والصـواب، وتـب علينـا يـا مولانا توبةً صادقـةً لا معصيـة بعدها إنّك أنـت الرحيـم الرحمـن التوّاب، وهـب لنا من لدنك رحمـة إنّك أنت الكريـم الوهّـاب، وتوّفنا تائبين مؤمنين مسـلمين، وأدخلنا دنيًا وأخرى في عبادك الصالحين، بجاه سـيّدنا ومولانا محمّد خاتم النبيّين وإمام المرسلين، صلّى اللّه وسلّم عليه وعلى آله وصحبه أجمعين.

O Allah, make us, O our Master, by Your grace among those endowed with sound intellects (*ulū al-albāb*); and guide us, O Most Merciful of the merciful, in our words, deeds, outward states, and inward realities to tread the path of truth and rightness.

And turn to us, O our Master, with a sincere repentance after which there is no sin – for indeed, You are the Merciful, the Compassionate, the Oft-Returning. And grant us from Your presence a mercy – for indeed, You are the Generous, the Bestower.

And cause us to die as repentant, believing, submitting servants; and admit us – both in this world and the next – among Your righteous servants, by the rank of our Master and Patron Muḥammad, the Seal of the Prophets and the Leader of the Messengers (may Allah bless him and give him peace, and his family and all his companions).

وآخر دعوانا أنّ الحمد لله ربي العالمين

And the last of our words is praise be to Allah, Lord of the worlds.

BIOGRAPHICAL NOTES

[التراجم]

noindent Basic information about scholars mentioned in this book is provided below to facilitate locating them in more comprehensive biographical works. Entries are in alphabetical order, ignoring the initial "al-" and diacritics. Each begins with the person's name and lineage, usually followed by their Hijri dates of birth and death (in parentheses, if known), and then brief biographical information. Titles and nicknames will come first in cases where an individual is best known through them. Cross references are also given (separated by an equals sign). Most honourifics have been omitted for the sake of brevity; readers are encouraged to add them as they read.

Abū al-Ḥasan al-Ashʿarī ʿAlī ibn Ismāʿīl ibn Isḥāq (260–324 AH/874–936 CE). Founder of the Ashʿarī school of theology. Born in Basra, he initially followed the Muʿtazilī school under his teacher Abū ʿAlī al-Jubbāʾī before publicly renouncing it and dedicating himself to refuting their doctrines. His works are said to number fifty-five, including *Maqālāt al-Islāmiyyīn*, *al-Ibānah ʿan Uṣūl al-Diyānah*, *al-Lumaʿ*, and *Istīḥsān al-Khawḍ fī al-Kalām*. He died in Baghdad.

Abū al-Maʿālī al-Juwaynī ʿAbd al-Malik ibn ʿAbd Allāh ibn Yūsuf, Imām al-Ḥaramayn (419–478 AH/1028–1085 CE). The most knowledgeable of all late scholars of the Shāfiʿī school. Born in Juwayn near Naysābūr, he travelled to Baghdad and the Ḥijāz before returning to Naysābūr, where Niẓām al-Mulk established the Niẓāmiyyah school under his leadership. He became a central figure in consolidating Ashʿarī theology. His principal works include *al-Irshād*, *al-Shāmil*, *al-Burhān*, *Ghiyāth al-Umam*, and *Nihāyat al-Maṭlab*.

Abū Ḥāmid al-Ghazālī Muḥammad ibn Muḥammad ibn Muḥammad al-Ṭūsī al-Shāfiʿī, Ḥujjat al-Islām (450–505 AH/1058–1111 CE). One of the foremost authorities in jurisprudence, legal theory, mysticism, and *kalām* in Islam. A prominent student of Imām al-Ḥaramayn, he taught at the Niẓāmiyyah in Baghdad before leaving to pursue asceticism and travel, later returning to Ṭūs to focus on writing and worship. His works include *Iḥyāʾ ʿUlūm al-Dīn*, *al-Mustaṣfā*, *Tahāfut al-Falāsifah*, and *al-Munqidh min al-Ḍalāl*.

Abū Isḥāq al-Isfarāyīnī Ibrāhīm ibn Muḥammad ibn Ibrāhīm, Rukn al-Dīn (d. 418 AH/1027 CE). A scholar of jurisprudence and legal theory, author of *al-Jāmiʿ fī Uṣūl al-Dīn* and a treatise on the principles of jurisprudence.

Abū Muḥammad ʿAbd al-Ḥaqq ibn Muḥammad ibn Hārūn al-Sahmī al-Qurashī al-Ṣiqillī (d. 466 AH/1073 CE). The leading Mālikī scholar of his generation, from Sicily. He studied under the jurists of Qayrawān and Sicily, among them Abū ʿImrān al-Fāsī and Ibn al-Ajdābī, and he studied alongside al-Tūnisī and al-Suyūrī. He performed the pilgrimage twice; on one occasion he met ʿAbd al-Wahhāb ibn Naṣr and Abū Dharr al-Harawī, and on the last — after his fame had spread — he met Imām al-Ḥaramayn Abū al-Maʿālī in Mecca around the year 450 AH. The two debated, and ʿAbd al-Ḥaqq put questions to al-Juwaynī whose answers were compiled into a well-known collection. ʿAbd al-Ḥaqq used to say of al-Juwaynī: "Were it not for my old age, I would never have left his doorstep," and al-Juwaynī in turn acknowledged his merit. He was described as a jurist of keen understanding, pious, devout, widely renowned, and elegant in his writing. His works include *al-Nukat wa-l-Furūq li-Masāʾil al-Mudawwanah* — one of the earliest such compositions, favoured by advanced students — and the larger *Tahdhīb al-Ṭālib*, a commentary on the *Mudawwanah* in which he corrected many of his earlier positions. He also wrote a creed and a treatise on the precise wording of the *Mudawwanah*. Ibn ʿAmmār al-Mutakallim described him as "a celebrated *imām* in every science, advanced in rank, who taught both *uṣūl* and *furūʿ*." He died in Alexandria.

Abū ʿImrān al-Fāsī Mūsā ibn ʿĪsā ibn Abī Ḥājj al-Ghafjūmī (368–430 AH/978–1038 CE). The leading jurist of Qayrawān in his time. Originally from Fez, he settled in Qayrawān where he attained pre-eminence in scholarship. He studied *fiqh* under Abū al-Ḥasan al-Qābisī in Qayrawān and Abū Muḥammad al-Aṣīlī in Cordoba, then travelled east, performing the pilgrimage and entering Iraq, where he studied *uṣūl* under al-Qāḍī Abū Bakr al-Bāqillānī and studied Qurʾānic recitation under Abū al-Ḥasan al-Ḥammāmī. Ḥātim ibn Muḥammad said of him: "He was among the most learned and retentive of people, combining mastery of *fiqh*, *ḥadīth*, narrators, and Qurʾānic recitation, with knowledge of *al-jarḥ wa-l-taʿdīl*." Students came to him from across the Maghrib, and his *fatwās* circulated in both east and west. He would hold sessions of study and audition at his home from morning until noon, and everything he said was written down. He died in Qayrawān on 13 Ramaḍān 430 AH.

al-ʿAnbarī ʿUbayd Allāh ibn al-Ḥasan ibn al-Ḥuṣayn al-Tamīmī (105–168 AH/723–785 CE). A jurist and *ḥadīth* scholar of Basra. Ibn Ḥibbān described him as among its leading figures in jurisprudence and knowledge. He served as judge of Basra from 157 AH until his dismissal in 166 AH, the year of his death.

Ashhab ibn ʿAbd al-ʿAzīz ibn Dāwūd ibn Ibrāhīm Abū ʿAmr al-Qaysī al-ʿĀmirī al-Jaʿdī (140 or 150–204 AH/757 or 767–819 CE). The leading jurist of Egypt in his time, and a companion of Imām Mālik. His real name was Miskīn, and Ashhab was a sobriquet. He studied under Mālik, al-Layth ibn Saʿd, and al-Fuḍayl ibn ʿIyāḍ among others. Al-Shāfiʿī said: "Egypt has not produced anyone more learned in *fiqh* than Ashhab." When Saḥnūn was asked whether Ibn al-Qāsim or Ashhab was the greater jurist, he said: "They were like two racehorses neck and neck." Ashhab died in Egypt in Rajab 204 AH, eighteen days after al-Shāfiʿī.

al-Bāqillānī Abū Bakr Muḥammad ibn al-Ṭayyib ibn Muḥammad ibn Jaʿfar (338–403 AH/950–1013 CE). A prominent judge and leading figure in the Ashʿarī school. Born in Basra and died in Baghdad. His notable works include *al-Inṣāf*, *al-Tamhīd*, *al-Hidāyah*, and *Iʿjāz al-Qurʾān*.

Dāwūd al-Ẓāhirī Dāwūd ibnʿAlī ibn Khalaf Abū Sulaymān al-Aṣbahānī (201–270 AH/816–884 CE). A *mujtahid imām* and founder of the Ẓāhirī school of jurisprudence. He adhered to the literal meaning of the Qurʾān and *Sunnah*, and avoided interpretation and analogical reasoning.

Ibn Dahhāq Ibrāhīm ibn Yūsuf ibn Muḥammad al-Dawsī Abū Isḥāq, known as Ibn al-Marʾah (d. after 620 AH/1223 CE). A scholar pre-eminent in *kalām*, well-versed in *tafsīr*, *ḥadīth*, *fiqh*, and history. He studied *kalām* under Ibn al-Shawdhī in Tlemcen. He travelled widely across al-Andalus and the Maghrib, rarely settling in one place. His works include a commentary on Imām al-Ḥaramayn's *al-Irshād*, which he dictated from memory, a commentary on the divine names, a work on the consensus of the jurists, and a commentary on Ibn al-ʿArīf's *Maḥāsin al-Majālis*. He was eloquent in speech and writing, well acquainted with Sufi teachings, and beloved by the common people. He resided for a long period at the congregational mosque of Malaga before being invited to Murcia, where he spent the remainder of his life. He was buried at Jabal Iyālah.

Ibn al-Ḥājib Jamāl al-Dīn AbūʿAmrʿUthmān ibnʿUmar ibn Abī Bakr ibn Yūnus (570–646 AH/1174–1249 CE). A Mālikī jurist and one of the foremost Arabic grammarians of his age. Of Kurdish origin, he was born in Usnā in Upper Egypt, where his father served as chamberlain (*ḥājib*) to the Ayyūbid commander ʿIzz al-Dīn Mūsak al-Ṣalāḥī. He studied in Cairo, taking Qurʾānic recitation from al-Shāṭibī and *fiqh* on the Mālikī school, then moved to Damascus, where he taught at the Mālikī corner of the congregational mosque and drew large numbers of students. He was of exceptionally sharp intellect, and his works — universally admired for their precision and elegance — include *al-Kāfiyah* in grammar, *al-Shāfiyah* in morphology, *Muntahā al-Sūl wa-l-Amal fī ʿIlmay al-Uṣūl wa-l-Jadal* and its *Mukhtaṣar* in legal theory, *Jāmiʿ al-Ummahāt* in Mālikī *fiqh* (compiled from sixty works), *al-Īḍāḥ* (a commentary on al-Zamakhsharī's *al-Mufaṣṣal*), and *al-Amālī al-Naḥwiyyah*. He later returned to Cairo, then settled in Alexandria, where he died.

Ibn Kullāb ʿAbd Allāh ibn Saʿīd ibn Kullāb al-Qaṭṭān al-Baṣrī, Abū Muḥammad (d. before 240 AH/854 CE). The leading *mutakallim* of Basra in his time. He was nicknamed Kullāb because he would draw his opponent to his own position by force of eloquence and argument. He authored works in refutation of the Muʿtazilah, including *Kitāb al-Ṣifāt*, *Khalq al-Afʿāl*, and *al-Radd ʿalā al-Muʿtazilah*. Dāwūd al-Ẓāhirī took *kalām* from him, and al-Ḥārith al-Muḥāsibī is said to have studied dialectics under him as well. Imām al-Ḥaramayn counted him among "our companions," and al-Subkī called him "one of the leading *imāms* of the *mutakallimūn*." His followers are known as the Kullābiyyah, and some of them were later met by Abū al-Ḥasan al-Ashʿarī.

al-ʿIrāqī Zayn al-Dīn Abū al-Faḍl ʿAbd al-Raḥīm ibn al-Ḥusayn ibn ʿAbd al-Raḥmān (725–806 AH/1325–1404 CE). The *ḥadīth* master of his age. Of Kurdish origin, he was born in Rāzanān near Irbil and moved as a child with his father to Egypt, where he studied and rose to pre-eminence. He travelled to Damascus, Aleppo, the Ḥijāz, and Alexandria in pursuit of *ḥadīth*. His works include *al-Mughnī ʿan Ḥaml al-Asfār fī* *al-Asfār*, a *takhrīj* of the *ḥadīths* cited in al-Ghazālī's *Iḥyā'*; the *Alfiyyah* in *ḥadīth* terminology and its commentary *Fatḥ al-Mughīth*; *al-Taḥrīr* in *uṣūl al-fiqh*; *Naẓm al-Durar al-Saniyyah* in the Prophetic biography; and *Nukat Minhāj al-Bayḍāwī* in *uṣūl*. He held the judgeship of Medina from 788 AH for approximately three years, then settled in Cairo. Ibn Ḥajar, his student, said: "We have not seen anyone more accomplished in this discipline," and when al-'Irāqī was asked on his deathbed who remained among the *ḥuffāẓ* after him, he named Ibn Ḥajar first. He died in Cairo.

al-Jāḥiẓ Abū 'Uthmān 'Amr ibn Baḥr ibn Maḥbūb al-Kinānī (163–255 AH/780–869 CE). Leader of the al-Jāḥiẓiyyah branch of the Mu'tazilah. He authored numerous works, including *al-Ḥayawān*, *al-Bayān wa-l-Tabyīn*, and *Akhlāq al-Mulūk*.

Mālik ibn Anas ibn Mālik al-Aṣbaḥī (93–179 AH/711–795 CE). The *imām* of Medina and founder of the Mālikī school. His *al-Muwaṭṭa'* is among the earliest *ḥadīth* collections.

al-Mughīrah ibn 'Abd al-Raḥmān ibn al-Ḥārith al-Makhzūmī al-Madanī. A Medinan jurist of the Quraysh. Ibn Ma'īn said of him: "There is no objection to him." He is not to be confused with al-Mughīrah ibn 'Abd al-Raḥmān ibn Abī Dhi'b al-Makhzūmī, who was the brother of the *muḥaddith* Muḥammad ibn 'Abd al-Raḥmān ibn Abī Dhi'b.

Ibn Kinānah 'Uthmān ibn 'Īsā ibn Kinānah Abū 'Amr (d. 186 AH/802 CE). A leading Medinan jurist and one of Mālik's closest companions. Kinānah was a *mawlā* of 'Uthmān ibn 'Affān. Mālik used to seat him at his right and would not part from him, and he would bring him to debate Abū Yūsuf before al-Rashīd. Yaḥyā ibn Bukayr said: "No one with Mālik was more precise or more diligent in study than Ibn Kinānah." When Mālik grew weary of holding the book for dictation, he would hand it to his scribe Ḥabīb, or sometimes to Ibn Kinānah. After Mālik's death, Ibn Kinānah succeeded him in his teaching circle. He died in Mecca while performing the pilgrimage.

al-Qalānisī Jamāl al-Dīn Abū al-ʿAbbās Aḥmad ibn Muḥammad ibn Muḥammad ibn Naṣr Allāh al-Tamīmī al-Dimashqī al-Shāfiʿī (669–731 AH/1270–1331 CE). A senior judge and scholar of Damascus. He memorised *al-Tanbīh* and then al-Rāfiʿī's *al-Muḥarrar*, and studied under Tāj al-Dīn al-Fazārī. He held the judgeship of the army, the trusteeship of the treasury, and taught at the Amīniyyah, Ẓāhiriyyah, and ʿAṣrūniyyah schools. Ibn Kathīr said of him: "He advanced in learning and leadership, and was unique in his time in prestige; he was humble, of good bearing, kind, and generous to scholars and the righteous." He died in Dhū al-Qaʿdah 731 AH and was buried at the family tomb on the slope of Qāsiyūn.

Saḥnūn Abū Saʿīd ʿAbd al-Salām ibn Saʿīd ibn Ḥabīb al-Tanūkhī (160–240 AH/777–854 CE). The foremost Mālikī jurist of the Maghrib in his time, through whom Mālik's school spread across North Africa. His family was originally from Ḥimṣ in Syria; his father came to Ifrīqiyah with the Ḥimṣī garrison. He studied under Ibn al-Qāsim, Ibn Wahb, and Ashhab. He compiled the *Mudawwanah* in Mālikī *fiqh*, which originated as questions that Asad ibn al-Furāt had put to Ibn al-Qāsim; Saḥnūn took these to Ibn al-Qāsim in 188 AH, had them corrected and revised, then returned to Qayrawān in 191 AH, where he reorganised and arranged the material with chapter headings and supporting traditions. The *Mudawwanah* became the foundational reference for Mālikī jurisprudence in the West. He was appointed judge of Qayrawān and attracted more students and companions than any other of Mālik's followers. He was nicknamed Saḥnūn after a sharp-sighted bird of the Maghrib, on account of his keen intellect. He died on Tuesday, 9 Rajab 240 AH.

al-Sanūsī Imām Abū ʿAbd Allāh Muḥammad ibn Yūsuf ibn ʿUmar al-Ḥasanī al-Tilmisānī (832–895 AH/1428–1490 CE). A master of outward and inward disciplines, he authored books in at least thirteen disciplines, primarily in creed, logic, and *taṣawwuf*, and is best known for his creedal works, especially *Umm al-Barāhīn*. His other writings include al-Kubrā, al-Wusṭā, al-Ṣughrā, and *Sughrā al-Ṣughrā*.

al-Subkī Tāj al-Dīn ʿAbd al-Wahhāb ibn ʿAlī ibn ʿAbd al-Kāfī (727–771 AH/1327–1370 CE). Born in Cairo, he emigrated as a child with his father to Damascus. He studied under al-Dhahabī and al-Mizzī, and held major scholarly and judicial positions in Egypt and the Levant. His prominent works include *Ṭabaqāt al-Shāfiʿiyyah al-Kubrā*, *Muʿīd al-Niʿam wa-Mubīd al-Niqam*, *Jamʿ al-Jawāmiʿ fī Uṣūl al-Fiqh*, and *al-Ashbāh wa-l-Naẓāʾir*. His writings combine rigorous foundation and investigation, marked by eloquence and extensive knowledge.

al-Taftāzānī Saʿd al-Dīn Masʿūd ibn ʿUmar (712–793 AH/1312–1390 CE). A foremost scholar of Arabic language, rhetoric, logic, and *kalām* in the post-classical Islamic tradition. Born in Taftāzān in Khurāsān, he lived in Sarakhs and was later taken to Samarqand by Tīmūr, where he died and was buried back in Sarakhs. In the field of *kalām*, his most important works include *Maqāṣid al-Ṭālibīn* and its commentary *Sharḥ al-Maqāṣid*, as well as the widely studied *Sharḥ al-ʿAqāʾid al-Nasafiyyah* and *Tahdhīb al-Manṭiq wa-l-Kalām*. His writings played a critical role in synthesising *kalām*, logic, and language, forming the backbone of Sunni *madrasah* curricula for centuries.

Thumāmah ibn Ashras al-Numayrī Abū Maʿn (d. 213 AH/828 CE). One of the leading figures of the Muʿtazilah and among the most eloquent orators of his time. He had close connections to the caliphs al-Rashīd and then al-Maʾmūn, who wished to appoint him vizier, but Thumāmah declined. Al-Jāḥiẓ was among his students. His followers are known as the Thumāmiyyah, and he held a number of distinctive positions: that generated effects (*mutawallidāt*) have no agent; that unbelievers, idolaters, and the children of believers will be turned to dust on the Day of Judgement rather than entering the Fire; and — as Ibn Ḥazm reported — that the world is God's act by its own natures (*bi-ṭibāʿihi*), which al-Shahrastānī noted resembled the philosophers' doctrine of necessitation by essence.

BIBLIOGRAPHY

[المَصادِرُ]

al-ʿAjlūnī, Ismāʿīl bin Muḥammad. *Kashf al-khafāʾ*. Cairo: Maktabat al-Qudsī, 1351.

al-Anṣārī, Zakariyā. *Asnā al-maṭālib*. Beirut: Al-Maktab al-Islāmī, n.d..

al-Asfahānī, Abū Nuʿaym. *Ḥilyat al-awliyāʾ*. Cairo: Al-Saʿādah, 1974/1394.

al-Ashʿarī, Abū Ḥasan. *Maqālāt al-islāmiyyīn*. n.p.: Al-Maktabah al-ʿAṣriyyah, 1426/2005.

Abū Dāwūd, Sulaymān bin al-Ashʿath al-Sajisānī.* Al-Sunan* ("Abū Dāwūd"). Edited by Muḥammad Muḥya al-Dīn ʿAbd al-Ḥamīd. Beirut: Dār al-Fikr, n.d.

Abū Yaʿlā al-Mawṣilī. *Musnad Abī Yaʿlā*. Edited by Ḥusayn Salīm Asad. Damascus: Dār al-Maʾmūn li-l-Turāth, 1984.

al-Bayhaqī, Abū Bakr. *Al-Biʿth wa al-nushūr*. Beirut: Markaz al-Khidamāt wa-l-Abḥāth, 1986/1406.

———. *Dalāʾil al-nabuwwah*. Beirut: Dār al-Kutub al-ʿIlmiyyah, 1405.

———. *Shuʿab al-īmān* ("al-Bayhaqī)". Edited by ʿAbd al-ʿAlī ʿAbd al-Ḥamīd Ḥāmid, et al. Riyadh: Maktabat al-Rushd, 2003/1423.

al-Bukhārī, Muḥammad bin Ismāʿīl Abū ʿAbd Allāh. *Al-Jāmiʿ al-ṣaḥīḥ al-mukhtaṣar min umūr rasūli Llāh⊠ wa sunanihi wa ayyāmihi* (*Ṣaḥīḥ al-Bukhārī*) ("al-Bukhārī"). Edited by Muḥammad Zuhayr bin Nāsir al-Nāṣir. n.a.: Dār Tawq al-Najāh, 1422AH.

al-Dhahabī, Shams al-Dīn. *Siyar aʿlām al-nubalāʾ*. Cairo: Dār al-Ḥadīth, 2006/1427.

al-Ḥākim, Abū ʿAbd Allāh Muḥammad. *Al-Mustadrak ʿalāl al-Ṣaḥīḥayn* ("al-Ḥākim"). Edited by Muṣṭafā ʿAbd al-Qādir ʿAṭā. Beirut: Dār al-Kutub al-ʿIlmiyyah, 1990/1411.

Ibn Ḥanbal, Aḥmed. *Al-Musnad* ("Aḥmad"). Edited by Shuʿayb al-Arnā'ūṭ, ʿĀdil Murshid, et al. Beirut: Mu'assisah al-Risālah, 2001/1421.

Ibn Ḥibbān, Muḥammad al-Bustī and al-Amīr ʿAlā' al-Dīn ʿAlī bin Balbān al-Fārasī. *Al-Iḥsān fī taqrīb Ṣaḥīḥ Ibn Ḥibbān* ("Ibn Ḥibbān"). Edited by Shūʿayb al-Arnā'ūṭ. ʿAmmān: Muʾassisat al-Risālah, 1988/1408.

Ibn Mājah, Abū ʿAbd Allāh Muḥammad bin Yazīd al-Qizwīnī. *Sunan Ibn Mājah* ("Ibn Mājah"). Edited by Muḥammad Fū'ād ʿAbd al-Bāqī. Aleppo: Dār Iḥā' al-Kutub alʿArabiyyah, n.d.

al-ʿIrāqī, Zayn al-Dāin. *Takhrīj aḥādīth Iḥyā' ʿulūm al-dīn*. Beirut: Dār Ibn Ḥazm, 2005/1426.

Muslim bin al-Ḥajjāj. *Al-Musnad al-ṣaḥīḥ al-mukhtaṣar bi-naql al-ʿadl ʿan al-ʿadl ilā rasūl Allāh* ☒ ("Muslim"). Edited by Muḥammad Fu'ād ʿAbd al-Bāqī. Beirut: Dār Iḥyā' al-Turāth, n.d.

al-Nasā'ī, Abū ʿAbd al-Raḥmān Aḥmed bin Shuʿayb. *Al-Mujtabā* ("al-Nasā'ī"). Edited by ʿAbd al-Fattāḥ Abū Ghuddah, 2nd ed. Aleppo: Maktab al-Maṭbūʿāt al-Islāmiyyah, n.d.

———. *Al-Sunan al-kubrā*. Edited by ʿAbd al-Ghaffār Sulayman al-Bandārī. Beirut: Dār al-Kutub al-ʿIlmiyyah, n.d.

al-Sanūsī, Abū ʿAbd Allāh Muḥammad ibn Yūsuf (d. 895/1490). *al-ʿAqīda al-wusṭā*. In *Sharḥ al-Wusṭā*, edited by Muḥammad Yūsuf Idrīs. Amman: al-Aṣlayn li-l-Dirāsāt wa-l-Nashr, 2017.

———. *Sharḥ al-ʿAqīda al-wusṭā*. Edited by Anas Muḥammad ʿAdnān al-Sharfāwī. Damascus: Dār al-Taqwā, 1440/2019.

———. *Sharḥ al-ʿAqīda al-wusṭā*. Edited by Muḥammad Yūsuf Idrīs. Amman: al-Aṣlayn li-l-Dirāsāt wa-l-Nashr, 2017.

———. *Sharḥ al-Muqaddimāt*. Edited by Anas Muḥammad ʿAdnān al-Sharfāwī. Damascus: Dār al-Taqwā, 1440/2019.

———. *Sharḥ al-Sanūsī ʿalā mukhtaṣarihi fī al-manṭiq*. N.p.: n.p., 1292/1875.

———. *Sharḥ al-Ṣughrā*. Edited by Anas Muḥammad 'Adnān al-Sharfāwī. Damascus: Dār al-Taqwā, 1440/2019.

———. *Al-Ṣughrā* ("*Umm al-barāhīn*"). In *Sharḥ al-Ṣughrā*, edited by Anas Muḥammad 'Adnān al-Sharfāwī. Damascus: Dār al-Taqwā, 1440/2019.

———. Umm al-barāhīn. In Majmū' Umm al-barāhīn, edited by Māhir Muḥammad 'Adnān 'Uthmān. Mardin: Dār Taḥqīq al-Kitāb, 2022.

al-Suyūṭī. *Jāmi' al-aḥādīth*. Cairo: n.p., 2002/1423.

———. *Jam' al-jawāmi'*. Cairo: al-Azhar al-Sharīf, 2005/1426.

———. *Al-Jāmi' al-ṣaghīr*. N.p: Al-Maktabah al-Shāmilah, n.d.

———. *Al-Tawshīḥ sharḥ Al-Jāmi' al-ṣaḥīh*. Riyāḍ: Maktabat al-Rusdh, 1998/1419.

al-Ṭabarānī, Sulaymān bin Aḥmed bin Ayyūb bin Muṭīr. *Al-Mu'jam al-kabīr*. Edited by Ḥamdī al-Salafī, 2nd ed. n.a.: Maktabat al-'Ulūm wa-l-Ḥikam, n.d.

al-Tirmidhī, Muḥammad bin 'Īsā bin Sawrah bin Mūsā. *Al-Sunan* ("al-Tirmidhī"). Edited by Aḥmed Muḥammad Shākir, et al, 2nd edition. Cairo: Sharikah Maktabah wa Maṭba'ah Muṣṭafā al-Bābī al-Ḥalabī, 1975/1395.

INDEX OF TECHNICAL TERMS

فهرس المصطلحا

INDEX OF PERSONS AND GROUPS

فهرس الأشخاص والفرق

ANALYTICAL TABLE OF CONTENTS

Also from Islamosaic

Ark of Salvation

Connecting to the Quran

Etiquette with the Quran

Infamies of the Soul

Hadith Nomenclature Primers

Hanbali Acts of Worship

Ibn Juzay's Sufic Exegesis

Sharḥ Al-Waraqāt

Shaykh al-Sulamī's Waṣiyyah

The Accessible Conspectus

The Correct Approach to 'Unpacking The Select Creed'

The Encompassing Epistle

The Evident Memorandum

The Ladder to Success in Truly Loving Allah Paperback

The Ultimate Conspectus

www.ingramcontent.com/pod-product-compliance
Ingram Content Group UK Ltd.
Pitfield, Milton Keynes, MK11 3LW, UK
UKHW040604210726
13854UKWH00009B/2522

9 781944 904272